Young spaces | Ambiances jeunes | Junges Ambiente

Coordination and text • Coordination et rédaction • Koordination und Redaktion
PATRICIA BUENO

Editorial Director • Directeur éditorial • Verlagsdirektor
NACHO ASENSIO

Design and layout • Conception et maquette • Design und Layout
KIKO NÚÑEZ

Cover design • Création de page de garde • Außengestaltung
NÚRIA SORDÉ ORPINELL

Translation • Traduction • Übersetzung
MARK HOLLOWAY (English)
ALINE RÉVOLTE (Français)
IRIS MOHR (Deutsch)

Production • Production • Produktion
JUANJO RODRÍGUEZ NOVEL

Cover image • Page de garde • Einband: Molteni & C.

Copyright © 2003 Atrium Group
Editorial Project: Books Factory, S.L.
e-mail: books@booksfactory.org

Published by: Atrium Group
de ediciones y publicaciones, S.L.
c/. Ganduxer, 112
08022 BARCELONA

Tel: +34 932 540 099
Fax: +34 932 118 139
e-mail: atrium@atriumgroup.org
www.atriumbooks.com

ISBN: 84-95692-50-3
National Book Catalogue Number:
B-36449-2003

Printed in Spain
Grabasa, S.L.

Copyright © 2003 Atrium Group
Projet éditorial : Books Factory, S.L.
e-mail : books@booksfactory.org

Publication : Atrium Group
de ediciones y publicaciones, S.L.
c/. Ganduxer, 112
08022 BARCELONA

Tel: +34 932 540 099
Fax: +34 932 118 139
e-mail: atrium@atriumgroup.org
www.atriumbooks.com

ISBN : 84-95692-50-3
Dépôt légal : B-36449-2003

Imprimé en Espagne
Grabasa, S.L.

Copyright © 2003 Atrium Group
Verlagsprojekt: Books Factory, S.L.
e-mail: books@booksfactory.org

Herausgegeben von: Atrium Group
de ediciones y publicaciones, S.L.
c/. Ganduxer, 112
08022 BARCELONA

Tel: +34 932 540 099
Fax: +34 932 118 139
e-mail: atrium@atriumgroup.org
www.atriumbooks.com

ISBN: 84-95692-50-3
Depot gesetzlicher Pflichtexemplare:
B-36449-2003

Druck in Spanien
Grabasa, S.L.

Young spaces | Ambiances jeunes | Junges Ambiente

|CONTENTS

INTRODUCTION   9

FUN AND COLORFUL   12
   Colorful living and dining rooms   14
   Stimulating kitchens   66
   Bathrooms with playful colors   90
   Colorful dreams   104
   Lights and tones   118

ECOLOGICAL AND NATURAL   134
   Nature in living and dining rooms   136
   Ecological kitchens   180
   Bathrooms inspired by nature   202
   Harmonious bedrooms   216
   Mimetic illumination   226

INNOVATORS AND THE AVANT-GARDE   236
   The latest fashions in living
   and dining rooms   238
   Metallic kitchens   274
   Bathroom design   298
   The avant-garde in the bedroom   310
   Creative illumination   324

THE TRADITIONAL AND NOSTALGIC   346
   Living and dining rooms
   with retro atmospheres   348
   Rustic kitchens   370
   Bathrooms with a style from the past   392
   Beds with canopies
   and more romanticism   406
   Cozy lighting   420

MINIMALISTS AND THE ESSENTIAL   430
   The basics in living and dining rooms   432
   Kitchens in white   458
   Transparent bathrooms   472
   Compact bedrooms   486
   Lights in search of simplicity   498

TRAVELERS AND CROSS-CULTURAL
SURROUNDINGS   508
   Ethnic living and dining rooms   510
   Lights and other objects
   that contain stories   534
   Bathrooms with an exotic touch   548
   Dreaming about other countries   560

DIRECTORY   572

|INDEX

INTRODUCTION   10

AMUSANTES ET COLORÉES   12

Des salons et des salles à manger
colorés   14
Des cuisines stimulantes   66
Des salles de bain
et des jeux chromatiques   90
Des rêves en couleurs   104
Des lumières et des tons   118

NATURELLES ET ÉCOLOGIQUES   134

La nature dans les salons
et les salles à manger   136
Des cuisines écologiques   180
Des salles de bain inspirées
de la nature   202
Des chambres harmonieuses   216
Un éclairage mimétique   226

INNOVATION ET AVANT-GARDE   236

La dernière mode en salons
et salles à manger   238
Des cuisines métalliques   274
Des salles de bain design   298
Un style d'avant-garde
pour la chambre   310
Un éclairage créatif   324

NOSTALGIQUES ET TRADITIONNELLES   346

Des salons et des salles à manger
avec des airs rétro   348
Des cuisines rustiques   370
Des salles de bain à l'ancienne   392
Des lits à baldaquin
et du romantisme   406
Un éclairage accueillant   420

MINIMALISTES ET ESSENTIELLES   430

L'essentiel en salons
et salles à manger   432
Des cuisines en blanc   458
Des salles de bain diaphanes   472
Des chambres aux lignes concises   486
Un éclairage en quête de simplicité   498

INTERCULTURELLES ET VOYAGEUSES   508

Des salons et des salles
à manger ethniques   510
Des éclairages et des objets
qui racontent...   534
Des salles de bain exotiques   548
Rêver d'autres pays   560

CARNET D'ADRESSES   572

|INHALTSVERZEICHNIS

EINLEITUNG 11

LUSTIGE, FARBENFREUDIGE INTERIEURS 13
Farben für Wohn- und Esszimmer 14
Stimulierend wirkende Küchen 66
Badezimmer und Farbenspiele 90
Träume und Farben 104
Licht und Farbtöne 118

NATURBEZOGENE UND ÖKOLOGISCHE
INTERIEURS 135
Natur und Wohn- und Esszimmer 136
Ökologische Küchen 180
Von der Natur inspirierte Badezimmer 202
Harmonisch eingerichtete
Schlafzimmer 216
Mimetische Beleuchtung 226

INNOVATE UND AVANTGARDISTISCHE
INTERIEURS 237
Aktuelle Trends für Wohn- und
Esszimmer 238
Küchen aus Stahl 274
Designerbadezimmer 298
Avantgardistische Interieurs
für Schlafzimmer 310
Erfindungsreiche Beleuchtung 324

INTERIEURS IM NOSTALGISCHEN
UND TRADITIONELLEN STIL 347

Wohn- und Esszimmer mit
dem Flair aus vergangenen Zeiten 348
Rustikale Küchen 370
Badezimmer mit einem Flair
aus vergangenen Zeiten 392
Himmelbetten und andere
romantische Details 406
Gemütliches Licht 420

MINIMALISTISCHE INTERIEURS 431
Grundelemente für Wohn- und
Esszimmer 432
Weiße Küchen 458
Badezimmer und Transparenz 472
Schlafzimmer mit konziser
Formgebung 486
Durch ihre Einfachheit geprägte
Lichtquellen 498

VON VERSCHIEDENEN KULTUREN UND
REISEEINDRÜCKEN GEPRÄGTE INTERIEURS 509
Wohn- und Esszimmer mit
ethnischem Flair 510
Licht und Objekte, von denen
Geschichten erzählt werden 534
Badezimmer mit einem
exotischen Flair 548
Der Traum von fremden Ländern 560

ADRESSEN 572

Introduction

How do the young live? This sounds like one of those trick questions because, not only are we sure to get innumerable answers and their corresponding nuances, but, maybe, we should also begin by defining what we really understand by young. When do we stop being young? The line that separates youth and maturity is becoming more and more indistinct, fading away with greater speed as we advance into the difficult terrain of the twenty-first century. It seems that the state of being young no longer has a great deal to do with age, but with attitudes and lifestyle. In more or less developed societies, each person can choose how he or she desires to live his or her life. One of the most evident consequences of this recently found freedom is the change in family structure and, therefore, the physiognomy of the home.

So in these pages, we are not going to establish any form of classification based on ages, which would be obsolete in its own conception, but we will speak of free spirits that have chosen to be young. We will speak of personalities.

"Tell me what your home is like and I will tell you what you are", could be, therefore, the heading of this piece of work. To try and reflect all of the possible personalities that can be restated in a definite decorative style in just one book would have been taking on an endless venture. Because of this, we have established a classification based on the main tendencies that presently reign in our society: **environments full of colors** for people who wish to transmit happiness, amusement and boldness. **Environments inspired in nature** are identified with those who are stable, harmonious and who make a bid to recover the values of the earth, of noble materials. **Avant-garde environments** for those of an innovative spirit, the pioneers, those who risk adopting the unknown. **More traditional environments** for the lovers of familiar things, the snug and cozy, crafted things. **Environments where a mixture of cultures dominates** for the traveling souls, yearning to share, to learn, to discover. And the **minimalist environments** for those who seek purity, essence, the intrinsic spirituality of each object.

The objective is for all those who feel young to be able to identify with some kind of environment, or with a mixture of various, offering an extensive collection of samples capable of transmitting emotions, even capable of inspiring love. Because at times, the dialogue established between a person and an object is that of authentic love at first sight, that of, "I cannot live without her."

It is undeniable that each piece of furniture, each object, each color, each texture, each small detail talks about us, communicating our inclinations, our desires, our fears of the outside world. For this reason, it is necessary that the home takes shape little by little at the rhythm we find those elements that are in tune with our style, that are a mirror with whose reflection we feel at home. In short, this is what it is about. To feel at home, comfortable, relaxed. To create one's own place, where the chaos of the world is as far from us as possible.

Each one of the articles that illustrate the different chapters of *Young Spaces* is directed towards creating a particular atmosphere, intended to awaken an irresistible attraction upon those who see it, offering itself as a guide and source of inspiration for future acquisitions. The selection that we are presenting has been made from among the latest proposals of the most prestigious specialists in the sector of decoration, those who know what characteristics a piece of furniture should combine so as not to defraud in the expectations that we may have of it: beauty, functionality, quality and personality.

Young Spaces establishes the guidelines for how to decorate according to what we are, proposing an imaginative kind of game, where each one of us should find what best defines him or her. From here on, intuition, fantasy and creativity enter the scene to stamp on each home the personal and nontransferable seal of whoever inhabits it, giving a thousand answers to the question that we formulated at the beginning, How do the young live?

Let all those who have chosen to exercise their freedom to be young give their own answer.

Introduction

De quelle façon les jeunes vivent-ils ? Voici une question à piège, car elle comporte d'innombrables réponses avec leurs nuances correspondantes ; mais, peut-être devrions-nous commencer par définir ce que signifie exactement le mot jeune. Quand cessons-nous d'être jeunes ? La limite séparant la jeunesse de la maturité devient de plus en plus floue : elle s'efface au fur et à mesure où nous avançons dans les méandres du 21e siècle. On pourrait dire que le fait d'être jeune n'a plus grandchose à voir avec l'âge, mais plutôt avec les attitudes et le style de vie. Dans les sociétés plus ou moins développées, chacun peut choisir la vie qu'il veut vivre. Une des conséquences les plus évidentes de cette nouvelle liberté réside dans le changement de la structure familiale classique et de la physionomie de la demeure.

De ce fait, nous n'établirons aucune classification basée sur les âges car elle serait obsolète de par sa propre conception, et nous parlerons plutôt de l'esprit libre des jeunes. Nous parlerons de personnalités.

"Décris-moi ta maison et je te dirai qui tu es ", cette expression pourrait donc être le titre de ce livre. Tenter de refléter en un seul livre toutes les personnalités pouvant être traduites par un style décoratif aurait été une tâche interminable. C'est pour cette raison que nous avons établi un classement basé sur les principales tendances régnant actuellement dans notre société : **des ambiances pleines de couleurs** pour les personnes qui veulent transmettre la joie, la distraction et l'audace. **Des ambiances inspirées de la nature**, équilibrées, harmonieuses et revendiquant la valeur de la terre et des matériaux nobles. **Des ambiances d'avant-garde** pour les esprits novateurs, les pionniers, ceux qui se risquent à l'inconnu. **Des ambiances plus traditionnelles** pour les amoreux de l'ambiance familiale, accueillante et des objets artisanaux. **Des ambiances où domine le mélange des cultures** pour les âmes voyageuses et désireuses de partager, d'apprendre, de connaître. Et des ambiances minimalistes pour ceux qui sont en quête de pureté, d'essence, et de la spiritualité intrinsèque de chaque objet.

L'objectif consiste à faire en sorte que tous ceux qui se sentent jeunes puissent s'identifier à un type d'ambiance bien défini, ou au mélange de plusieurs styles, à leur offrir un vaste étalage d'articles capables de transmettre des émotions, et même, de les faire tomber amoureux. Car parfois, le dialogue qui s'établit entre une personne et un objet se trouve être un authentique coup de cœur, un "je ne peux pas vivre sans lui".

Il est indéniable que chaque meuble, chaque objet, chaque couleur, chaque texture, chaque petit détail parle de nous et révèle nos goûts, nos souhaits ou nos peurs. C'est pour cette raison même qu'il est nécessaire de donner un caractère à notre demeure de trouver des éléments en harmonie avec notre style, des éléments et qui seront le miroir dont le reflet nous fera nous sentir bien. C'est de cela qu'il s'agit, en définitive: de se sentir bien, à l'aise, décontracté. Créer un endroit à soi où le chaos du monde extérieur nous atteigne le moins possible.

Chacun des articles illustrant les différents chapitres de Ambiances Jeunes, est destiné à créer une certaine atmosphère qui devra provoquer une attraction irrésistible sur le lecteur et qui sera le guide et l'inspirateur de ses futures acquisitions. La sélection que nous présentons a été effectuée parmi les dernières propositions des spécialistes les plus connus dans le secteur de la décoration, les spécialistes qui savent quelles sont les caractéristiques que doit réunir un meuble pour ne pas manquer aux espérances de l'acheteur: la beauté, la fonctionnalité, la qualité et la personnalité.

Ambiances Jeures établit les lignes maîtresses définissant la façon de décorer notre maison en fonction de notre moi et propose une sorte de jeu imaginatif dans lequel chacun pourra trouver ce qui le définit le mieux. L'intuition, la fantaisie et la créativité entrent alors en scène pour donner à la demeure la touche personnelle correspondante à la personne qui y habite, et donnent des milliers de réponses à la question que nous nous posions : comment les jeunes vivent-ils ?

Que tous ceux qui ont choisi la liberté d'être jeune donnent leur propre réponse.

Einleitung

Wie wohnt die junge Generation heutzutage? Diese scheinbar einfache Frage ist gar nicht so leicht zu beantworten, die Aussagen hierzu können vielfältig und sehr differenziert ausfallen. Vielleicht sollte deshalb zunächst einmal abgeklärt werden, was wir unter jungen Generation zu verstehen haben. Ab wann gehören wir nicht mehr zur Jugend? Die Grenze zwischen Jugend und reiferem Alter verwischt sich zunehmend, und in Folge der das XXI. Jh. prägenden Ereignisse scheint sich dieser Prozeß immer schneller zu vollziehen. Jung zu sein hat heute anscheinend nicht mehr sehr viel mit dem biologischen Alter zu tun, sondern vielmehr mit Lebensauffassung und –stil. In unserer heutigen Industriegesellschaft steht es jedem frei, sein Leben nach eigenen Wünschen zu gestalten. Diese neue Freiheit hat u.a. zu einer Umstrukturierung des klassischen Familienverbandes geführt; für das Konzipieren und die Gestaltung der Wohnungen haben sich somit neue Kriterien ergeben. .

Da es von der Konzeption her nicht zeitgemäß wäre, werden wir also dieses Buch nicht in nach Altersgruppen gegliederte Kapitel unterteilen, sondern vielmehr von freien Menschen sprechen, die sich dafür entschieden haben, jung zu sein. Wir werden deshalb also über Persönlichkeiten reden.

"Zeige mir dein Haus, und ich sage dir, wie du bist" – so könnte der Buchtitel eigentlich lauten. Es wäre ein kaum zu bewältigendes Unterfangen, in einem einzigen Buch die verschiedenen Persönlichkeitsstrukturen darstellen zu wollen und zu zeigen, wie sich diese in dem jeweils gewählten Wohnstil ausdrücken.

Wir haben uns deshalb für eine Einteilung entschieden, die sich an den wichtigsten, heute in unserer Gesellschaft zu beobachtenden Trends ausrichtet.

Farbenfreudige Interieurs für alle, die damit ihrer Lebensfreude, ihrer Lust an Spaß und ihrer Experimentierfreudigkeit Ausdruck verleihen wollen. Unter den von der **Natur inspirierten Interieurs** sind ausgewogene Räume voller Harmonie zu verstehen, bei deren Ausstattung Ök... edle Materialien eine wichtige Rolle spi... **stische Interieurs** entscheid... der Suche nach In... Wege z...

Suche nach der reinen Form, der Essenz, des Wesentlichen eines jeden Objektes sind.

Mit diesem Buch beabsichtigen wir, dass sich jeder, der sich jung fühlt, mit einem bestimmten Interieur oder der Mischung aus verschiedenen Stilen identifizieren kann. Dazu zeigen wir eine große Auswahl an Gegenständen, die Gefühle auslösen und übertragen können, und in die man sich sogar verlieben kann, denn manchmal entsteht zwischen dem Betrachter und dem Gegenstand etwas, was man als Liebe auf den ersten Blick bezeichnen könnte, woraus sich dann zwangsläufig das „ich kann nicht mehr ohne ihn leben" ergibt.

Es steht außer Zweifel, dass jedes Möbelstück, jeder Gegenstand, jede Farbe, jede Textur, jedes kleinste Detail über uns Auskunft gibt und Außenstehende über unseren Geschmack, unsere Wünsche, unsere Ängste informiert. Nach und nach werden wir also unsere Wohnung ganz individuell gestalten und dazu Elemente einsetzen, die unserem Stil entsprechen und Zeugnis darüber ablegen, dass wir uns in dem so geschaffenen Raum wohlfühlen. Denn darum geht es schließlich: Man soll sich wohlfühlen, Bequemlichkeit und Relax genießen. Einen eigenen Raum schaffen, der uns so gut wie möglich Schutz vor der oft chaotischen Außenwelt bietet.

In den einzelnen Kapiteln von Wohnen der jungen Generation werden jeweils Interieurs mit einem ganz bestimmten Ambiente vorgestellt, von denen sich der Betrachter unwiderstehlich in Bann gezogen fühlen soll. Was er hier sieht, kann ihm als Kriterium und Inspiration für spätere Akquisitionen dienen. Bei der von uns getroffenen Auswahl haben wir die neusten Projekte der renommiertesten Innenarchitekten berücksichtigt, da wir sicher sein könne... genau wissen, wie ein Möbelstück... mit ihm verbundenen En... muss sich durch... und R...

FUN AND COLORFUL
Colors and states of mind

The introduction of strong colors into the decoration of interiors signifies, to begin with, boldness and challenge. We do not know what will happen when we put a blue sofa next to some red chairs, or when we paint the kitchen wall yellow. Each color exerts a specific power over our state of mind, as well as contributing to the image we project of ourselves to others. Many psychologists maintain that color has the capacity to explain some of our personality traits. What is indisputable is its aptness to enrich life, as it acts directly upon our emotions or, in the words of Kandinsky, "influencing directly on our souls". It can create happiness or induce melancholy, awaken desire or aversion, stimulate or relax.

An adequate use of color can enrich any space, breaking with monotony and boredom and improving, consequently, our quality of life. Although, used unwisely, it can tire quickly, and, even, generate tension in the atmosphere.

Each one of the colors of the spectrum is associated with particular emotional effects. It is neccesary to be aware of this before choosing paint for the walls or the color of the curtains:

–RED: associated with joy and happiness, as well as with the heart, the flesh, emotion and passion. A prolonged exposure to large quantities of red speeds up our heartbeat and favors the discharge of adrenaline into the blood flow, as well as generating a certain sense of heat. When it tends toward rose, it becomes kinder and more feminine.

–BLUE: the color of the soul. It is associated with a noble character. A blue ambience exerts a soothing effect, to the extent, even, of lowing blood pressure. Although it is fundamentally a healthy color, from time to time, it can denote melancholy or sadness. It is especially recommended for bedrooms or places of rest.

–YELLOW: the color traditionally associated with intelligence. The color of the sun and of spring, of joy, able to stimulate and energize. In its purest form it radiates heat and inspiration. It is used especially in rooms for the young.

–GREEN: the color of life, of the power of nature. It is credited with a restful effect and associated with qualities of stability and security and with emotional equilibrium. It is used to give perspective. A very old belief exists that attributes beneficial and relaxing effects upon the sight of it.

–VIOLET: born from the union of opposites, red and blue. This contrast generates color schemes that can provoke desire or aversion. It is related to intimacy and excellence, and indicates deep feelings. Purple, in turn, functions as a synonym of sensuality.

–ORANGE: an unmistakably warm color associated with the fall and the earth. It stimulates and generates energy. Psychologically it acts like yellow, lively, expansive, rich and extrovert. It is a color well adjusted to all that signifies food, therefore, it is especially used in kitchens.

AMUSANTES ET COLORÉES
Des couleurs et des états d'âme

...ion de couleurs vives dans la décoration d'in-
...esprit audacieux et provocateur.
...l'effet produit si nous met-
...fauteuils rouges,
...jaune.

Chacune des couleurs du spectre est associée à des effets émotionnels bien définis qu'il est conseillé de prendre en compte avant de choisir la peinture des murs ou la couleur des rideaux :

–ROUGE : il est associé à la joie et au bonheur, au cœur, à la chair, à l'émotion et à la passion. Une exposition ...ongée à une grande quantité de couleur rouge ...battements cardiaques, provoque la ...dans le flux sanguin et génère ... lorsqu'il tire sur le ...sin.

emps, de la joie, elle est capable de stimuler et de donner du courage. Lorsqu'il s'agit d'un jaune pur, cette couleur diffuse la chaleur et l'inspiration. Elle est spécialement utilisée dans les chambres des enfants.

–VERT : il s'agit de la couleur de la vie, du pouvoir de la nature. On lui attribue un effet reposant et des qualités de stabilité et de sécurité liées à l'équilibre émotionnel. On l'utilise pour donner de la perspective. Il existe une croyance très ancienne lui attribuant des effets bénéfiques et tranquillisants pour la vue.

–VIOLET : il naît du mélange entre deux opposés, le rouge et le bleu. Ce contraste génère des tonalités pouvant provoquer le désir ou l'aversion. Il est lié à la timidité et à la sublimation, et indique des sentiments profonds. Le pourpre, pour sa part, fonctionne comme synonyme de sensualité.

–ORANGE : il s'agit d'une couleur indéniablement chaude, associée à l'automne et à la terre. Elle est stimulante et génère de l'énergie. Psychologiquement, elle agit comme le jaune, elle donne du courage, elle nous rend expansif, riche et extraverti. C'est une couleur orientée vers la nourriture elle spécialement utilisée pour décorer les cuisines.

LUSTIGE, FARBENFREUDIGE INTERIEURS
Farben und Stimmung

Bei der Innenausstattung lebhafte Farben einzusetzen ist zunächst einmal ein kühnes und gewagtes Unternehmen. Wir können nicht abschätzen, welche Wirkung hervorgerufen wird, wenn wir ein blaues Sofa mit roten Sesseln zusammenstellen, oder wenn wir die Küchenwand gelb anstreichen. Jede Farbe beeinflußt in einer ganz bestimmten Weise unsere Stimmung; außerdem läßt sich von Außenstehenden aus den Farben viel über unsere Persönlichkeit ablesen.

Von vielen Psychologen wird die Aussagekraft der Farben bei Persönlichkeitsanalysen eingesetzt. Unbestritten ist, dass Farben ein großes Potential in ﹏gen: Sie können unser Leben versch﹏ direkten Einfluss auf unser﹏ mit Kandinsky z﹏ auf uns﹏

–BLAU: Sie ist die Farbe der Seele und des Geistes. Man verbindet mir ihr einen edlen Charakter. Ein in Blau gehaltenes Interieur strahlt Ruhe aus und kann sogar eine blutdrucksenkende Wirkung hervorrufen. Es handelt sich hier zwar um eine vitale Farbe, dennoch kann﹏ mit ihr manchmal Melancholie oder Triste﹏ drückt werden. Besonders empfoh﹏ immer oder sonstige O﹏

–GELB: Von jeh﹏ so﹏

Colorful living and
rooms

Des salons et des salles à manger colorés

Farben für Wohn– und Esszimmer

Color is life. It is happiness. It is letting yourself be carried away by the emotions of the moment. It is feeling. It is communication. It is not the same to contemplate the passing of time, chat, embrace, read, paint or dream from a red sofa, as from one of neutral tones. Red will allow all associated with passion fall upon the environment. And who says sit on red, says rest in a blue chair, put a book on a yellow shelf, eat in tones of orange or walk over an intensely colored carpet. It is a question of knowing which colors to put into a cocktail shaker and to let them flow, creating surprising or harmonic chromatic combinations, dependant on the rapport each of us has with the world of colors. Because in life, everything depends on the shade of the lens we look through....

La couleur, c'est la vie. C'est la joie. C'est se laisser aller aux émotions du moment. C'est le sentiment. C'est la communication. Ce n'est pas la même chose de contempler le passage des heures, de discuter, de s'étreindre, de lire, de peindre ou de rêver sur un canapé rouge que sur un canapé aux tons neutres. Le rouge remplira à l'atmosphère des connotations passionnelles. Et qui dit s'asseoir sur du rouge, dit se reposer sur une chaise bleue, poser un livre sur une étagère jaune, manger sur des tons orangés ou marcher sur un tapis aux couleurs intenses. La question est de savoir comment mélanger les couleurs appropriées afin de créer des combinaisons chromatiques surprenantes ou harmonieuses, en fonction des affinités de chacun. Tout dépend du regard que l'on porte sur la vie...

Farbe ist Synonym für Leben, für Freude. Mit ihr geben wir uns den Emotionen des Moments hin. Sie bedeutet Kommunikation. Es ist schon ein Unterschied, ob wir in unseren Mußestunden, beim Unterhalten, Umarmen, Lesen, Malen oder Träumen auf einem roten oder auf einem in neutralen Farben gehaltenen Sofa sitzen. Das Rot gibt dem Ambiente etwas von seiner Konnotation (Leidenschaft) ab. Und wer sich auf ein rotes Sofa setzt, der wird sich auch auf einem blauen Stuhl ausruhen, das Buch in ein gelbes Regal zurückstellen, seine Mahlzeiten in einem orangenfarbenen Essbereich einnehmen oder über einen in kräftigen Farben gehaltenen Teppich gehen. Worum es hier geht, ist, die geeigneten Farben zu einer richtigen Mischung zusammenzustellen, sie frei in dem Raum zu verteilen, und zu erreichen, dass daraus eine Farbkombination entsteht, die überraschende Effekte hervorruft oder harmonisch auf uns wirkt. Die Zusammenstellung der Farben erfolgt dabei ganz individuell in Funktion der von den einzelnen Bewohnern bevorzugten Farbtöne, denn im Leben liegt die Schönheit im Auge des Betrachters ...

Stefano Giovannoni was inspire
of the 60's in the design
"Bombo". P

Stefano Giovan
des années 60 pou
"Bomb

Stefano Giovannor
"Bombo" vom Stil
lass

Composition of the collection
"Occa" from Club 8 Company.

Composition de la collection
"Occa" du Club 8 Company.

Zusammenstellung aus der Serie
"Occa" von Club 8 Company.

Sofa "Tuamutu" and container system "The Wall", by Roche Bobois.

Canapé "Tuamutu" et rangement "The Wall", de Roche Bobois.

Sofa "Tuamutu" und Containersystem "The Wall" von Roche Bobois.

Peter Keler designed the easy chairs "Bauhaus Cube" in 1925. Produced by Tecta.

Peter Keler a créé les fauteuils "Bauhaus Cube" en 1925. Fabriqué par Tecta.

Peter Keler entwarf im Jahre 1925 die Sessel "Bauhaus Cube" Hergestellt von Tecta.

"Icon" is a design by Nana Ditzel for Fredericia Furniture.

"Icon" est une création de Nana Ditzel pour Fredericia Furniture.

"Icon" ist ein Design von Nana Ditzel für Fredericia Furniture.

Mobi i by Fredericia proposes this armchair with footrests, model "900".

Mobi i by Fredericia propose ce fauteuil avec repose-pieds, modèle "900".

Mit Mobili von Fredericia wird dieser Sessel mit Fußstütze angeboten, Modell "900".

The easy chair "Nemo" is presented in bold colors.
A design by Peter Maly for Cor.

Le fauteuil "Nemo" est présenté avec des couleurs audacieuses.
Il s'agit d'une création de Peter Maly pour Cor.

Der Sessel "Nemo" präsentiert sich in auffallenden
Farben. Design von Peter Maly für Cor.

Sofa "2300", designed by Christian Werner for Rolf Benz.

Canapé "2300", création de Christian Werner pour Rolf Benz.

Sofa "2300", Design von Christian Werner für Rolf Benz.

Georg Appeltshauser is the author of the design of sofa "6700". From Rolf Benz.

Georg Appeltshauser signe la création du canapé "6700". De Rolf Benz.

Georg Appeltshauser zeichnet für das Design des Sofas "6700". Hergestellt von Rolf Benz.

Table and sofa with rounded lines,
designed by Gijs Papavoine for Montis.

Table et canapé aux lignes arrondies,
créés par Gijs Papavoine pour Montis.

Tisch und Sofa mit runder Linienführung.
Entworfen von Gijs Papavoine für Montis.

Sideboard from the collection
"Do it", from Viccarbe.

Buffet de la collection
"Do it", de Viccarbe.

Büfett der Serie "Do it"
von Viccarbe.

The chaise-longue "VK Chaise", designed by Vladimir Kagan, forms part of the Kagan New York Collection Line.

La chaise-longue "VK Chaise", créée par Vladimir Kagan, fait partie de la ligne Kagan New York Collection.

Die Chaiselongue "VK Chaise", entworfen von Vladimir Kagan, gehört zu der Kagan New York Collection.

"The Serpentine Sofa", created in 1949, is also included in the Kagan New York Collection.

"The Serpentine Sofa", créé en 1949, fait également partie de la Kagan New York Collection.

"The Serpentine Sofa", entworfen im Jahre 1949, ist ebenfalls Teil der Kagan New York Collection.

Antonio Citterio is the author of the sofa design
"George", from B&B Italia.

Antonio Citterio signe la création du canapé "George",
de B&B Italia.

Antonio Citterio zeichnet für das Design des Sofas
"George" von B&B Italia.

Sofas from the collection "Boa"
designed by Gil Coste for Cor.

Canapés de la collection "Boa",
créés par Gil Coste pour Cor.

Sofas der Modellreihe "Boa",
Design von Gil Coste für Cor.

An original design by Roberto Lazzeroni.
This is the model "It" from Insa.

Création originale de Roberto Lazzeroni.
Il s'agit du modèle "It" de Insa.

Originelles Design von Roberto Lazzeroni.
Hier wird das Modell "It" von Insa gezeigt.

This easy chair from the "Serie Up" reminds us of ancient representations of fertility goddesses. This is a design by Gaetano Pesce for B&B Italia.

Ce fauteuil de la "Serie Up" rappelle les anciennes représentations des déesses de la fertilité. Il s'agit d'une création de Gaetano Pesce pour B&B Italia.

Dieser Sessel der Serie „Up" erinnert an die alten Darstellungen der Fruchtbarkeitsgöttinnen. Das Design hat Gaetano Pesce für B&B Italia übernommen.

Massimo Losa Ghini is the author of this design from the collection "Pop Art". From Roche Bobois.

Massimo Iosa Ghini signe la création de la collection "Pop Art". De Roche Bobois.

Massimo Iosa Ghini zeichnet für das Design der Serie "Pop Art" von Roche Bobois.

On the left, the easy chair "Love" by F. Scansetti and M.Paul. Bottom, sofas from the collection "It" by R. Lazzeroni. All from Insa.

À gauche, le fauteuil "Love" de F. Scansetti et M.Paul. En bas, les canapés de la collection "It", de R. Lazzeroni. Ensemble de Insa.

Links, Sessel "Love" von F. Scansetti und M.Paul. Unten: Sofas der Serie "It" von R. Lazzeroni. Alle Möbel werden von Insa hergestellt.

Marcel Breuer designed the chair
"D4" in 1928. Produced by Tecta.

Marcel Breuer a créé la chaise "D4"
en 1928. Fabriqué par Tecta.

Marcel Breuer entwarf im Jahr 1928
den Stuhl "D4". Hergestellt von
Tecta.

Werner Aisslinger has designed this
group of container furniture
"Plus Unit". From Magis.

Werner Aisslinger a créé le
rangement "Plus Unit". De Magis.

Werner Aisslinger hat die Gruppe
der Containermöbel "Plus Unit"
für Magis entworfen.

"Air Chair" is a design by Jasper
Morrison for Magis.

"Air Chair" est une création de
Jasper Morrison pour Magis.

"Air Chair" ist ein Design
von Jasper Morrison für Magis.

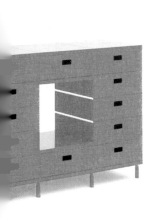

Sofa from the collection "Bauhaus Cube",
designed by Peter Keler. From Tecta.

Canapé de la collection "Bauhaus Cube",
créé par Peter Keler. De Tecta.

Sofa der Serie "Bauhaus Cube",
Design von Peter Keler. Hergestellt von Tecta.

Sofa designed by Walter Gropius in 1920.
Produced by Tecta.

Canapé créé par Walter Gropius en 1920.
Fabriqué par Tecta.

Ein 1920 von Walter Gropius entworfenes Sofa.
Hergestellt von Tecta.

Carpet designed by Sybilla for the firm Nani Marquina.

Tapis créé par Sybilla pour la marque Nani Marquina.

Von Sybilla für die Firma Nani Marquina entworfener Teppich.

The designer El Lissitzski created this easy chair in 1928. Produced by Tecta.

Le créateur El Lissitzski a présenté ce fauteuil en 1928. Fabriqué par Tecta.

Dieser Sessel ist von El Lissitzski im Jahre 1928 entworfen worden. Hergestellt von Tecta.

On the left, modular sofas from the series "Cubist" designed by Massimo Morozzi for Edra. Above these lines, seat "Monster" by Krd Shona Kitchen and Ab Rogers for Edra.

À gauche, canapés convertibles de la série "Cubista", créés par Massimo Morozzi pour Edra. Dans la même ligne, siège "Monster" de Krd Shona Kitchen et Ab Rogers pour Edra.

Links, Sofas aus Moduls der Serie "Cubista", Design von Massimo Morozzi für Edra. Direkt über diesem Text: Sitz "Monster" von Krd Shona Kitchen und Ab Rogers für Edra.

Cupboard with metallic doors from Maisa.

Armoire à portes métalliques de Maisa.

Schrank mit Metalltüren von Maisa.

On the left, sofa "Arco" from Misura Emme. On the right, sideboard "Hey Gi" from Misura Emme.

À gauche, canapé "Arco" de Misura Emme. À droite, buffet "Hey Gi" de Misura Emme.

Links das Sofa "Arco" von Misura Emme. Rechts die Anrichte "Hey Gi" von Misura Emme.

"Tempo" can be used as a stall and as an auxiliary table. A design from Prospero Rasulo for Zanotta. Below, chest of drawers from the program Rolf Benz Evolution. From Rolf Benz.

"Tempo" peut être utilisé comme tabouret ou comme table d'appoint. Il s'agit d'une création de Prospero Rasulo pour Zanotta. En bas, commode de la gamme Rolf Benz Evolution. De Rolf Benz.

"Tempo" kann sowohl als Hocker als auch als Beistelltisch dienen. Das Design hat Prospero Rasulo für Zanotta erstellt. Unten eine Kommode aus der Modellreihe Rolf Benz Evolution von Rolf Benz.

The modular group "Niki" allows for an infinite number of combinations. From Ennio Arosio for Mobileffe.

Ensemble convertible "Niki" permettant d'obtenir de nombreuses combinaisons. De Ennio Arosio pour Mobileffe.

Das Modulsystem "Niki" bietet unzählige Kombinationsmöglichkeiten. Von Ennio Arosio für Mobileffe.

The sofa "Bohemien" is a design by
Emaf Progetti for Zanotta.

Le canapé "Bohemien" est une création
de Emaf Progetti pour Zanotta.

Das Sofa "Bohemien" ist ein Design
von Emaf Progetti für Zanotta.

Container furniture from the firm Montana.

Rangement de la marque Montana.

Containermöbel der Firma Montana.

Modular shelving "Soho",
by Emaf Progetti for Zanotta.

Étagère convertible "Soho",
de Emaf Progetti pour Zanotta.

Modulregal "Soho"
von Emaf Progetti für Zanotta.

Stalls "Tri-Symmetric". From Kagan New York
Collection. Bottom image, sofa "Rooby" from Leolux.

Tabourets "Tri-Symmetric". De Kagan New York
Collection. Image du bas, canapé "Rooby" de Leolux.

Hocker "Tri-Symmetric" von Kagan New York
Collection. Unten das Sofa "Rooby" von Leolux.

A group of shelves and container
furniture from Maisa.

Ensemble d'étagères et de
rangements de Maisa.

Regalsystem mit Containermöbeln
von Maisa.

Auxiliary table "Querubino" from Leolux.

Table d'appoint "Querubino" de Leolux.

Der Beistelltisch "Querubino" von Leolux.

Design for Use and Sergio Suchomel are the authors of the design for the shelving system "Joggle" from Magis.

Design for Use et Sergio Suchomel signent la création de l'étagère "Joggle", de Magis.

Design for Use und Sergio Suchomel zeichnen für das Design des Regals "Joggle" von Magis.

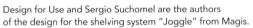

Sofa bed and puff upholstered in vivid colors in stripes from Innovation.

Canapé-lit et pouf à rayures de couleurs vives de Innovation.

Schlafsofa und gepolsterter Hocker mit Bezug in lebhaften Farben von Innovation.

"Meditation Pod" is a seat with evocative lines. A design from Steven Blaess for Edra.

"Meditation Pod" est un siège aux lignes suggestives. Il s'agit d'une création de Steven Blaess pour Edra.

"Meditation Pod" – ein Sitzmöbel mit suggestiver Linienführung. Das Design hat Steven Blaess für Edra erstellt.

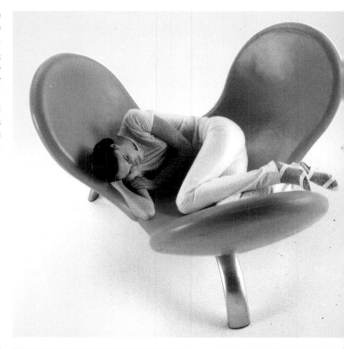

Tables "Brighella" designed by L. Arosio for Glas. On the right, proposal from the firm Maisa.

Tables "Brighella", créées par L. Arosio pour Glas. À droite, proposition de la marque Maisa.

Die Tische "Brighella", vom L. Arosio für Glas entworfen. Rechts ein Vorschlag der Firma Maisa.

Maisa proposes a combination
based on green tones.

Maisa propose une combinaison
basée sur des tons de verts.

Maisa schlägt eine in Grüntönen
gehaltene Kombination vor.

Container furniture "Morgana" with drawers in intense colors. From Lago.

Rangement "Morgana" à tiroirs colorés intenses. De Lago.

Containermöbel "Morgana" mit in kräftigen Farben gehaltenen Schubladen von Lage.

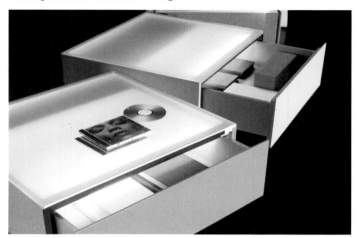

Mirco Pallecchi has created the armchair "Momma" for Giovannetti Collezioni d'Arrendamento.

Mirco Pallecchi a créé le fauteuil "Momma" pour Giovannetti Collezioni d'Arrendamento.

Mirco Pallecchi hat den Sessel "Momma" für Giovannetti Collezioni d'Arrendamento entworfen.

Cairoli and Donzelli are the authors of the design for the sofa "Reform" from Bodema.

Cairoli et Donzelli signent la création du canapé "Reform" de Bodema.

Cairoli und Donzelli zeichen für das Design des Sofas "Reform" von Bodema.

Sofa "Continental" from Perobell designed by Lievore, Altherr & Molina.

Canapé "Continental" de Perobell, créé par Lievore, Altherr & Molina.

Sofa "Continental" von Perobell, Design von Lievore, Altherr & Molina.

Zanotta presents the sofa "Bohemien",
designed by Emaf Progetti.

Zanotta présente le canapé "Bohemien",
créé par Emaf Progetti.

Zanotta präsentiert das Sofa "Bohemien",
Design von Emaf Progetti.

On the left, sideboards from Montis and from Klenk.

À gauche, buffets de Montis et de Klenk.

Büffets von Montis und von Klenk.

Easy chair "Rooby" from Leolux.

Fauteuil "Rooby" de Leolux.

Sessel "Rooby" von Leolux.

Chairs with colored backs
from Vibiemme.

Chaises à dossiers colorés
de Vibiemme.

Stühle mit farbigen Rückenlehnen
von Vibiemme.

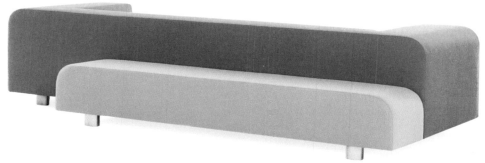

Top, seating group from Montis, designed
by Gijs Papavoine.

En haut, ensemble de sièges de Montis,
créé par Gijs Papavoine.

Oben eine Sitzgruppe von Montis,
Design von Gijs Papavoine.

Container furniture from the collection "Odeon" from Klenk.

Rangement de la collection "Odeon" de Klenk.

Containermöbel aus der Modellreihe "Odeon" von Klenk.

On the left, model "Acrobat", by J. Armgardt for
Styling. On the right, easy chair "Moon" designed
by F. Estela for Perobell.

À gauche, modèle "Acrobat", de J. Armgardt pour
Styling. À droite, fauteuil "Moon" créé par
F. Estela pour Perobell.

Links: Modell "Acrobat" von J. Armgardt für Styling.
Rechts der Sessel "Moon", Design von
F. Estela für Perobell.

On the left, sofa "Alfa" by Emaf Progetti for Zanotta.
On the right, "Sanctus" from Perobell, created by Diego Fortunato.

À gauche, canapé "Alfa" de Emaf Progetti pour Zanotta.
À droite, "Sanctus" de Perobell, créé par Diego Fortunato.

Links: Sofa "Alfa" von Emaf Progetti für Zanotta.
Rechts: "Sanctus" von Perobell, Design von Diego Fortunato.

"Agua" is a sofa with sinuous lines, designed by Diego Fortunato for Perobell.

"Agua" est un canapé aux lignes sinueuses, créé par Diego Fortunato pour Perobell.

"Agua" ist ein Sofa mit geschwungener Linienführung, Design von Diego Fortunato für Perobell.

Magazine rack "Karui"
from the firm Viccarbe.

Porte-revues "Karui"
de la marque Viccarbe.

Der Zeitungsständer "Karui"
von der Firma Viccarbe.

Left, easy chair "Isa" by A. Scarpitta and N. Delfinetti for Giovannetti. Middle, collection "Millenium" designed by Dalter for Andreu World. Right, Pablo Gironés has designed this carpet "Pop" from Gandía Blasco.

À gauche, fauteuil "Isa" de A. Scarpitta et N. Delfinetti pour Giovannetti. Au centre, collection "Millenium" créée par Dalter pour Andreu World. À droite, Pablo Gironés a créé le tapis "Pop", de Gandía Blasco.

Links, Sessel "Isa" von A. Scarpitta und N. Delfinetti für Giovannetti. Mitte: Modellreihe "Millenium", Design von Dalter für Andreu World. Rechts: Pablo Gironés hat für Gandía Blasco den Teppich "Pop" entworfen.

Original chaise-longue designed by
Flavia Alves de Souza. This is the
model "Pororoca" from Edra.

Chaise-longue originale créée
par Flavia Alves de Souza.
Il s'agit du modèle "Pororoca" de Edra.

Originelle, von Flavia Alves de Souza
entworfene Chaiselongue, es handelt
sich hier um das Modell "Pororoca"
von Edra.

Modular furniture from the collection "Kronos" by Ennio Arosio for Verardo.

Meubles convertibles de la collection "Kronos", de Ennio Arosio pour Verardo.

Modulmöbel aus der Serie "Kronos", von Ennio Arosio für Verardo entworfen.

Humberto and Fernando Campana are the creators
of "Anemone". From Edra.

Humberto et Fernando Campana sont les créateurs
de "Anemone". De Edra.

Humberto und Fernando Campana haben
"Anemone" entworfen. Hergestellt von Edra.

"Verde" and "Vermelha" are designs by H. and F. Campana for Edra.

"Verde" et "Vermelha" sont des créations de H. et F. Campana pour Edra.

"Verde" und "Vermelha" sind ein Design von H. und F. Campana für Edra.

The easy chair "Roly Poly" is produced in more
than 300 colors. By Guido Rosati for Giovannetti.

Le fauteuil "Roly Poly" est fabriqué dans une variété de
plus de 300 couleurs. De Guido Rosati pour Giovannetti.

Der Sessel "Roly Poly" wird in über 300 Farben angeboten.
Design von Guido Rosati für Giovannetti.

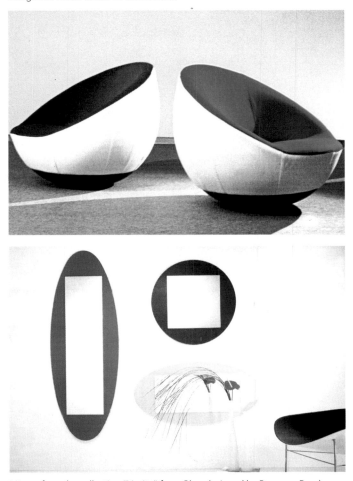

Mirrors from the collection "Vanity" from Glas, designed by Prospero Rasulo.

Miroirs de la collection 'Vanity" de Glas, crées par Prospero Rasulo.

Spiegel der Serie "Vanity" von Glas, Design von Prospero Rasulo.

Top image, sofa "Mr. Koala" by Nicola Adami and the piece of furniture "Olo" by Chi Wing Lo. From Giorgetti. Bottom, interior furnished with products from Edra.

Image du haut, canapé "Mr. Koala" de Nicola Adami et meuble "Olo" de Chi Wing Lo. De Giorgetti. En bas, meublé par Edra.

Oben: Sofa "Mr. Koala" von Nicola Adami und Möbelstück "Olo" von Chi Wing Lo für De Giorgetti entworfen. Unten: das Mobiliar stammt von Edra.

The sofa "Elysee" permits multiple combinations. From Christophe Pillet for Edra.

Le canapé "Elysee" permet d'obtenir de nombreuses combinaisons. De Christophe Pillet pour Edra.

Das Sofa "Elysee" kann in verschiedensten Kombinationen zusammengestellt werden. Design von Christophe Pillet für Edra.

The color and the innovative design are the predominant aspects of these interiors, furnished with products from Edra.

La couleur et le caractère innovateur dominent dans ces séjours, meublés par Edra.

Diese Interieurs zeichnen sich durch Farbe und innovatives Design aus, das Mobiliar stammt von Edra.

"Gala" is a design by Dalter for Andreu World.

Le canapé "Gala" est une création de Dalter pour Andreu World.

Das Sofa "Gala" ist ein Design von Dalter für Andreu World.

Enzo Mari is the author of the design "Delfina", produced by Robots.

Enzo Mari signe la création de "Delfina", fabriquée par Robots.

Enzo Mari zeichnet für das Design von "Delfina", hergestellt von Robots.

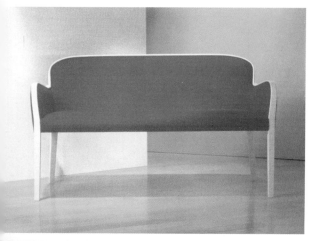

Sofas from the collection "Igirovaghi" from Giovannetti.

Canapés de la collection "Igirovaghi" de Giovannetti.

Sofas der Modellreihe "Igirovaghi" von Giovannetti.

"Bubba" is a design by A. Scarpitta and N. Delfinetti for Giovanetti. •

"Bubba" est une création de A. Scarpitta et N. Delfinetti pour Giovanetti.

"Bubba" ist ein Design von A. Scarpitta und N. Delfinetti für Giovanetti.

Philippe Starck is the author of "Minimum Table" and the chairs "Miss C.o.c.o.". From Cassina (photo: A. Ferrari).

Philippe Starck signe la création de la table "Minimun Table" et des chaises "Miss C.o.c.o.". De Cassina (photo: A. Ferrari).

Philippe Starck zeichnet für das Design des Tischs "Minimun Table" und der Stühle "Miss C.o.c.o.". Hergestellt von Cassina (Foto: A. Ferrari).

The chair "Myto high" is one of the new proposals from Leolux. Below on the left, chair "Eina" designed by Josep Lluscà for Enea.

La chaise "Myto high" est une des nouvelles propositions de Leolux. En bas à gauche, chaise "Eina" créée par Josep Lluscà pour Enea.

Der Stuhl "Myto high" gehört zu dem neuen Angebot von Leolux. Unten links der Stuhl "Eina", der von Josep Lluscà für Enea entworfen wurde.

Table "Dry" by Arquivolto and chairs "Anna" by J. Broente. From Bonaldo.

Table "Dry", de Arquivolto, et chaises "Anna", de J. Broente. De Bonaldo.

Tisch "Dry" von Arquivolto und Stühle "Anna" von J. Broente. Hergestellt von Bonaldo.

The model "Dune" is a design
from Misura Emme.

Le modèle "Dune" est une création
de Misura Emme.

Das Modell "Dune" ist ein Design
von Misura Emme.

"La Diva" is a design by
Jaime Bouzaglo for Andreu World

"La Diva" est une création de
Jaime Bouzaglo pour Andreu World.

"La Diva" ist ein Design von
Jaime Bouzaglo für Andreu World.

Chairs from the program "890" designed by Lievore, Altherr & Molina for Thonet.

Chaises de la gamme "890", créées par Lievore, Altherr & Molina pour Thonet.

Stühle aus der Modellreihe "890", Design von Lievore. Altherr & Molina für Thonet.

Sofa from the collection "Silver"
by Leonardo Volpi for Edra.

Canapé de la collection "Silver",
de Leonardo Volpi pour Edra.

Sofa der Modellreihe "Silver"
von Leonardo Volpi für Edra.

On the left, modular composition "Kronos", by Ennio
Arosio for Verardo. On the right, proposal from the
collection "Silver" by L. Volpi for Edra.

À gauche, composition convertible "Kronos", de Ennio
Arosio pour Verardo. À droite, proposition de la collection "Silver", de L. Volpi pour Edra.

Links: Modulsystem "Kronos" von Ennio Arosio für
Verardo. Rechts: Angebot aus der Serie "Silver" von L.
Volpi für Edra.

Simone Micheli is the author of the design "Nuca"
from Adrenalina.

Simone Micheli signe la création de "Nuda",
de Adrenalina.

S mone Micheli zeichnet für das Design von "Nuda"
für Adrenalina.

Bottom left, container system "Paessaggi italiani"
designed by Massimo Morozzi for Edra. Bottom right,
television stand from Porada designed by M.
Marconato and T. Zappa.

En bas à gauche, rangement "Paessaggi italiani", créé
par Massimo Morozzi pour Edra. En bas à droite, meuble
télévision de Porada, créé par M. Marconato et T. Zappa.

Unten links: Containersystem "Paessaggi italiani",
Design von Massimo Morozzi für Edra. Unten rechts:
TV-Möbel von Porada, Design von M. Marconato
und T. Zappa.

| Stimulating kitchens

Stalls "Yuyu"
by Stefano Giovannoni for Magis.

Tabourets "Yuyu",
de Stefano Giovannoni pour Magis.

Hocker "Yuyu"
von Stefano Giovannoni für Magis.

Des cuisines
stimulantes

Stimulierend
wirkende Küchen

Let's welcome kitchen furniture that seemingly wants to blend with the colors of strawberries, lemons, oranges, apples, mint, vegetables or with the color of the sky. Kitchens that are blue, orange, yellow, green, red... a colorist's setting to give rhythm to the heart of the home. Combining cupboards or lively colored details with wooden or metal surfaces is a wager destined for success. In contrast to the old, aseptic, monochromatic kitchens, endless esthetic possibilities arise to create our own personal spaces. Spaces in which storing food, preparing it and gathering with the family or friends around the table become more pleasant tasks, more comfortable and, above all, more entertaining.

Nous souhaitons la bienvenue aux meubles de cuisine qui semblent vouloir combiner les couleurs de la fraise, du citron, de l'orange, de la pomme, de la mente, des légumes ou du ciel. Des cuisines bleues, oranges, jaunes, vertes, rouges... un environnement coloré pour donner du rythme au cœur de la demeure. Combiner les armoires ou les détails de couleurs vives avec les surfaces de bois ou de métal est un pari dont le succès est assuré. Face aux anciennes cuisines monochromatiques et aseptiques, surgit une infinité de possibilités esthétiques pour créer des espaces à caractère personnel et unique. Des espaces dans lesquels le rangement et la préparation des aliments, les réunions en famille ou entre amis deviendront des activités plus faciles, plus agréables et surtout, plus amusantes.

Wir möchten Küchenmöbel vorstellen, bei deren Design die Farben der Erdbeeren, Zitronen, Orangen, Äpfel, Pfefferminze, Gemüsesorten oder des Himmels Pate gestanden haben. Blaue, orange, gelbe, grüne, rote Küchen – farbig gestaltete Räume, um so dem Herzstück der Wohnung Leben und Rhythmus zu verleihen. Werden in lebhaften Farben gehaltene Schränke oder Details mit Holz- oder Metallflächen kombiniert, ist das Ergebnis garantiert erfolgversprechend. Im Vergleich zu den alten, keimfrei wirkenden Küchen, in denen eine einzige Farbe vorherrschte, ergeben sich hier unzählige Möglichkeiten, einen Raum individuell zu gestalten.

There is an intense contrast of colors in this proposal from Bis Bis Imports Boston.

Intenses contrastes de couleurs pour cette proposition de Bis Bis Imports Boston.

Kräftiger Farbkontrast bei diesem Vorschlag von Bis Bis Imports Boston.

Alno proposes the installation of the water zone
in a central island.

Alno propose l'installation du système d'eau
courante centrale.

Alno schlägt vor, die Nasszone in einem zentral
gelegenen Bereich anzuordnen.

Modular furniture permits the creation of compositions
that adapt to different spaces. Model "Techno" from
Alno.

Les meubles convertibles permettent la création
de compositions qui s'adaptent à l'espace. Modèle
"Techno" de Alno.

Die Modulmöbel können an den zur Verfügung
stehenden Raum angepasst werden. Mode l "Techno"
von Alno.

Practical independent cupboards
from Alno.

Système pratique d'armoire et de
rangement indépendants, de Alno.

Praktischer Containerschrank
von Alno.

The wall has been covered with vitrified mosaic in various colors. The extractor hood is from Alno.

Le mur est recouvert d'une mosaïque de couleurs. La hotte est de Alno.

Die Wand ist mit Glasmosaik in verschiedenen Farben verkleidet. Die Abzugshaube ist von Alno.

Bottom left, shelves with incorporated lights from Alno. Bottom, a contemporary design for extractor hood from Alno.

En bas à gauche, étagères avec éclairage incorporé de Alno. Hotte aspirante de design contemporain, de Alno.

Unten links Regal mit Beleuchtung von Alno. Unten: Abzughaube in modernem Design von Alno.

The combination of blue and yellow creates a highly stimulating atmoshere. This is the model "Jet" from Alno.

La combinaison du bleu et du jaune crée une atmosphère très stimulante. Modèle "Jet" de Alno.

Mit der Farbkombination Blau-Gelb wirkt das Ambiente höchst anregend. Es handelt sich um das Modell "Jet" von Alno.

Zengiaro Associati is responsible for the design of this kitchen. It is the model "Joker" from Febal.

Zengiaro Associati est à l'origine de la création de cette cuisine. Modèle "Joker" de Febal.

Zengiaro Associati haben das Design dieser Küche übernommen. Gezeigt wird das Modell "Joker" von Febal.

The rounded profiles stand out on the model "Lemon", designed by Zengiaro Associati for Febal.

Les contours arrondis sont mis en valeur dans le modèle "Lemon", créé par Zengiaro Associati pour Febal.

Das Modell "Lemon" zeichnet sich durch seine abgerundeten Profile aus. Design von Zengiaro Associati für Febal.

An elegant composition designed by Zengiaro
Associati. This is the model "Flipper" from Febal.

Élégante composition créée par Zengiaro Associati.
Modèle "Flipper" de Febal.

Elegantes, von Zengiaro Associati entworfenes Ambiente.
Es handelt sich um das Modell "Flipper" von Febal.

On the left, the model "Lime" designed by Zengiaro Associati for Febal. Bottom image, detail of glass-fronted drawers from Alno.

À gauche, modèle "Lime", créé par Zengiaro Associati pour Febal. Image du bas, détail des tiroirs en verre de Alno.

Links: Modell "Lime", Design von Zengiaro Associati für Feba. Unteres Foto: Detail der Schubladen mit Fronten aus Glas, hergestellt von Alno.

Febal go for blue in this combination of the model "Orange".

Febal joue sur le bleu dans cette combinaison du modèle "Orange".

Bei dieser Kombination des Modells "Orange" setzt Febal auf die Farbe Blau.

This composition incluys a small breakfast bar. Model "Plan" from Alno.

Cette composition comprend un bar pour les petits-déjeunés. Modèle "Plan" de Alno.

Zu dieser Zusammenstellung gehört eine kleine Frühstückstheke. Modell "Plan" von Alno.

Composition from the series "Trend" from Nobilia.

Composition de la série "Trend" de Nobila.

Kombination aus der Serie "Trend" von Nobilia.

Luca Meda is the author of the design of this kitchen
with an avant-garde line. It is the model "Nuvola" from Dada.

Luca Meda signe la création de cette cuisine aux lignes d'avant-garde.
Il s'agit du modèle "Nuvola" de Dada.

Luca Meda zeichnet für das Design dieser in avantgardistischen
Linien gehaltenen Küche. Hier das Modell "Nuvola" von Dada.

On the left, composition from the program "Nuvola", from Dada.
On the right, a detail of the model "Vega" from Scavolini.

À gauche, composition de la gamme "Nuvola", de Dada.
À droite, détail du modèle "Vega" de Scavolini.

Oben links: Kombination aus der Modellreihe "Nuvola" von Dada.
Rechts: Detail des Models "Vega" von Scavolini.

Kitchen from the program "Vega", from Scavolini.

Cuisine de la gamme "Vega", de Scavolini.

Küche der Modellreihe "Vega" von Scavolini.

In this proposal from Alno, the co or of the natural wood combines perfectly with red.

Dans cette proposition de Alno, la couleur naturelle du bois est en parfaite harmonie avec le rouge.

Bei diesem Vorschlag von Alno wird die Farbe des Naturholzes auf ideale Weise mit der Farbe Rot kombiniert.

Rustic and contemporary styles fuse in this composition.
This is the model "Jet" from Alno.

Les styles rustiques et contemporains se complètent
dans cette composition. Modèle "Jet" de Alno.

Der rustikale und moderne Stil verschmelzen bei dieser Kombination
miteinander. Gezeigt wird das Modell "Jet" von Alno.

Luca Meda designed these two models from Dada: "Vela" and "Tempera".

Luca Meda est le créateur de ces deux modèles de Dada : "Vela" et "Tempera".

Luca Meda hat das Design dieser beiden Modelle von Dada "Vela" und "Tempera" übernommen.

A contemporary style composition from the program "Jet" from Alno.

Composition de style contemporain de la gamme "Jet" de Alno.

Moderne Kombination aus der Modellreihe "Jet" von Alno.

A well-conceived combination of materials in this kitchen with a layout in the form of an "L". From Alno.

Très belle combinaison de matériaux pour cette cuisine disposée en forme ce "L". De Alno.

In der L-förmig angeordneten Küche von Alno sind die verschiedenen Materialien geschickt miteinander kombiniert worden.

Proposal from Bis Bis Imports Boston.

Proposition de Bis Bis Imports Boston.

Vorschlag von Bis Bis Imports Boston.

Calligaris proposes a unified kitchen and dining room. The table is the model "Cube" and the chairs are the model "Sonica". Design from Arkiline.

Calligaris propose de réunir cuisine et salle à manger dans une même pièce. La table "Cube" et les chaises "Sonica", sont une création de Arkiline.

Von Calligaris wird die Zusammenlegung von Küche und Esszimmer vorgeschlagen. Der Tisch "Cube" und die Stühle "Sonica" sind ein Design von Arkiline.

The program "Onda" is a design from Studio Phoem for Febal.

La gamme "Onda" est une création de Studio Phoem pour Febal.

Die Modellreihe "Onda" ist ein Design von Studio Phoem für Febal.

Bathrooms with playful colors

Model "Pluvia" from Toscoquattro, with a Carrara marble surface.

Modèle "Pluvia" de Toscoquattro, avec surface en marbre de Carrara.

Modell "Pluvia" von Toscoquattro, mit Deckplatte aus Carrara-Marmor.

Des salles de bain et des jeux chromatiques

Badezimmer und Farbenspiele

The glass itself is full of colors, the walls are covered with gresite, tiles or paint of all tones imaginable, the furniture creates interesting combinations of materials and colors, the accessories see to introducing small explosions of color. The result is a place that transmits energy and helps us start the day in the right way. Colorful bathrooms are a goodbye to the sadness of old bathrooms, which were generally relegated to the smallest and darkest room of the house and where ideas of design and esthetics were conspicuous by their absence. Now the coloristic spirit has countless options at its disposal to completely change the aspect of this area, which has now become a sanctuary where we can give free rein to our imagination.

Du verre aux reflets colorés, des murs recouverts de grès, de faïence ou de peinture aux tons inimaginables, des meubles créant d'intéressantes combinaisons de matériaux et de couleurs, des accesoires se chargeant d'introduire de petites explosions de couleurs. Le résultat est un espace qui transmet de l'énergie et qui nous aide à nous lever du bon pied. Les salles de bain en couleurs sont un adieu à la tristesse des anciennes installations qui étaient généralement de petites pièces sombres où le design et l'esthétique brillaient par leur absence. Aujourd'hui, les esprits coloristes ont à leur disposition d'innombrables options leur permettant de changer entièrement l'aspect de cette pièce maintenent devenue un sanctuaire où nous pouvons laisser aller notre imagination.

Spiegel in verschiedenen Farben, mit Seidenleim erstellte Wände, Fliesen und Wände in allen nur vorstellbaren Farben, Möbel, bei denen Material und Farben auf interessante Weise kombiniert werden, und sonstige Accessoires sorgen dafür, dass kleine Farbexplosionen erzeugt werden. Das Ergebnis ist ein Raum, von dem Energie ausgeht, und der uns hilft, dem Tag optimistisch entgegenzusehen. Durch die farbig gestalteten Bäder werden die tristen, alten Badezimmer verdrängt, für die man normalerweise den kleinsten und dunkelsten Raum der ganzen Wohnung vorsah, und für die Design und Ästhetik ein Fremdwort waren. Sollen diese Räume farbig gestaltet werden, so kann man heute unter unzähligen Varianten wählen, um dem Badezimmer ein völlig neues Aussehen zu geben, denn es ist zu einem Ort geworden, bei dessen Gestaltung man seiner Phantasie freien Lauf lassen kann.

A glass washbasin, mode "Metropolis" from Toscoquattro.

Lavabo en verre du modèle "Metropolis" de Toscoquattro.

Waschbecken aus Glas aus der Modellreihe "Metropolis" von Toscoquattro.

Left, proposal from Bis Bis Imports Boston. Middle,
original bathtub from Bis Bis Imports Boston. Right,
a blue glass surface from Toscoquattro.

À gauche, proposition de Bis Bis Imports Boston.
Au centre, baignoire originale de Bis Bis Imports Boston.
A droite, surface en verre bleu de Toscoquattro.

Links: Vorschlag von Bis Bis Imports Boston. Mitte:
Originelle Badewanne von Bis Bis Imports Boston.
Rechts: Deckplatte aus blauem Glas von Toscoquattro.

A hanging washbasin from the series
"Podium" from Gama-Decor.

Lavabo mural de la série "Podium"
de Gama-Decor.

Aufgehängtes Waschbecken aus der
Modellreihe "Podium" von Gama-Decor.

Rounded forms in this proposal
from Bis Bis Imports Boston.

Formes arrondies pour cette proposition
de Bis Bis Imports Boston.

Abgerundete Formen bei diesem Vorschlag
von Bis Bis Imports Boston.

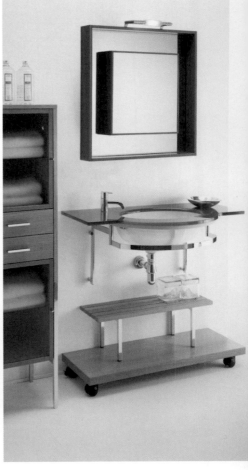

A composition from the program "Metropolis" from Toscoquattro.

Composition de la gamme "Metropolis" de Toscoquattro.

Zusammenstellung aus der Modellreihe "Metropolis" von Toscoquattro.

A proposal from
Bis Bis Import Boston.

Proposition de
Bis Bis Import Boston.

Vorschlag von
Bis Bis Import Boston.

Mirror "Eta" and washbasin
"Beta" designed by G. Landoni
for Nito.

Miroir "Eta" et lavabo "Beta",
créés par G. Landoni para Nito.

Spiegel "Eta" und Waschbecken
"Beta", entworfen
von G. Landoni für Nito.

Colored doors and natural wood
alternate in this composition
from Bis Bis Imports Boston.

Alternance de bois et de coleurs
pour les portes de cette composition de
Bis Bis Imports Boston.

Farbig gehaltene Türen und Holz werden
bei diesem Vorschlag von Bis Bis Imports
Boston miteinander kombiniert.

The faucets "Tip Tap" by Dornbracht are designs
from Sieger Design.

Le robinet "Tip Tap" de Dornbracht est une création
de Sieger Design.

Die Armaturen "Tip Tap" von Dornbracht sind
ein Design von Sieger Design.

A composition from the program "Breezy"
from Toscoquattro.

Composition de la gamme "Breezy"
ce Toscoquattro.

Zusammenstellung aus der Modellreihe "Breezy"
von Toscoquattro.

Model "Miro" from Rapsel designed
by Mauri and Studio Rapsel.

Modèle "Miro" de Rapsel,
créé par Mauri et Studio Rapsel.

Modell "Miro" von Rapsel,
entworfen von Mauri und Studio Rapsel

On the left, washbasin "Homage to Sheila", designed by Studio Rapsel and Gianluigi Landoni, and shower screen "Mimi", designed by Peter Büchele. All from Rapsel. Bottom image, model "Pluvia" from Toscoquattro.

À gauche, "Homage a Sheila", création de Studio Rapsel et Gianluigi Landoni, et porte de douche "Mimi", création de Peter Büchele. De Rapsel. Image du bas, modèle "Pluvia" de Toscoquattro.

Waschbecken "Homage a Sheila", Design von Studio Rapsel und Gianluigi Landoni und Duschwand "Mimi", Design von Peter Büchele. Alles hergestellt von Rapsel. Unteres Foto: Modell "Pluvia" von Toscoquattro.

Composition "1009" from Axia. Bottom, illustrated ceramic designed by Rubén Toledo. Model "Cuban Veranda" from Cerámica Bardelli.

Composition "1009" de Axia. En bas, céramique illustrée créée par Rubén Toledo, modèle "Cuban Veranda" de Cerámica Bardelli.

Modellreihe "1009" von Axia. Dekorkacheln, Design von Rubén Toledo, Ausführung "Cuban Veranda" von Cerámica Bardelli.

Stefano Cavazzana has designed
this furniture for the bathroom "Pop"
from Nito.

Stefano Cavazzana a créé les meubles
pour la salle de bain "Pop", de Nito.

Stefano Cavazzana hat die
Badezimmermöbel "Pop" für Nito
entworfen.

On the left, washbasins "Ninfo" designed by Ramón Úbeda
for Rapsel. On the right, Regia presents the washbasin
"Quadrotto". Design from Bruna Rapisarda.

À gauche, lavabos "Ninfo", créés par Ramón Úbeda pour
Rapsel. À droite, Regia présente le lavabo "Quadrotto",
une création de Bruna Rapisarda.

Links die von Ramón Úbeda für Rapsel entworfene
Waschbecken "Ninfo". Rechts stellt Regia das Waschbecken
"Quadrotto" vor, Design von Bruna Rapisarda.

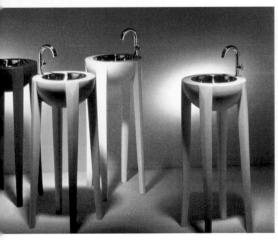

Model "Positano"
designed by Matteo Thun for Rapsel.

Modèle "Positano",
créé par Matteo Thun pour Rapsel.

Modell "Positano",
von Matteo Thun für Rapsel entworfen.

Washbasin and surface in one piece of stainless steel.
Composition "1022" from Axia.

Lavabo et surface d'une seule pièce en acier inoxydable.
Composition "1022" de Axia.

Waschbecken und Deckplatte aus einem
Stück in rostfreiem Stahl. Modellreihe "1022" von Axia.

| Colorful dreams

Chest of drawers "Intu" from
Niels Bendtsen for Montis.

Meuble à tiroirs "Intu",
de Niels Bendtsen pour Montis.

Kommode "Intu"
von Niels Bendtsen für Montis.

Des rêves en couleurs

Träume und Farben

We do not know if inducing sleep in a colorful environment is a sufficient guarantee to having beautiful dreams capable of recreating the rainbow, but what we can be assured of is that the introduction of colors into the bedroom stamps character onto this area. In this case, fabrics tend to be the main elements responsible for introducing harmonic shades of color: we find them on upholstered bed-heads, filtering the light that enters through the windows and, at the same time, pigmenting it with smooth color schemes, adorning the bed with intense contrasts that are full of life… In general, the object is to add visually impacting brushstrokes, which bring vitality to the whole room. Care must be taken, however, not to abuse and to avoid acute combinations, as they may make it difficult for us to get to sleep.

Wir können zwar nicht mit Sicherheit behaupten, dass Farben im Schlafzimmer wunderbare Träume bescheren, aber dass sie diesem Raum einen gewissen Charakter verleihen, darüber kann kein Zweifel bestehen. Die harmonisch wirkenden Farbtupfer werden in erster Linie von den verwandten Stoffen gesetzt. Wir denken da an die stoffverkleideten Kopfteile der Betten, Gardinen, die die Sonnenstrahlen filtern und den Raum in sanftes Licht hüllen und Bettwäsche in kräftigen Farben, die lebendige Kontraste herstellen … Es geht also darum, farbige Elemente mit großer visueller Ausdruckskraft vorzusehen, die dem ganzen Raum Leben verleihen. Es sollte jedoch darauf geachtet werden, nicht zu schrille Farbkombinationen zu wählen, damit wir von ihnen in unserem Ruhebedürfnis und beim Einschlafen nicht gestört werden.

Nous ne savons pas si le fait de trouver le sommeil dans une atmosphère colorée peut garantir de beaux rêves capables de recréer l'arc-en-ciel, mais ce que nous pouvons affirmer avec certitude, c'est que l'introduction des couleurs dans une chambre donnera du caractère à vos nuits. Dans ce cas, les principales responsables des nuances harmonieuses sont, en général, les tissus : ils peuvent couvrir la tête du lit, filtrer avec la lumière du l'exterieur et lui donner de douces tonalités colorées, recouvrir le lit d'intenses contrastes pleins de vie… Généralement, l'objectif est d'ajouter des coups de pinceaux d'un important impact visuel assez fort pour donner de la vitalité à la chambre. Mais il faut veiller à ne pas abuser des combinaisons pouvant résulter stridentes car elles risqueraient de déranger le calme nécessaire pour trouver le sommeil.

Chairs "Mafalda" by T. Colzani for Porada.
Chaises "Mafalda", de T. Colzani pour Porada.
Stühle "Mafalda", von T. Colzani für Porada.

Bedroom "Tao" from Misura Emme.

Chambre "Tao" de Misura Emme.

Schlafzimmer "Tao" von Misura Emme.

There is room for everything in this dressing room designed by Ennio Arosio for Mobileffe.

Chaque chose trouve sa place dans cette penderie créée par Ennio Arosio pour Mobileffe.

Alles hat in diesem von Ennio Arosio für Mobileffe entworfenen Ankleideraum seinen Platz.

Bedroom "Maggie" from Misura Emme.

Chambre "Maggie" de Misura Emme.

Schlafzimmer "Maggie" von Misura Emme.

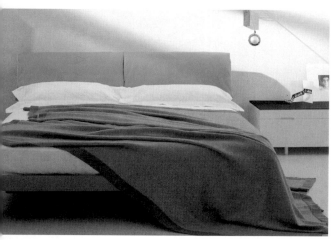

Model "Marlo" from A. and T. Scarpa for Molteni & C. Bottom image, program "Global System" from Lluís Codina for Perobell.

Modèle "Marlo" de A. et T. Scarpa pour Molteni & C. Image du bas, gamme "Global System" de Lluís Codina pour Perobell.

Modell "Marlo" von A. und T. Scarpa für Molteni & C. entworfen. Unten Modellreihe "Global System", von Lluís Codina für Perobell entworfen.

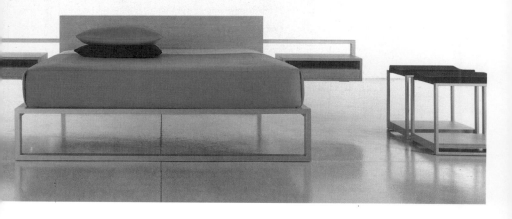

Two models from the collection
"Iron Line"™ from Domus.

Deux modèles de la collection
"Iron Line"™ de Domus.

Zwei Stücke aus der Modellreihe
"Iron Line"™ von Domus.

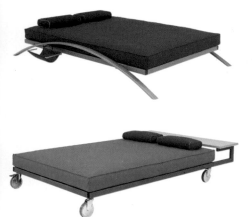

Top left, model "Zen" from Innovation. Bottom left, model "Wheel" from Innovation. On the right, chest of drawers "Street" from Klenk.

En haut à gauche, modèle "Zen" de Innovation. En bas à gauche, modèle "Wheel" de Innovation. À droite, commode "Street" de Klenk.

Oben links das Modell "Zen" von Innovation. Unten links das Modell "Wheel" von Innovation. Rechts die Kommode "Street" von Klenk.

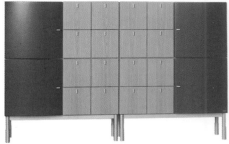

Bedroom from the program "Ross". Design from Ennio Arosio for Mobileffe.

Chambre de la gamme "Ross", création de Ennio Arosio pour Mobileffe.

Ein Schlafzimmer aus der Modellreihe "Ross", Design von Ennio Arosio für Mobileffe.

From left to right: bed "Douglas" and side tables "Rialto" from Paco Camus for Interi; "Gilda Pouf" from T. Colzani for Porada; sofa bed "Anfibio" from A. Becchi for Giovannetti.

De gauche à droite : lit "Douglas" et tables "Rialto", de Paco Camus pour Interi ; "Gilda Pouf" de T. Colzani pour Porada ; canapé-lit "Anfibio", de A. Becchi pour Giovannetti.

Von links nach rechts: Das Bett "Douglas" und die Nachttische "Rialto", von Paco Camus für Inter entworfen; "Gilda Pouf" von T. Colzani für Porada; Schlafsofa "Anfibio", von A. Becchi für Giovannetti entworfen.

On the left, composition from the series "Star". On the right, model "Tosca". Designed by Ennio Arosio for Verardo.

À gauche, composition de la série "Star". À droite, modèle "Tosca". Créé par Ennio Arosio pour Verardo.

Links eine Zusammenstellung aus der Modellreihe "Star". Rechts das Modell "Tosca". Design von Ennio Arosio für Verardo.

Marco Acerbis is the author of the design "Lys" from Acerbis International.

Marco Acerbis signe la création de "Lys", de Acerbis International.

Marco Acerbis zeichnet für das Design von "Lys", hergestellt von Acerbis International.

Bed "Deimos" designed by R. & S. Verardo, and aluminum side table "Braian". From Verardo.

Lit "Deimos, création de R. et S. Verardo, et table de nuit en aluminium "Braian". De Verardo.

Bett "Deimos, Design von R. und S. Verardo, und Nachttisch "Braian" aus Aluminium, hergestellt von Verardo.

"Invisible" is one of the latest
proposals from Zanotta
designed by I. Bride.

"Invisibile" est une des dernières
propositions de Zanotta,
création de I. Bride.

"Invisibile" ist einer der neusten
Vorschläge von Zanotta,
Design von I. Bride.

"Alfa" is a design by Emaf Progetti
for Zanotta.

"Alfa" est une création
de Emaf Progetti pour Zanotta.

"Alfa" ist ein Design
von Emaf Progetti für Zanotta.

Composition from the collection "Basic"
from Club 8 Company.

Composition de la collection "Basic"
de Club 8 Company.

Zusammenstellung aus der Modellreihe "Basic"
von Club 8 Company.

Model "Mill" from the collection TM L ne. From Domus.

Modèle "Mill" de la collection TM Line. De Domus.

Modell "Mill" der Modellreihe TM Line. von Domus.

Bedroom from the collection "Inzoni"
from Club 8 Company.

Chambre de la collection "Inzoni"
de Club 8 Company.

Schlafzimmer aus der Modellreihe "Inzoni"
von Club 8 Company.

Model "Paoletto" designed by G. Canavese for Methodo.

Modèle "Paoletto", création de G. Canavese pour Methodo.

Modell "Paoletto", Design von G. Canavese für Methodo.

| Lights and tones

Suspended lamp "Yoohoodoo"
from Ingo Maurer.

Plafonnier "Yoohoodoo",
de Ingo Maurer.

Hängelampe "Yoohoodoo"
von Ingo Maurer.

Des lumières et des tons

Licht und Farbtöne

According to Chromothera-py, a natural therapeutic technique that consists of activating the organism's defense mechanisms with the use of specific colors, many sensations and emotions vital to maintaining our essential and organic harmony have a lot to do with light and colors. Used properly, color can provoke positive psychological reactions on people. In this way, for example, red is used to stimulate blood circulation, against depression and melancholy; blue is used as a sedative and antibiotic or against insomnia and migraine; green as a painkiller and anti-inflammatory and against hypertension, etc. For this reason, each of us should choose the illumination that is most suitable to his or her character or state of mind, that which, in addition to decorating, makes us feel comfortable.

Selon la Chromothérapie, une technique thérapeutique naturelle consistant à activer les mécanismes de défense de l'organisme grâce à l'utilisation de couleurs bien définies, de nombreuses sensations et émotions essentielles à l'équilibre de notre harmonie organique et vitale sont liées à la lumière et aux couleurs. Si elle est utilisée correctement, la couleur peut provoquer des réactions psychologiques positives. De cette façon, le rouge est utilisé pour stimuler la circulation sanguine, contre la dépression et la mélancolie ; le bleu est employé comme calmant et antibiotique ou contre l'insomnie et les maux de tête ; le vert comme analgésique et anti-inflammatoire et contre l'hypertension, etc. C'est pour cette raison que chacun doit choisir la couleur qui convient à son caractère ou à son humeur, la couleur qui ne se limitera pas à décorer son univers, et qui pourra lui apporter le bien-être.

Laut der Chromotherapie, bei der es sich um eine Technik handelt, die darin besteht, den Abwehrmechnismus unseres Organismus durch den Einsatz bestimmter Farben zu aktivieren, haben viele zur Herstellung unseres inneren Gleichgewichts wichtige Gefühle und Emotionen mit Licht und Farben zu tun. Richtig eingesetzt, können durch Farben bei den Menschen auf psychologischer Ebene positive Reaktionen hervorgerufen werden. So wird zum Beispiel die Farbe Rot zur Anregung des Blutkreislaufes und zur Bekämpfung von Depressionen und Melancholie zu Hilfe genommen; dem Blau wird eine beruhigende und antibiotische Wirkung zugeschrieben und gleichzeitig wird es bei Schlaflosigkeit und hartnäckigem Kopfschmerz verwandt; und Grün wird als schmerzstillendes und entzündungshemmendes Mittel als auch gegen Bluthochdruck eingesetzt. Jeder muß also Farben und Beleuchtung wählen, die am ehesten seinem Charakter oder Seelenzustand entsprechen. Sie sind nicht nur Teil der Innenausstattung geworden, sondern tragen auch wesentlich zu unserem Wohlbefinden bei.

Suspended lamp "Ilde" designed by David Abad for Dab.

Plafonnier "Ilde", créée par David Abad pour Dab.

Lampe "Ilde", Ausführung als Tisch- und Stehlampe. Design von David Abad für Dab.

From left to right: "Relax" by Dafne Koz; two versions of "Colour" by R. Giovanetti. All from Fontana Arte.

De gauche à droite: "Relax" de Dafne Koz ; deux versions de "Colour" de R. Giovanetti. Ensemble de Fontana Arte.

Von links nach rechts: "Relax" von Dafne Koz; zwei Ausführungen von "Colour" von R. Giovanetti. Alle Modelle hergestellt von Fontana Arte.

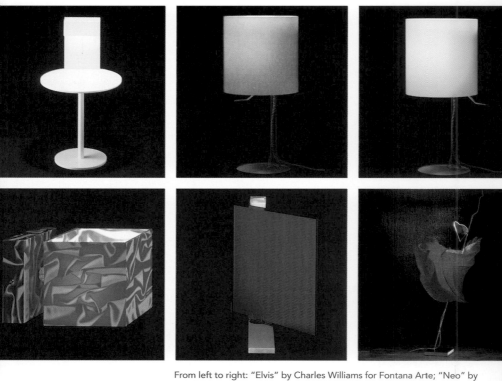

From left to right: "Elvis" by Charles Williams for Fontana Arte; "Neo" by L. Calvi, M. Merlini and C. Moya for Fontana Arte; "Kokoro" from Ingo Maurer.

De gauche à droite : "Elvis", de Charles Williams pour Fontana Arte ; "Neo", de L. Calvi, M. Merlini et C. Moya pour Fontana Arte ; "Kokoro", de Ingo Maurer.

Von links nach rechts: "Elvis" von Charles Williams für Fontana Arte; "Neo" von L. Calvi, M. Merlini und C. Moya für Fontana Arte; "Kokoro" von Ingo Maurer.

Table lamps "Elisabeth Glase" from Domus.

Lampes de table "Elisabeth Glase" de Domus.

Tischlampen "Elisabeth Glase" von Domus.

"Ilde" in its table and standard lamp versions. Designed by David Abad for Dab.

Lampe "Ilde" version lampe de table et version lampadaire. Création de David Abad pour Dab.

Tischlampe "Ilde", entworfen von David Abad für Dab.

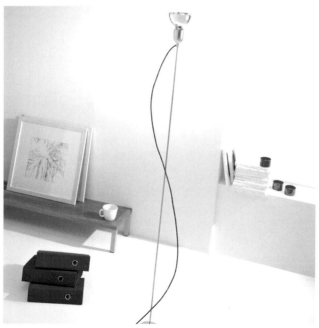

"One from the Heart" is one of the magnificent creations from Ingo Maurer.

"One from the Heart" est une des magnifiques créations de Ingo Maurer.

"One from the Heart" gehört zu den wunderbaren Entwürfen von Ingo Maurer.

The lamp "Hara" is presented in different colors. It is a design by Carlotta de Bevilacqua for Artemide.

La lampe "Hara" est présentée dans des versions de différentes couleurs. Il s'agit d'une création de Carlotta de Bevilacqua pour Artemide.

Die Lampe "Hara" präsentiert sich mit in verschiedenen Farben. Entworfen von "Braian"Carlotta de Bevilacqua für Artemide.

Innovation propose these amusing standard lamps: from left to right, "Cross", "Shine", "Glow" and "Stripe".

Innovation propose ces amusants lampadaires : de gauche à droite, "Cross", "Shine", "Glow" et "Stripe".

Innovation bietet diese lustigen Stehlampen an. Von links nach rechts: "Cross", "Shine", "Glow" und "Stripe".

From top to bottom: "Duplex" by
C. Tamborini; "Elvis" by C. Williams;
"Sag" by C. Tamborini. All from
Fontana Arte.

De haut en bas : "Duplex", de C.
Tamborini ; "Elvis", de C. Williams ;
"Sag", de C. Tamborini. Ensemble
de Fontana Arte.

Von oben nach unten: "Duplex" von
C. Tamborini; "Elvis" von C.
Williams; "Sag" von C. Tamborini.
Alle Lampen werden von Fontana
Arte angeboten.

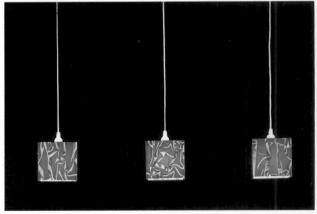

On the right, standard lamp
"Ying Flu" designed by
Carlotta Bevilacqua for Artemide.

À droite, lampadaire "Ying Flu",
créé par Carlotta Bevilacqua
pour Artemide.

Stehlampe "Ying Flu",
Design von Carlotta Bevilacqua
für Artemide.

Standard lamp "Sag" by Carlo Tamborini
for Fontana Arte.

Lampadaire "Sag", de Carlo Tamborini
pour Fontana Arte.

Stehlampe "Sag" von Carlo Tamborini
für Fontana Arte.

Two versions of the lamp "Neo" by L. Calvi,
M. Merlini and C. Moya for Fontana Arte.

Deux versions de la lampe "Neo", de L. Calvi,
M. Merlini et C. Moya pour Fontana Arte.

Zwei Modelle der Lampe "Neo" von L. Calvi,
M. Merlini und C. Moya für Fontana Arte.

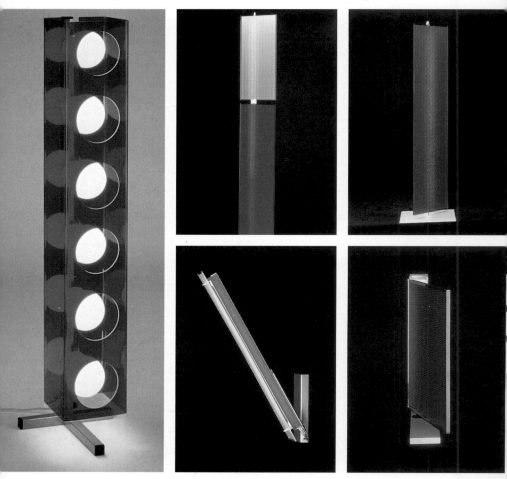

On the left, wall lamp "One" by L. Calvi, M. Merlini and C. Moya. On the right, "Neo"
in its wall lamp version. From Fontana Arte.

À gauche, applique "One", de L. Calvi, M. Merlini et C. Moya. À droite "Neo" en version applique. De Fontana Arte.

Links: Wandlampe "One" von L. Calvi, M. Merlini und C. Moya. Rechts: "Neo"
als Wandlampe. Hergestellt von Fontana Arte.

"Románica" is a design by Mariví Calvo for Luzifer.

"Románica" est une création de Mariví Calvo pour Luzifer.

"Románica" ist ein Design von Mariví Calvo für Luzifer.

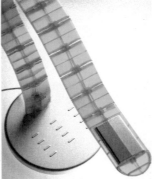

On the left, "Tatiana" from Estudi de Disseny Blanc for Tramo. Middle, "Soon" from Tobias Grau. Right, Artemide presents "Brezza Note" designed by Andrea Anastasio.

À gauche, "Tatiana" de Estudi de Disseny Blanc pour Tramo. Au centre, "Soon" de Tobias Grau. À droite, Artemide présente "Brezza Note", création de Andrea Anastasio.

Links: "Tatiana", von Estudi de Disseny Blanc für Tramo entworfen. Mitte: "Soon" von Tobias Grau. Rechts: Artemide präsentiert "Brezza Note", Design von Andrea Anastasio.

"Trípode" from Santa & Cole (photo: Carmen Masiá).

"Trípode" de Santa & Cole (photo : Carmen Masiá).

"Trípode" von Santa & Cole (Foto: Carmen Masiá).

"Bicho" from Pascal Frot for Luzifer (collection Luzitroniks).

"Bicho" de Pascal Frot pour Luzifer (collection Luzitroniks).

"Bicho" von Pascal Frot für Luzifer (Modellreihe Luzitroniks).

From left to right: "Domine" from X. Mariscal for Santa & Cole (photo: Carmen Masia); "Venezia" from Marcello Furlan for Itre; "Metacolor" from Ernesto Gismondi for Artemide.

De gauche à droite : "Domine" de X. Mariscal pour Santa & Cole (photo : Carmen Masia) ; "Venezia" de Marcello Furlan pour Itre; "Metacolor" de Ernesto Gismondi pour Artemide.

Von links nach rechts: "Domine", von X. Mariscal für Santa & Cole entworfen (Foto: Carmen Masia); "Venezia" von Marcello Furlan für Itre entworfen; "Metacolor" von Ernesto Gismondi für Artemide.

ECOLOGICAL AND NATURAL
The colors and raw materials of the earth

All day running around town. Trying not to fail in our attempt to get to the office or make our professional dreams come true. A traffic jam holds us up while we are engulfed by gray asphalt, contamination and the deafening noise of the horns of the more impatient. And upon opening the front door, you need to be received by a breath of fresh air, a remnant of nature that makes you feel alive.

For those who feel this need, this is the style that best suits them. Harmonious atmospheres, ordered and free of obstruction, where everything has a place.

The dominating colors are neutrals or those taken directly from nature: the white of pure light, the yellow of a ray from the sun, ocher, the grays and browns of the ground, the greens of plants. These are the colors of life, introduced into the home to imitate, as far as possible, the color schemes we find in nature.

As with the colors, the materials that we find in these environments also try to eliminate contrivance as far as can be done and are obtained, basically, from raw materials that are given to us by nature and the animal kingdom: wood, osier, rattan, stone, linen, cotton, silk, wool, leather, etc.

Textures are also given a special importance for their innate capacity to transmit sensations. The feel of untreated wood, the smoothness of a few linen sheets, the roughness of a stone surface, the delicate rustle of a few silk cushions, the pleasant harshness of a rug or fitted carpet made of coconut fiber... all of this is able to connect us with nature, filling our homes with freshness.

This tendency to incorporate natural elements into the home is related, in a way, to the manner some oriental philosophies understand life, that emphasizes contact with nature as something indispensable in our lives, starting with a indispensable respect for what we find around us.

Here, in the West, our main objective is to feel at home with everything that surrounds us: the comfort and well being with which an intelligently distributed space provides us combined with a reasonable election of furniture and complements that all together transmits harmony and calmness.

This way of understanding decoration implies a return to authenticity, to that which has roots, as opposed to the dehumanization and the excess of contrivance that extends over large cities. It could be said that this tendency has arisen as a result of present worries over what we eat, due to the adoption of basically vegetarian diets, and due to a search for enlightenment in the religions or philosophies of oriental origins, such as Buddhism or Zen.

Equilibrium is what we are trying to achieve. To live in a space that transmits peacefulness and conveys nature, making us feel alive in our homes.

NATURELLES ET ECOLOGIQUES
Les couleurs et les matériaux de la terre

Nous courons toute la journée à travers la ville, pour arriver à l'heure au bureau et pouvoir acomplir nos rêves professionnels. Mais nous voilà bloqués dans un embouteillage et nous nous retrouvons entourés d'asphalte, de pollution et du bruit assourdissant du klaxons des conducteurs les plus impatients. Lorsque nous ouvrons la porte de notre maison, nous avons besoin d'un souffle d'air frais, d'un morceau de nature qui nous sentir vivants.

Pour les personnes qui ressentent ce besoin, voici le style qui les définira le mieux. Des contextes harmonieuses, spacieux et ordonnés, où chaque élément trouvera sa place.

Les couleurs dominantes sont les couleurs neutres ou directement tirée de la nature : le blanc de la lumière pure, les jaunes des rayons du soleil, les ocres, les pourpres et les marrons de la terre, les verts des plantes. Ce sont les couleurs de la vie que nous introduisons dans notre demeure pour imiter, dans la mesure du possible, les tonalités qui se trouvent dans la nature.

Tout comme les couleurs, les matériaux qui se trouvent dans ce genre de contextes tentent d'éliminer le plus grand nombre possible d'artifices et offrent essentiellement des matières premières présentes dans le monde naturel et animal : le bois, l'osier, le ratanhia, la pierre, le lin, le coton, la soie, la laine, la peau...

Les textures ont également une importance spéciale de par leur capacité à transmettre es sensations. Le touché de la matière à l'état nature , la douceur des draps de lin, la rugosité de la surface d'une pierre, le délicat froissement des coussins de soie, l'agréable rudesse d'un tapis ou d'une moquette en fibre de coco... tout ceci nous permet d'entrer en contact avec la nature et de remplir notre maison de fraîcheur.

Cette tendance à incorporer des éléments naturels dans la demeure est liée, d'une certaine manière, à des philosophies orientales qui mettent en avant le contact avec la nature et le présentent comme un élément indispensable à une certain approche de la vie selon laquelle il nous fait respecter tout ce qui nous entoure.

Ici, en Occident, notre principal objectif, c'est de nous sentir bien avec notre environnement : la commodité et le bien-être que nous fournit une distribution intelligente associée à des meubles et des compléments habilement choisis, formeront un ensemble qui nous transmettra harmonie et tranquillité.

Cette façon de comprendre la décoration suppose un retour à l'authentique, aux racines, pour faire face à la déshumanisation et à l'excès d'artifices des grandes villes. On pourrait dire que cette tendance est liée à la préoccupation que nous avons maintenant pour ce que nous mangeons, pour les régimes essentiellement végétariens, pour la quête de l'inspiration vitale dans les religions ou philosophies orientales comme le Bouddhisme ou le Zen

L'équilibre est le résultat que nous voulons obtenir : vivre dans un espace transmettant la tranquillité et nous plongeant dans la beauté de la nature, pour nous faire sentir vivants dans notre propre demeure.

Naturbezogene und Ökologische Interieurs
Farben und der Natur entliehene Elemente

Den ganzen Tag hetzen wir durch die Stadt, versuchen zu überleben, unser Büro zu erreichen oder unsere beruflichen Träume Realität werden zu lassen. Wir bleiben in einem Stau stecken, umgeben von grauem Asphalt sind wir der Luftverpestung und dem ohrenbetäubenden Hupen der ungeduldigen Autofahrer ausgesetzt. Wenn man dann endlich zu Hause ankommt und die Tür aufschließt, sollte uns ein frischer Luftzug empfangen, ein Stück Natur, durch das unsere Lebensgeister wiederbelebt werden.

Alle, die dieses Bedürfnis verspüren, werden sich mit diesem Stil am besten identifizieren können. Harmonisches Interieur, übersichtlich und aufgeräumt, wo jedes Ding seinen Platz hat.

Die Räume werden vorzugsweise in neutralen oder der Natur entliehenen Farbtönen gehalten: Weiß des puren Lichts, Gelb der Sonnenstrahlen, graue und braune Erdfarben und Grüntöne der Pflanzen. Es sind die Farben, die Leben symbolisieren und in unseren Wohnbereich übernommen werden, um die in der Natur vorkommenden Farbtöne bis zu einem gewissen Grad auf unsere Einrichtung zu übertragen.

Ebenso wie bei den Farben, legt man auch bei den für diese Interieurs verwandten Materialien Wert darauf, möglichst auf alles Künstliche zu verzichten und greift deshalb auf Rohstoffe zurück, die uns von der Natur angeboten werden: Holz, Weide, Rattan, Stein, Leinen, Baumwolle, Seide, Wolle, Leder etc.

Da Texturen dazu beitragen können, Sinneseindrücke zu übermitteln, kommt ihnen eine ganz besondere Bedeutung zu. Das Berühren eines unbehandelten Holzes, das weiche Gewebe eines Leinenlakens, die unebene Oberfläche eines Steins, das feine Rascheln eines Seidenkissens, die angenehme Rauhigkeit eines Teppichs oder einer Auslegware aus Kokosfaser, ... das alles vermag, dass wir uns der Natur verbundener fühlen und unser Haus Frische ausstrahlt.

Diese Tendenz, Elemente aus der Natur in den Wohnbereich aufzunehmen, ist in gewisser Weise in Zusammenhang mit der von einigen orientalischen Philosophien beschriebenen Lebensweise zu sehen. Diese betrachten den Kontakt mit der Natur als etwas Essentielles, das aus unserem Lebensbereich nicht wegzudenken ist. Voraussetzung hierfür ist, dass wir Respekt für alles empfinden, was uns in der Natur umgibt.

Hier, in unserer westlichen Welt, sind wir in erster Linie darauf ausgerichtet, im Einklang mit den uns umgebenden Dingen zu leben. Eine auf intelligente Weise vorgenommene Raumaufteilung soll uns Bequemlichkeit und Wohlbefinden verschaffen. Mit einer geschickten Auswahl der entsprechenden Möbel und Accessoires erreichen wir, daß unser Wohnbereich Harmonie und Ruhe ausstrahlt.

Bei der Innenausstattung diese Kriterien zugrundezulegen, bedeutet eine Rückkehr zu den authentischen, den ursprünglichen Werten, zu dem, was tief verwurzelt ist – im Gegensatz zu der in den Großstädten zunehmenden Dehumanisation und Überbewertung alles Künstlichen. Diese Tendenz drückt sich sicherlich auch darin aus, daß die Ernährung heute für uns zu einem wichtigen Thema geworden ist, und sich immer mehr Leute für die vegetarianische Küche entscheiden. Hinzu kommt die Suche nach Inspiration für unser Leben, wie sie von orientalischen Religionen oder Philosophien – wie z.B. dem Budismus oder dem Zen – versprochen werden.

Wir sind darauf ausgerichtet, ein ausgewogenes Interieur herzustellen. Wir möchten in Räumen leben, die uns Ruhe vermitteln, uns in die Natur zurückversetzen und uns so ein gutes Lebensgefühl in unserem Haus vermitteln.

Nature in living and dining rooms

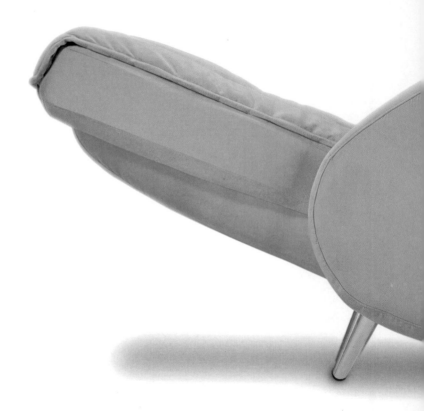

Massage armchair "Mounamar" from Keyton.

Fauteuil de massage "Mounamar", de Keyton.

Massagesessel "Mounamar" von Keyton.

La nature dans les salons et les salles à manger

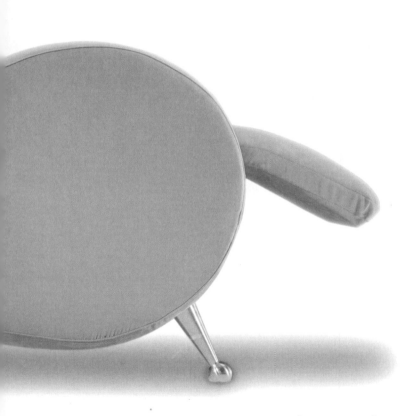

Natur und Wohn- und Esszimmer

In environments such as these, wood takes the leading role, in its different color schemes and kinds: cherry, beech, pine, oak, wengé, etc., it is transformed into shelving, tables, chairs and into the structures of seats and sofas, stamping its particular qualities on these living and dining rooms. The furniture and wooden objects accompany with their natural and luminous colors, principally browns, oranges, yellows and whites, the greenness of the plants used as a backdrop. One flees from artificial materials or from those that could alter the ecological balance, since the objective is to enter into fellowship with nature, enjoy it, taste it, respect it and, why not, let's take advantage of it as well, using its capacity to transmit harmony, balance and, principally, comfort to the maximum in our living and dining rooms.

In diesen Räumen dominiert Holz in seinen verschiedensten Farben und Klassen: Kirschbaum, Buche, Pinie, Eiche, Wengé etc., das zu Regalen, Tischen, Stühlen und für Sessel- und Sofauntergestelle verarbeitet wird. Ihre jeweiligen Eigenschaften tragen dazu bei, diesen Wohn– und Esszimmern ihren besonderen Charakter zu geben. Für die Möbel und Objekte werden lichte Naturfarben vorgesehen, vorzugsweise Braun–, Orange– und Gelbtöne sowie Weiß, damit sie einen guten Kontrast zu der Kulisse der Grünpflanzen bilden. Da beabsichtigt wird, einen Kontakt mit der Natur herzustellen, sie zu genießen und gleichzeitig zu respektieren, verzichtet man auf die Verwendung von Kunststoffen oder Materialien, die das ökologische Gleichgewicht stören könnten. Gleichzeitig nutzen wir die Natur aber auch zu unseren Zwecken, wenn wir versuchen, mit ihr Harmonie, Ausgeglichenheit und vor allen Dingen Wohlbefinden in unsere Räume zu bringen.

Le bois est le rotagoniste de ce type de contexte, avec ses différentes tonalités et ses différentes classes : le cerisier, le hêtre, le pin, le chêne, le wengé, etc., se transforment en étagères, en tables, en chaises, en structures de fauteuils ou de canapés, mettant en valeur leurs propriétés respectives dans les salons et les salles à manger. Les meubles et les objets en bois sont accompagnés de couleurs naturelles et lumineuses, comme les bruns, les orangés, les jaunes et les blancs, avec pour toile de fond, la couleur verte des plantes. Les matériaux artificiels, ou ceux qui pourraient altérer l'équilibre écologique, ont été mis de côté, car le but est d'entrer en communion avec la nature, de la savourer, de la respecter et, pourquoi pas, de l'utiliser en mettant en évidence, dans nos salons et nos salles à manger, sa capacité à transmettre l'harmonie, l'équilibre et le bien-être.

Easy chair "Savoy" by Nancy Robbins for Andreu World.

Fauteuil "Savoy" de Nancy Robbins pour Andreu World.

Sessel "Savoy" von Nancy Robbins für Andreu World.

Composition in natural tones
from the firm Montis.

Composition aux tons naturels
de la marque Montis.

In Naturfarben gehaltene
Zusammenstellung von der
Firma Montis

Model "Sit on lounge"
from Lambert.

Modèle "Sit on lounge"
de Lambert.

Modell "Sit on lounge"
von Lambert.

On the left, dining room set "Milano" from Lambert.
On the right, sofa "Maui" from Vincent Sheppard.

À gauche, ensemble salle à manger "Milano"
de Lambert. À croite, canapé "Maui"
de Vincent Sheppard.

Links: Esszimmer "Milano" von Lambert.
Rechts: das Scfa "Maui" von Vincent Sheppard.

Proposal for dining room from Misura Emme.
Model "Mallu".

Proposition de salle à manger de Misura Emme,
modèle "Mallu".

Vorschlag für ein Esszimmer von Misura Emme,
Modell "Mallu".

Chairs with armrests "Sydney" from Vincent Sheppard.

Chaises avec accoudoirs "Sydney", de Vincent Sheppard.

Stühle "Sydney" mit Armlehnen von Vincent Sheppard.

Table "Plano" designed by M. Marconato and T. Zappa for Porada.

Table "Plano", créée par M. Marconato et T. Zappa pour Porada.

Tisch "Plano", Design von M. Marconato und T. Zappa für Porada.

Giulio Dalto has designed the modular composition "Millennium" for Rattan Wood.

Giulio Dalto a créé la composition convertible "Millennium" pour Rattan Wood.

Giulio Dalto hat das Modulsystem "Millennium" für Rattan Wood entworfen.

Composition "Tenderness" from Roche Bobois.

Composition "Tenderness" de Roche Bobois.

Die Modellreihe "Tenderness" von Roche Bobois.

Top image, console "Millennium" by G. Dalto for Rattan Wood. Bottom, computer table from Nils Holger Moorman.

Image du haut, console "Millennium" de G. Dalto pour Rattan Wood. En bas, table pour ordinateur de Nils Holger Moorman.

Oben Konsole "Millennium" von G. Dalto für Rattan Wood. Unten: Computertisch von Nils Holger Moorman.

Top image, composition from the program "Odeon" from klenk. Bottom, sofa "Stanhope" from Lambert.

Image du haut, composition de la gamme "Odeon" de klenk. En bas, canapé "Stanhope" de Lambert.

Oben: Zusammenstellung aus der Modellreihe "Odeon" von klenk. Unten: Sofa "Stanhope" von Lambert.

Sofas "Svevo" designed
by Giulio Dalto for Rattan Wood.

Canapés "Svevo" créés
par Giulio Dalto pour Rattan Wood.

Scfas "Svevo", Design
von Giulio Dalto für Rattan Wood.

Composition from the program
"Quatro" from Organica.

Composition de la gamme
"Quatro" de Organica.

Zusammenstellung aus der
Modellreihe "Quatro" von Organica.

Table "Tape" with acid etched top, lacquered in white.
Designed by M. Marconato and T. Zappa for Porada.

Table "Tape" en acier laqué blanc avec plateau en verre.
Créée par M. Marconato et T. Zappa pour Porada.

Der Tisch "Tape" mit weißlackierter Glasplatte.
Von M. Marconato und T. Zappa für Porada entworfen.

On the left, table "Millennium"
by G. Dalto for Rattan Wood.
On the right, mirror "Oblio"
by P. Salvadé for Porada.

À gauche, table "Millennium"
de G. Dalto pour Rattan Wood.
À droite, miroir "Oblio",
de P. Salvadé pour Porada.

Links: Tisch "Millennium"
von G. Dalto für Rattan Wood.
Rechts: Spiegel "Oblio"
von P. Salvadé für Porada.

On the following page, easy chairs "Lineal" from Bonestil.

Sur la page suivante, fauteuils "Lineal" de Bonestil.

Auf der nachfolgenden Seite der Sessel "Lineal"
von Bonesti.

Top image, composition from the collection "Caleidos" from Studio Opera Work in Progress for Insa. On the left, table from the series "Giro" from Rafemar.

Image du haut, composition de la collection "Caleidos", de Studio Opera Work in Progress pour Insa. À gauche, table de la série "Giro" de Rafemar.

Oben: Zusammenstellung aus der Modellreihe "Caleidos" von Studio Opera Work in Progress für Insa. Links: Tisch aus der Serie "Giro" von Rafemar.

On the following page, center table from "In Linea" de Rafemar.

Sur la page suivante, table basse "In Linea" de Rafemar.

Auf der nächsten Seite: Tisch "In Linea" von Rafemar.

Table "Aura" from Rafemar.

Table "Aura" de Rafemar.

Tisch "Aura" von Rafemar.

Furniture from the collection "Ampolla" from Lago.

Meubles de la collection "Ampolla" de Lago.

Möbel aus der Modellreihe "Ampolla" von Lago.

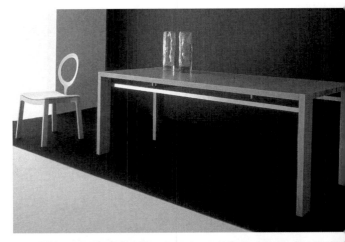

On the left, table "Max" from Rafemar. On the right, bookcase "Crossline" from the group Tissetanta.

À gauche, table "Max" de Rafemar. À droite, bibliothèque "Crossline" du groupe Tissetanta.

Links: Tisch "Max" von Rafemar. Rechts: Regal "Crossline" der Gruppe Tissetanta.

"Metropolis" is a spectacular modular bookcase
from the group Tissetanta.

"Metropolis" est une superbe bibliothèque convertible,
du groupe Tissetanta.

"Metropolis" – ein aufsehenerregendes, aus Modulen
zusammengestelltes Regal der Gruppe Tissetanta.

Container system "505 Cd"
by Luca Meda for Molteni & C.

Rangement "505 Cd",
de Luca Meda pour Molteni & C.

Containersystem "505 Cd"
von Luca Meda für Molteni & C.

Modular bookcase "Teca" by E.
Tonucci, and divan "Sigmund" by
Enzo Mari. Produced by Triangolo.

Bibliothèque "Teca", de E. Tonucci,
et divan "Sigmund", de Enzo Mari.
Fabriqués par Triangolo.

Modulregal "Teca" von E. Tonucci
und Diwan "Sigmund" von Enzo
Mari. Hergestellt von Triangolo.

Composition "Oblio" design by
P. Salvadé for Porada.

Composition "Oblio", création de
P. Salvadé pour Porada.

Zusammenstellung "Oblio",
Design von P. Salvadé für Porada.

Modular Composition from the
program "Atres" from Arlex.

Composition convertible de la
gamme "Atres" de Arlex.

Zusammenstellung von Modulen aus
der Modellreihe "Atres" von Arlex.

Chest of drawers from the program "Atres" from Arlex.

Commode de la gamme "Atres" de Arlex.

Kommode aus der Modellreihe "Atres" von Arlex.

On the left, proposal from Bis Bis Imports Boston.
On the right, container furniture from the program
"Atres" from Arlex.

À gauche, proposition de Bis Bis Imports Boston.
À droite, rangement de la gamme "Atres" de Arlex.

Links: Vorschlag von Bis Bis Imports Boston. Rechts:
Containermöbel aus der Modellreihe "Atres" von Arlex.

Container system "505 Cd"
contrived by Luca Meda for Molteni & C.

Rangement "505 Cd",
sur une idée de Luca Meda pour Molteni & C.

Containersystem "505 Cd",
von Luca Meda für Molteni & C entworfen.

On the following page,
dining room set "Ballara"
from Trip-Trap Denmark.

Sur la page suivante,
ensemble salle à manger "Ballara"
de Trip-Trap Denmark.

Auf der nächsten Seite:
Esszimmer "Ballara"
von Trip-Trap Denmark.

On the left, composition
"Columbus" from Trip-Trap
Denmark. On the right, bookcase
"Wall to Wall" from Poliform.

À gauche, composition
"Columbus" de Trip-Trap Denmark.
À droite, bibliothèque
"Wall to Wall" de Poliform.

Zusammenstellung "Columbus"
von Trip-Trap Denmark. Rechts:
Bücherregal "Wall to Wall"
von Poliform.

Proposal for a terrace dining area from Trip-Trap Denmark. On the following page, chaise-longue "2000" designed by Mauro Lipparini for Rolf Benz.

Proposition de salle à manger pour terrasse de Trip-Trap Denmark. Sur la page suivante, chaise-longue "2000" créée par Mauro Lipparini pour Rolf Benz.

Vorschlag für eine Essgruppe auf der Terrasse von Trip-Trap Denmark. Auf der nächsten Seite: Die Chaiselongue "2000", von Mauro Lipparini für Rolf Benz entworfen.

Luca Meda is the author of the design "Ho" from Molteni & C.

Luca Meda signe la création de "Ho" de Molteni & C.

Luca Meda zeichnet für das Design von "Ho" von Molteni & C.

Easy chair "Verona" by Nancy Robbins for Andreu World.

Fauteuil "Verona" de Nancy Robbins pour Andreu World.

Sessel "Verona" von Nancy Robbins für Andreu World.

On the left, chaise-longue from the series "Caleidos" design from Studio Opera Work in Progress for Insa. On the right, sofa "Billy" from Kelly Hopen.

À gauche, chaise-longue de la série "Caleidos", création de Studio Opera Work in Progress pour Insa. À droite, canapé "Billy", de Kelly Hopen.

Links: Chaiselongue aus der Serie "Caleidos", Design von Studio. Opera Work in Progress für Insa. Rechts: Sofa "Billy" von Kelly Hopen.

Peter Maly has designed
the collection "Cirrus" for Cor.

Peter Maly a créé la collection
"Cirrus" pour Cor.

Peter Maly hat die Modellreihe
"Cirrus" für Cor entworfen.

The sofa "Circum" is a design
from Peter Maly for Cor.

Le canapé "Circum" est une
création de Peter Maly pour Cor.

Sofa "Circum" handelt es sich
um ein Design von Peter Maly für Cor.

On the following page, easy chairs "Malena".
Design from Jon Gasca for Stua.

Sur la page suivante, fauteuils "Malena",
création de Jon Gasca pour Stua.

Auf der nachfolgenden Seite sind die von Jon Gasca
für Stua entworfenen Sessel "Malena" zu sehen.

On the left, sofa "Milord" from Biccapa Italia.
On the right, model "Spencer" from Insa,
design from Studio Opera Work in Progress.

À gauche, canapé "Milord" de Biccapa Italia.
À droite, modèle "Spencer", de Insa,
création de Studio Opera Work in Progress.

Links: Sofa "Milord" von Biccapa Italia.
Rechts: Modell "Spencer" von Insa,
Design von Studio Opera Work in Progress.

On the left, sofa "Mixer" from Insa.
On the right, sofa "Cortese" from Biccapa Italia.

À gauche, canapé "Mixer" de Insa.
À droite, canapé "Cortese" de Biccapa Italia.

Links: Sofa "Mixer" von Insa.
Rechts: Sofa "Cortese" von Biccapa Italia.

On the left, model "Classic" from Trip-Trap Denmark.
Right, chaise-longue and puff "Stoccolma" from Biccapa Italia.

À gauche, modèle "Classic" de Trip-Trap Denmark.
À droite, chaise-longue et pouf "Stoccolma" de Biccapa Italia.

Links das Modell "Classic" von Trip-Trap Denmark.
Rechts Chaiselongue und Hocker "Stoccolma" von Biccapa Italia.

On the previous page, the easy chair "Manila '. A design from Lievore, Altherr and Molina for Andreu World.

Sur la page précédente, le fauteuil "Manila" est une création de Lievore, Altherr y Molina pour Andreu World.

Auf der vorangegangenen Seite ist der Sessel "Manila" zu sehen, der von Lievore, Altherr und Molina für Andreu World entworfen wurde.

On the left, chaise-longue "Spencer". On the right, sofa "Portofino". These are designs from Studio Opera Work n Progress for Insa.

À gauche, chaise-longue "Spencer". À droite, canapé "Portofino". Il s'agit d'une création de Studio Opera Work in Progress pour Insa.

Links die Chaiselongue "Spencer". Rechts das Sofa "Portofino" Entworfen wurden sie vom Studio Opera Work in Progress für Insa.

Two models from Perobell: "Oberon" and "Florence", designed by Lievore, Altherr and Molina.

Deux modèles de Perobell : "Oberon" et "Florence", créés par Lievore, Altherr et Molina.

Zwei Modelle von Perobell: "Oberon" und "Florence", entworfen von Lievore, Altherr und Molina.

Shelving and television stand
from the program "Atres" from Arlex.

Étagère et meuble télévision
de la gamme "Atres" de Arlex.

Regal und TV-Tisch aus der Modellreihe
"Atres" von Arlex.

Occasional table "Nautic"
from Trip Trap Denmark.

Table d'appoint "Nautic"
de Trip Trap Denmark.

Beistelltisch "Nautic"
von Trip Trap Denmark.

The shelves "Pontaccio" allow for the creation
of multiple combinations. From Lago.

Les étagères "Pontaccio" permettent de créer
de nombreuses combinaisons. De Lago.

Das Regalsystem "Pontaccio" kann auf verschiedenste
Weise zusammengesetzt werden. Hergestellt von Lago.

Tables "Base" from Rafemar.

Tables "Base" de Rafemar.

Die Tische "Base" von Rafemar.

Carpets from the model "Losas".
Design from Ramón Esteve for Gandía Blasco.

Tapis modèle "Losas",
création de Ramón Esteve pour Gandía Blasco.

Teppiche der Serie "Losas",
Design von Ramón Esteve für Gandía Blasco.

On the left, center table "Zen" from Rafemar.
On the right, sofa "Spencer" from Studio Opera Work in Progress for Insa.

À gauche, table basse "Zen" de Rafemar.
À droite, canapé "Spencer" de Studio Opera Work in Progress pour Insa.

Links: Tisch "Zen" von Rafemar. Rechts: Sofa "Spencer",
vom Studio Opera Work in Progress für Insa entworfen.

The model "Justin" is a proposal from Möller Design.

Le modèle "Justin" est une proposition de Möller Design.

Modell "Justin" ist eine Anregung von Möller Design.

Sofa with high backrest designed by Borge Mogensen for Fredericia Furniture.

Canapé à dossier haut, créé par Bcrge Mogensen pour Fredericia Furniture.

Sofa mit hoher Lehne, Design von Borge Mogensen für Fredericia Furniture.

Sofa bed "Drifter" from Innovation. On the right, set upholstered in leather "Loveseat" from Möller Design.

Canapé-lit "Drifter" de Innovation. À droite, ensemble revêtement cuir "Loveseat", de Möller Design.

Schlafsofa "Drifter" von Innovation. Rechts die Sitzgruppe "Loveseat" aus Leder von Möller Design.

On the left, sideboard "Sapporo" and chair "Gas" designed by Jesús Gasca for Stua.

À gauche, buffet "Sapporo" et chaise "Gas", création de Jesús Gasca pour Stua.

Links Anrichte "Sapporo" und Stuhl "Gas", Design von Jesús Gasca für Stua.

Puff upholstered in leather "Ursel" from e15.

Pouf revêtement cuir "Ursel", de e15.

Gepolsterter Lederhocker "Ursel" von e15.

Model "Sydney" from Vincent Sheppard.

Modèle "Sydney" de Vincent Sheppard.

Das Modell "Sydney" von Vincent Sheppard.

Bench "Taro" from e15.

Banc "Taro" de e15.

Die Bank "Taro" von e15.

Chairs "Paris" from Vincent Sheppard.

Chaises "Paris" de Vincent Sheppard.

Stühle "Paris" von Vincent Sheppard.

Dining room set proposed
by Vibiemme.

Ensemble de salle à manger
proposé par Vibiemme.

Eine von Vibiemme vorgeschlagene
Lösung für das Esszimmer.

Original rocking chair
from Vibiemme.

Rocking-chair original
de Vibiemme.

Origineller Schaukelstuhl
von Vibiemme.

Jaime Bouzaglo is the author of the design
"Toi & Moi" from Andreu World.

Jaime Bouzaglo signe la création de
"Toi & Moi", de Andreu World.

Jaime Bouzaglo zeichnet für das Design von
"Toi & Moi" von Andreu World.

On the left, table "Sistema". Right,
composition from the collection
"Cool". All from Gandía Blasco.

À gauche, table "Sistema".
À droite, composition de la
collection "Cool". Ensemble
de Gandía Blasco.

Links der Tisch "Sistema",
rechts Zusammenstellung
aus der Modellreihe "Cool". Alle
Möbelstücke von Gandía Blasco.

Easy chairs "Malindi".
Design from O. Moon for Porada.

Fauteuils "Malindi",
création de O. Moon pour Porada.

Sessel "Malindi",
Design von O. Moon für Porada.

From left to right: television
stand "Olona" and trolley
"Matiz" from Rizza Design; stool
"Sister" from Giacomo Pascal for
Andreu World.

De gauche à droite : meuble
télévision "Olona" et desserte
"Matiz" de Rizza Design ;
tabouret "Sister" de Giacomo
Pascal pour Andreu World.

Von links nach rechts: TV-Möbel
"Olona" und Wagen "Matiz" von
Rizza Design; Hocker "Sister"
von Giacomo Pascal für
Andreu World.

Sofa "Overdrive" from Molteni & C, designed by G. Van Der Berg.

Canapé "Overdrive" de Molteni & C, création de G. Van Der Berg.

Sofa "Overdrive" von Molteni & C, Design von G. Van Der Berg.

Container system "Pass" by Luca Meda for Molteni & C.

Rangement "Pass" de Luca Meda pour Molteni & C.

Containersystem "Pass" von Luca Meda für Molteni & C.

Sofa "Pascia"
by Antonello Mosca for Giorgetti.

Canapé "Pascia"
de Antonello Mosca pour Giorgetti.

Das von Antonello Mosca für
Giorgetti entworfene Sofa "Pascia".

Composition from the program
"Pass". Design from Luca Meda
for Molteni & C.

Composition de la gamme "Pass",
création de Luca Meda pour
Molteni & C.

Zusammenstellung aus der
Modellreihe "Pass", Design
von Luca Meda für Molteni & C.

| Ecological kitchens

Stools "Europa" from Bonestil.

Tabourets "Europa" de Bonestil.

Hocker "Europa" von Bonestil.

Des cuisines écologiques

Ökologische Küchen

Welcoming and uniform tend to be the first perceptions that we receive upon entering these types of kitchens. Generally, all of the furniture is made of wood and it has been unified by the use of one single color. In kitchens of the most contemporary design, it is also frequent to find wood combined with glass or steel surfaces, which creates a pleasant sensation of amplitude and order. Comfort, ergonomics, the use of recycled materials, esthetics concerned with the detail and the creation of an open space where we are able to move freely are the main solutions that new ecological and natural kitchens should provide us with, recovering this area's past function as that of being the center of life in the home.

Gemütlich und homogen – das ist der erste Eindruck, den wir beim Betreten dieser Küchen haben. Normalerweise sind sie mit Holzmöbeln ausgestattet, die alle in derselben Farbe gehalten sind. Aber auch in den modernen Designer–Küchen wird Holz häufig mit Glas– und Stahlflächen kombiniert und somit ein Gefühl der Weite und Ordnung hervorgerufen. Bequemlichkeit, Ergonomie, der Einsatz von wiederverwendtbaren Materialien, eine auf Details wertlegende Ästhetik sowie das Zurverfügungstellen eines freien Raums mit viel Bewegungsfreiheit sind die wichtigsten Kriterien, die bei der Einrichtung der neuen naturbezogenen und ökologischen Küche zu berücksichtigen sind, damit dieser Raum seine ehemalige Funktion als neuralgisches Zentrum der Wohnung zurückgewinnt.

Accueillantes et homogènes, ce sont souvent les premiers mots qui nous viennent à l'esprit lorsque nous entrons dans ce type de cuisines. La plupart du temps, tous les éléments du mobilier sont fabriqués dans un bois de même couleur. Dans les cuisines design les plus contemporaines, il est fréquent de trouver le bois combiné avec des surfaces de verre ou d'acier, créant ainsi une agréable sensation de grandeur et d'ordre. La commodité, l'ergonomie, l'utilisation de matériaux recyclables, une esthétique tournée vers les détails et la création d'un espace vaste où l'on peut se déplacer librement, sont les principales solutions que doivent apporter les nouvelles cuisines naturelles et écologiques, récupérant ainsi leur ancienne fonction de centre vital de la demeure.

Furniture from the collection "Mixer".
Design from Zengiaro Associati for Febal.

Meubles de la collection "Mixer",
création de Zengiaro Associati pour Febal.

Möbel aus der Modellreihe "Mixer",
Design von Zengiaro Associati für Febal.

Model "Avium", in cherry wood, from Leicht.

Modèle "Avium" en bois de cerisier, de Leicht.

Modell "Avium" aus Kirschbaum von Leicht.

Composition from the program "Class"
from Alno.

Composition de la gamme "Class"
de Alno.

Zusammenstellung aus der Modellreihe "Class"
von Alno.

On the left, program "Class" from Alno.
On the right, model "Alura" from Oster.

À gauche, gamme "Class" de Alno.
À droite, modèle "Alura" de Oster.

Links, die Modellreihe "Class" von Alno.
Rechts, das Modell "Alura" von Oster.

Proposal from Alno.

Proposition de Alno.

Eine Anregung von Alno.

Stool "Edward" from Vincent Sheppard.

Tabouret "Edward" de Vincent Sheppard.

Hocker "Edward" von Vincent Sheppard.

Alno includes a breakfast bar in this proposal.

Alno introduit dans cette proposition un bar pour les petits déjeuners.

Zu dem Vorschlag von Alno gehört eine kleine Frühstückstheke.

Composition "Contura" from Nobilia.

Composition "Contura" de Nobilia.

Zusammenstellung "Contura" von Nobilia.

Two compositions from the program "Amarena".
Designed by Luca Meda for Dada.

Deux compositions de la gamme "Amarena",
création de Luca Meda pour Dada.

Zwei Zusammenstellungen aus der Modellreihe
"Amarena", Design von Luca Meda für Dada.

Kitchen "Cosmo" from Nobilia.

Cuisine "Cosmo" de Nobilia.

Küche "Cosmo" von Nobilia.

Detail from a composition from Leicht.

Détail d'une composition de Leicht.

Detail aus einer Zusammenstellung von Leicht.

Composition from the program "Mixer" from Febal.
Design from Zengiaro Associati.

Composition de la gamme "Mixer" de Febal,
création de Zengiaro Associati.

Zusammenstellung aus der Modellreihe "Mixer"
von Febal, Design von Zengiaro Associati.

Composition from the program "Jet" from Alno.

Composition de la gamme "Jet " de Alno.

Zusammenstellung aus der Modellreihe "Jet" von Alno.

Bottom and center images:
details of compositions from Alno.

Image du bas et du centre :
détails des compositions de Alno.

Unten und in der Mitte
Details der Zusammenstellungen von Alno.

Composition from the program
"Ontario Line" from Leicht.

Composition de la gamme
"Ontario Line" de Leicht.

Zusammenstellung aus der
Modellreihe "Ontario Line" von Leicht.

Composition from Alno
of rural inspiration.

Composition de Alno
d'inspiration champêtre.

Zusammenstellung von Alno
mit rustikalem Flair.

Model "Style" from Alno.

Modèle "Style" de Alno.

Das Modell "Style" von Alno.

On the left, composition "Tell" from Alno.
On the right, model "Natura" from Nobilia.

À gauche, composition "Tell" de Alno.
À droite, modèle "Natura" de Nobilia.

Links eine Zusammenstellung aus der Modellreihe
"Tell" von Alno. Rechts Modell "Natura" von Nobilia.

Model "Rondo" from Nobilia.

Modèle "Rondo" de Nobilia.

Das Modell "Rondo" von Nobilia.

Composition from the program "Genua" from Oster.

Composition de la gamme "Genua" de Oster.

Eine Zusammenstellung aus der Modellreihe "Genua" von Oster.

Composition in a rustic style from
the program "Cosmo" from Nobilia.

Composition de style rustique
de la gamme "Cosmo" de Nobilia.

Eine Zusammenstellung in rustikalem Stil
aus der Modellreihe "Cosmo" von Nobilia.

Program "Montana" from Oster.

Gamme "Montana" de Oster.

Die Modellreihe "Montana"
vor Oster.

Model "Lido" from Nobilia"

Modèle "Lido" de Nobilia"

Das Modell "Lido" von Nobilia"

Compositions from the program
"Natura" from Nobilia.

Autre combinaison de la gamme
"Natura" de Nobilia.

Eine Zusammenstellung aus der
Modellreihe "Natura" von Nobilia.

Below, on the left, composition "Look" from Alno.
On the right, chest of drawers from the series
"Street" from Klenk.

En bas, à gauche, composition "Look" de Alno.
À droite, commode de la série "Street" de Klenk.

Unten links die Zusammenstellung "Look" von Alno.
Rechts eine Kommode aus der Modellreihe
"Street" von Klenk.

There is a certain romantic air in this proposal from Bulthaup.

Une petite note romantique pour cette proposition de Bulthaup.

Ein Vorschlag von Bulthaup mit einem gewissen romantischem Flair.

"Orlando" is one of the latest proposals from Leicht.

"Orlando" est une des dernières propositions de Leicht.

"Orlando" gehört zu den neuesten Vorschläge von Leicht.

Composition from the program
"Ontario Line" from Leicht.

Composition de la gamme "Ontario
Line" de Leicht.

Eine Zusammenstellung aus
der Modellreihe "Ontario Line"
von Leicht.

Stall "Move", Designed by
Per Øie for Stokke.

Tabouret "Move", créé par
Per Øie pour Stokke.

Der von Per Øie für Stokke
entworfene Hocker "Move".

Composition "Pia" from Nobilia.

Composition "Pia" de Nobilia.

Eine Zusammenstellung aus der Modellreihe "Pia" von Nobilia.

Bathrooms inspired by nature

Furniture from the collection
"Replay" from Toscoquattro.

Meubles de la collection
"Replay" de Toscoquattro.

Möbelstücke aus der Modellreihe
"Replay" von Toscoquattro.

Des salles de bain inspirées de la nature

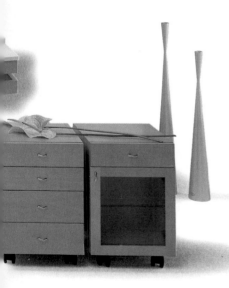

Von der Natur inspirierte Badezimmer

A puff of fresh air and comfort invades us upon entering the bathroom, the most intimate and private space of the home which, little by little, is receiving the same importance as that given to the public spaces. It is a question of transforming the moment we dedicate to our daily washing into a first-class excuse to spend some time taking care of ourselves, spoiling ourselves and relaxing. The bathroom furniture becomes welcoming: we find ourselves encircled by the warmth of the wood that creates smooth and discrete forms. The ceramic and glass also come into play with their natural tones, refreshing the atmosphere with their presence. These proposals are directed to the creation of spaces that are modern and timeless, those that transform the bathroom into a temple to water, where one can escape, although only for a brief interim of time, from the day to day anxieties.

Un souffle d'air frais et de bien-être nous envahit lorsque nous entrons dans la salle de bain, l'espace le plus intime et privé de la demeure qui prend, peu à peu, autant d'importance que les autres espaces communs. Il s'agit de transformer le moment de la toilette quotidienne en un bon prétexte pour nous consacrer à nous-mêmes, pour prendre soin de notre corps et pour nous relaxer. Les meubles de la salle de bain deviennent accueillants : la chaleur du bois, avec ses formes discrètes et douces, nous enveloppe. La céramique et le verre participent également au jeu des tons naturels et leur présent aide à rafraîchir l'atmosphère. Les propositions se tournent vers la création d'espaces intemporels et modernes, permettant de transformer la salle de bain en un temple de l'eau grâce auquel il nous sera facile de nous évader, pour quelques minutes, loin des préoccupations de la vie quotidienne.

Beim Betreten des Badezimmers empfängt uns ein frischer Luftzug, und wir empfinden ein gewisses Wohlbehagen in diesem Raum, der zu dem intimsten und privatesten Bereich der Wohnung gehört, und dem im Laufe der Zeit zunehmend dieselbe Bedeutung zugeschrieben wird wie dem Rest der Zimmer. Die für die tägliche Körperpflege aufgewandte Zeit gibt uns Gelegenheit, uns einige Minuten auf uns selber zu konzentrieren, uns zu pflegen, zu verwöhnen und uns zu entspannen. Die Badezimmermöbel haben ihren sterilen Charakter verloren: Die Wärme des Holzes, das zu weichen, harmonischen Formen verarbeitet worden ist, überträgt sich auf uns. Auch Kacheln und Glas sind an diesem Spiel der Naturfarben beteiligt und verleihen dem Raum eine gewisse Frische. Ziel ist es, zeitlose, moderne Räume zu schaffen, die das Badezimmer in einen Wassertempel verwandeln, in dem man – wenn auch nur für kurze Zeit – Zuflucht vor dem Alltag mit allen seinen Problemen findet.

Faucets "Dreamworks" wall version.
Designed by Sieger Design for Dornbracht.

Robinet encastrée "Dreamworks", version murale.
Création de Sieger Design pour Dornbracht.

Armaturen "Dreamworks" als Wandausführung.
Design von Sieger Design für Dornbracht.

Mirror "Oblio" by P. Salvadé for Porada.

Miroir "Oblio", de P. Salvadé pour Porada.

Spiegel "Oblio" von P. Salvadé für Porada.

Washbasin "Lisboa" suspended. From Gama-Decor.

Lavabo mural "Lisboa", de Gama-Decor.

Aufgehängtes Waschbecken "Lisboa" von Gama-Decor.

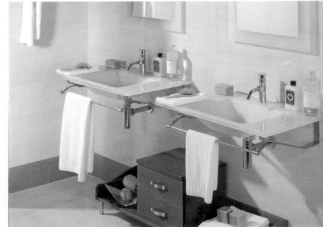

On the left, washbasin "Gran Qubik" with a birch base from Altro.
On the right, bathroom furniture "Tokyo" in wenge, from Gama-Decor.

À gauche, lavabo "Gran Qubik" avec structure en bois de bouleau, de Altro.
À droite, meubles de salle de bain "Tokyo" en bois de wengé, de Gama-Decor.

Links das Waschbecken "Gran Qubik" von Altro mit Unterbau aus Birke.
Rechts Badezimmermöbel "Tokyo" aus Wengé von Gama-Decor.

Faucets from the collection "Obina"
from Sieger Design for Dornbracht.

Robinet de la collection "Obina",
de Sieger Design pour Dornbracht.

Armaturen aus der Modellreihe
"Obina" von Sieger Design
für Dombracht.

Bathroom furniture "Flash" finished
in beech from Roca.

Meuble de salle de bain "Flash"
avec finition hêtre, de Roca.

Badezimmermöbel "Flash" von
Roca mit Buchenholzverarbeitung.

Two possible combinations from the program
"Metropolis" from Toscoquattro.

Deux combinaisons possibles pour la gamme
"Metropolis", de Toscoquattro.

Zwei Kombinationsmöglichkeiten mit Elementen
aus der Modellreihe "Metropolis" von Toscoquattro.

Furniture from the collection
"Replay Naturale" from Toscoquattro.

Meubles de la collection
"Replay Naturale" de Toscoquattro.

Möbelstücke aus der Modellreihe
"Replay Naturale" von Toscoquattro.

The collection "Metropolis" from Toscoquattro allows
for multiple combinations.

La collection "Metropolis" de Toscoquattro permet
d'obtenir de nombreuses combinaisons.

Mit der Modellreihe "Metropolis" von Toscoquattro
können die verschiedensten Zusammenstellungen
vorgenommen werden.

Composition from the program "Cotta"
from Keramag.

Composition de la gamme "Cotta"
de Keramag.

Zusammenstellung aus der Modellreihe "Cotta"
von Keramag.

Another composition of "Replay"
from Toscoquattro.

Une autre composition de "Replay"
Toscoquattro.

Ein andere Zusammenstellung von "Replay"
von Toscoquattro.

On the right, composition "Metropolis" from
Toscoquattro. Below, composition "3006" from Axia.

À droite, composition "Metropolis" de Toscoquattro.
En bas, composition "3006" de Axia.

Rechts die Zusammenstellung "Metropolis"
von Toscoquattro. Unten die Zusammenstellung
"3006" vom Axia.

Left, proposal from Bis Bis Imports Boston. Bottom right, furniture from the series "Tokyo"
in cherry wood from Gama-Decor.

À gauche, proposition de Bis Bis Imports Boston. En bas à gauche, meubles de la série "Tokyo"
en bois de cerisier, de Gama-Decor.

Links ein Vorschlag von Bis Bis Imports Boston. Unten rechts Möbel aus Kirschbaum aus der Modellreihe "Tokyo"
von Gama-Decor.

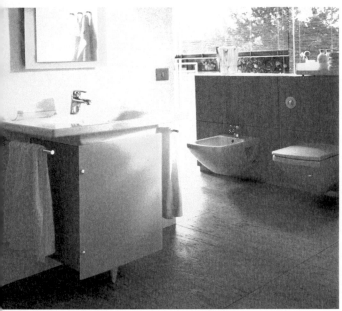

Series "Caro" from Duravit
designed by Phoenix Product
Design.

Série "Caro" de Duravit,
créée par Phoenix Product Design.

Modellreihe "Caro" von Duravit,
entworfen von Phoenix Product
Design.

Left, double washbasin "Kapp" from
Gama-Decor. On the right, proposal
from Bis Bis Imports Boston.

À gauche, lavabo double "Kapp" de
Gama-Decor. À droite, proposition
de Bis Bis Imports Boston.

Links das Doppelwaschbecken
"Kapp" von Gama-Decor. Rechts ein
Vorschlag von Bis Bis Imports
Boston.

Composition "Millennium"
from Gama-Decor.

Composition "Millennium"
de Gama-Decor.

Zusammenstellung "Millennium"
von Gama-Decor.

Various compositions from Axia.

Autres compositions de Axia.

Verschiedene Zusammenstellungen
von Axia.

Model "Cubico" from Gama-Decor.

Modèle "Cubico" de Gama-Decor.

Das Modell "Cubico" von Gama-
Decor.

Left: Composition "1012" in cherry, from Axia.
Right: Composition "1011" in maple, from Axia.

À gauche: Composition "1012" en bois de cerisier, de Axia.
À droite: Composition "1011" en bois d'érable, de Axia.

Links: Die Modellreihe "1012" aus Kirsch von Axia.
Rechts: Die Modellreihe "1011" aus Ahorn von Axia

On the left, composition from the series "Lisboa" from Gama-Decor.
On the right, furniture from the program "System" from Industrias Cosmic.

À gauche, composition de la série "Lisboa" de Gama-Decor.
À droite, meubles de la gamme "System" de Industrias Cosmic.

Links eine Zusammenstellung aus der Modellreihe "Lisboa" von Gama-Decor.
Rechts Möbel aus der Modellreihe "System" von Industrias Cosmic.

| Harmonious bedrooms

Bed "Alero" from J. M. Andrés and auxiliary furniture
"Diva" from P. Martínez. From Interi.

Lit "Alero" de J. M. Andrés et meubles d'appoint
"Diva" de P. Martínez. De Interi.

Das Bett "Alero" von J. M. Andrés und Beistellmöbel
"Diva" von P. Martínez. Angeboten von Interi.

Des chambres harmonieuses

Harmonisch eingerichtete Schlafzimmer

It would be ideal if we could always wake up in a good mood and find ourselves in possession of numerous incentives to get up enthusiastically to begin a new day. Although it isn't the absolute solution, an important step toward obtaining this goal is to sleep in a place that emits harmony, a place that establishes an intense dialogue with nature. One of the principal forces that stimulates us to act is light, therefore, it is important to install the bedroom in the area of the building that receives the maximum amount of natural light possible. Some linen or gauze curtains that wave in the breeze, a bed with simple forms and a wooden base, light furniture made of high quality materials and some decorative accessories that integrate into the whole, these would be a good choice to provide us with happy awakenings.

L'idéal serait de toujours nous réveiller de bonne humeur et avec l'enthousiasme nécessaire pour commencer une nouvelle journée. Même s'il ne s'agit pas de la solution définitive, le fait de dormir dans un endroit plein d'harmonie et capable d'établir un dialogue intense avec la nature peut être une aide importante. Une des principales forces qui nous pousse à bouger est la lumière ; il est donc important que la chambre se trouve dans une pièce recevant la plus grande quantité de lumière naturelle possible. Des rideaux en toile de lin ou en toile de crêpe accompagnant de leurs ondulations un lit aux formes simples sur une structure en bois, un mobilier léger mais de qualité et des accessoires décoratifs s'intégrant parfaitement à cet ensemble : tous ces éléments nous procurerons, sans aucun doute, des réveils en beauté.

Es wäre wunderbar, wenn wir immer gut gelaunt aufwachen und gleich den Impuls verspüren, den neuen Tag voller Enthusiasmus zu beginnen. Natürlich kann es keine definitive Lösung sein, aber wir kämen unserem Ziel vielleicht schon ein ganzes Stück näher, wenn wir in einem Raum schlafen, von dem ein Gefühl der Harmonie hervorgerufen wird und in dem ein intensiver Dialog mit der Natur stattfindet. Licht ist für uns eine vitale Antriebskraft, deshalb sollte dem Schlafzimmer ein Raum zugewiesen werden, der von allen Zimmern das meiste Tageslicht empfängt. Gardinen aus Leinen und Gaze, die sich leicht im Wind bewegen, ein schlichtes Bett mit einem Holzuntergestell, leicht wirkendes, aus gutem Material hergestelltes Mobiliar und einige sich in das Ambiente einfügende dekorative Elemente werden sicher die richtige Wahl sein, damit wir morgens fröhlich gestimmt aufwachen.

Program "Tobia" from Poliform.
Gamme "Tobia" de Poliform.
Die Modellreihe "Tobia" von Poliform.

Composition "Tosca" from Ennio Arosio for Verardo.
Below, collection "Apta" from Antonio Citterio for
Maxalto.

Composition "Tosca" de Ennio Arosio pour Verardo.
En bas, collection "Apta" de Antonio Citterio pour
Maxalto.

Die von Ennio Arosio für Verardo entworfene
Modellreihe "Tosca". Unten die Serie "Apta",
von Antonio Citterio für Maxalto entworfen.

Bed "Grace" from Kelly Hoppen
Below, program "Ares" from Poliform

Lit "Grace" de Kelly Hoppen
En bas, gamme "Ares" de Poliform

Das Bett "Grace" von Kelly Hoppen
Unten die Modellreihe "Ares" von Poliform

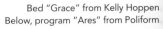

L. Gorgoni is the author of this design from the program "Vanity".
From the collection Los Contemporáneos from Roche Bobois.

L. Gorgoni signe la création de la gamme "Vanity",
de la collection Los Contemporáneos de Roche Bobois.

L. Gorgoni zeichnet für das Design der Serie 'Vanity'
aus der Modellreihe Los Contemporáneos von Roche Bobois.

On the left, bed "Dolceluna" from Luca Meda for Molteni & C. Bottom, bed "Giorgia" from Misura Emme.

À gauche, "Dolceluna" de Luca Meda pour Molteni & C. En bas, lit "Giorgia" de Misura Emme.

Links: das Bett "Dolceluna", von Luca Meda für Molteni & C. entworfen. Unten das Bett "Giorgia" von Misura Emme.

On the right, model "Sydney" from Domus. Bottom, wardrobe "7 volte 7" from L. Meda for Molteni & C.

À droite, modèle "Sydney" de Domus. En bas, armoire "7 volte 7" de L. Meda pour Molteni & C.

Rechts das Modell "Sydney" von Domus. Unten der Schrank "7 volte 7". von L. Meda für Molteni & C.

Bedroom "Eden" from Roche Bobois.

Chambre "Eden" de Roche Bobois.

Das Schlafzimmer "Eden" von Roche Bobois.

Bed "Dolcenotte" in walnut.
From L. Meda for Molteni & C.

Lit "Dolcenotte" en bois de noyer.
De L. Meda pour Molteni & C.

Das Bett "Dolcenotte"
aus Nussbaum, von L. Meda
für Molteni & C entworfen.

On the left, collection "Basic" from
Club 8 Company. In the center,
proposal from Prealpi. On the right
composition "Onda" from Zanette.

À gauche, collection "Basic"
de Club 8 Company. Au centre,
proposition de Prealpi. À droite,
composition "Onda" de Zanette.

Links die Modellreihe "Basic" von
Club 8 Company. In der Mitte ein
Vorschlag von Prealpi. Rechts eine
Zusammenstellung aus der
Modellreihe "Onda" von Zanette.

Model "Quadro" from the collection TM Line, from Domus. Below, on the left, "Dodicesima Notte" from L. Meda for Molteni & C. In the center, wardrobe "Millennium" from G. Dalto for Rattan Wood. On the right, program "Quatro" from Organica.

Modèle "Quadro" de la collection TM Line, de Domus. En bas à gauche, "Dodicesima Notte" de L. Meda pour Molteni & C. Au centre, armoire "Millennium" de G. Dalto pour Rattan Wood. À droite, gamme "Quatro" de Organica.

Das Modell "Quadro" aus der Modellreihe TM Line von Domus. Unten links "Dodicesima Notte", von L. Meda für Molteni & C. erstellt. In der Mitte der Schrank "Millennium", von G. Dalto für Rattan Wood entworfen. Rechts die Modellreihe "Quatro" von Organica.

| Mimetic illumination

Suspended lamp "Chandler"
from Lambert.

Plafonnier "Chandler" de Lambert.

Die Hängelampe "Chandler"
von Lambert.

Un éclairage mimétique

Mimetische Beleuchtung

The general atmosphere of an area can change drastically according to the type of lighting used. Each room requires a specific type of light to help the functions to which it is dedicated be carried out. For example, in a living room inspired in nature, it would be advisable to have different sources of light of different intensities: some table lamps with linen or cotton shades will create an intimate atmosphere, conducive to confidential remarks and long conversations; a standard lamp to illuminate the hours of reading; a ceiling lamp that covers the dining area; perhaps, a wall lamp to emphasize the colors and textures of our favorite painting... What we are trying to do is copy the quality and shades of sunlight, helped by natural materials and technological resources.

L'atmosphère générale d'une pièce peut se transformer totalement en fonction de l'éclairage utilisé. Chaque pièce demande un type de lumière bien défini, qui s'adaptera à toutes les occupations pour lesquelles elle a été pensée. Par exemple, il est conseillé de disposer différentes sources d'éclairage dans un salon s'inspirant de la nature : des lampes à abat-jour en lin ou en coton pour créer une ambiance intime, propice aux confidences et aux longues conversations ; un lampadaire pour éclairer les heures de lecture ; un plafonnier pour couvrir la zone de la salle à manger ; une applique mettant en relief les couleurs et les textures de notre tableau préféré… Tout ce qui sera nécessaire pour copier la qualité et les nuances de la lumière du soleil à l'aide de matériaux naturels et de ressources technologiques.

Die in einem Zimmer herrschende Stimmung ist in hohem Maße von der Art der gewählten Beleuchtung abhängig. Für jedes einzelne Zimmer muß eine geeignete Beleuchtung vorgesehen werden, die in Funktion der Nutzung des Raumes ausgewählt wird. So wird zum Beispiel für ein von der Natur inspiriertes Wohnzimmer die Anordnung verschieden starker Lichtquellen empfohlen: Tischlampen mit Leinen– oder Baumwollschirmen werden für ein gemütliches Ambiente sorgen, das zu langen, vertraulichen Gesprächen einlädt; eine Stehlampe gibt das richtige Licht, um sich in eine Lektüre zu vertiefen; über der Essecke wird eine Deckenlampe passen und ein Wandstrahler rückt die Farben und Textur unseres Lieblingsgemäldes in das richtige Licht...Mit all diesen Optionen wird beabsichtigt, das Tageslicht mit allen seinen Nuancen zu kopieren; Produkte aus der Natur und Mittel der modernen Technologie helfen uns dabei.

Lamp "Románica" with a shade in veneer or parchment. Design from Mariví Calvo for Luzifer

Lampe "Románica" avec diffuseur plaqué bois ou papier-parchemin. Création de Mariví Calvo pour Luzifer

Die Lampe "Románica" mit Diffusor aus Holz oder Pergament. Design von Mariví Calvo für Luzifer

Above, two versions of the model "Tip Toe" with leather support. Design from Ramón Isern for Vibia. Below, on the left, "Torre" from Diemo Alfons. On the right, "Maite", suspended lamp, from M. A. Ciganda for B. Lux.

En haut, deux versions du modèle "Tip Toe", avec support en cuir, création de Ramón Isern pour Vibia.
En bas à gauche, "Torre" de Diemo Alfons. À droite, "Maite" lampe suspendue, de M. A. Ciganda pour B. Lux.

Oben zwei Ausführungen des Modells "Tip Toe" mit Ledergestell, Design von Ramón Isern für Vibia.
Unten links "Torre" von Diemo Alfons. Rechts Hängelampe "Maite" von M. A. Ciganda für B. Lux entworfen.

"Balance" is a standard lamp and a ceiling lamp.
A design from Jordi Vilardell for Vibia.

"Balance" est un lampadaire ou un plafonnier.
Il s'agit d'une création de Jordi Vilardell pour Vibia.

"Balance" gibt es als Steh- und Deckenlampe.
Das Design hat Jordi Vilardell für Vibia erstellt.

Extendable lamp "Vol"
from Ramón Valls for Taller Uno.

Lampe extensible "Vol",
de Ramón Valls pour Taller Uno.

Die ausziehbare Lampe "Vol",
cie von Ramón Valls für Taller Uno entworfen wurde.

On the left, "Básica" from S. Roqueta and Equipo Santa & Cole. In the center, "Timy" from Domus. On the right, "Nórdica" from Santa & Cole.

À gauche, "Básica" de S. Roqueta et Equipo Santa & Cole. Au centre, "Timy" de Domus. À droite, "Nórdica" de Santa & Cole.

Links "Básica" von S. Roqueta und Equipo Santa & Cole. In der Mitte "Timy" von Domus. Rechts "Nórdica" von Santa & Cole.

"Dórica" from J. Miralbell and M. Raventós for Santa & Cole.

"Dórica" de J. Miralbell et M. Raventós pour Santa & Cole.

"Dórica" von J. Miralbell und M. Raventós für Santa & Cole.

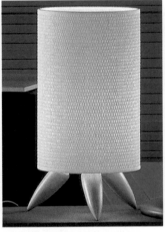

On the left, "3 eran 3" from Mariví Calvo for Luzifer. In the center, "Gigantic" has a minimum height of 1,55m. From Tramo.

À gauche, "3 eran 3" de Mariví Calvo pour Luzifer. Au centre, la hauteur minimum de "Gigantic" est de 1,55 m, de Tramo.

Links "3 eran 3", von Calvo für Luzifer entworfen. In der Mitte "Gigantic" mit einer Mindesthöhe von 1,55 m von Tramo.

On the left, "Spring" from Jorge Pensi for B. Lux. On the right, "Alhambra Oval", a table lamp. Design from Ray Power for Luzifer.

À gauche, "Spring" de Jorge Pensi pour B. Lux. À droite, "Alhambra Oval", lampe de bureau, création de Ray Power pour Luzifer.

Links "Spring", von Jorge Pensi für B. Lux entworfen. Rechts die Tischlampe "Alhambra Oval", von Ray Power für Luzifer entworfen.

Bottom, on the left "Moragas" from A. de Moragas. In the center, "Sólida" from J. Miralbell and M. Raventós. Both are from Santa & Cole (photo: C. Masiá). On the right, "Duplo" from J. Vilardell for Vibia.

À gauche, "Moragas" de A. de Moragas. Au centre, "Sólida" de J. Miralbell et M. Raventós. Les deux lampes sont de Santa & Cole (photo : C. Masiá). À droite, "Duplo" de J. Vilardell pour Vibia.

Links "Moragas" von A. de Moragas. In der Mitte "Sólida" von J. Miralbell und M. Raventós. Beide Modelle von Santa & Cole (Foto: C. Masiá). Rechts "Duplo", von J. Vilardell für Vibia. entworfen.

"Lino" from Helena Poch for Taller Uno. On the right, "Arquímedes' from Gemma Bernal and Ramón Isern for Tramo.

Au centre, "Lino" de Helena Poch pour Taller Uno. À droite, "Arquímedes" de Gemma Bernal et Ramón Isern pour Tramo.

In der Mitte "Lino" von Helena Poch für Taller Uno. Rechts "Arquímedes", von Gemma Bernal und Ramón Isern für Tramo entworfen.

Bottom, "Atlas" from Massana and Tremoleda for Mobles 114. In the center, Model "Willy" from Carpyen. On the right, appliance "Trio" from Joan Augé and Helena Poch for Taller Uno.

En bas, "Atlas" de Massana et Tremoleda pour Mobles 114. Au centre, modèle "Willy" de Carpyen. À droite, applique "Trio" de Joan Augé et Helena Poch pour Taller Uno.

Unten: "Atlas" von Massana und Tremoleda für Mobles 114 entworfen. In der Mitte: das Modell "Willy" von Carpyen. Rechts die Wandlampe "Trio", die von Joan Augé und Helena Poch für Taller Uno entworfen wurde.

INNOVATORS AND THE AVANT-GARDE
Metal, daring designs and new materials

Do you feel a tickle of emotion in your stomach when you contemplate something new, a surprising form, an ingenious solution to an everyday problem, a design of impacting simplicity, a display of creativity which resolves a functional necessity? If your answer is affirmative, then welcome to the group of the innovators and the avant-garde.

To innovate means to introduce a breakthrough into something, to change, to discover, to explore, to invent. It means, in short, to be original, to go beyond the established or the conventional. To dare try something new.

Innovators are the people who have stimulated, from the first who dared use fire, evolution by promoting the changes in our surroundings.

In this way, the figure of the industrial designer, as a magician capable of inventing new forms, becomes vital in these environments. The majority of objects have a name, that of their creator. The limit is drawn by the designer's own imagination that should be adapted to fulfilling a specific function and to the technical restraints that, on the other hand, are being overcome with increasing speed.

They are environments, therefore, where technology also plays an important role. The tendency of creating spaces with a technological atmosphere, reminiscent of industry, has its origins in the 70's when the style called "high-tech" arose. Its main inheritance is the introduction of materials such as metals and industrial synthetics, the reflections and sparkles of which offer interesting contrasts with any color, into domestic spaces.

People who live in environments of this type are those who feel a special attraction to the most advanced tendencies of the time, challenging conventions. This does not mean that they follow fashion, but that they go beyond it. From here comes the term "avant-garde" in its meaning of being before others.

Although we may think that we are speaking of a minority, there are an increasing number of followers of avant-garde design. This is reflected by the fact that there are currently many businesses dedicating their efforts to the development of this type of furniture wagering for pure creativity, for contours that flow freely, by prompting investigation and the introduction of new materials, by supporting young creators.

The challenge is to find those designs that really bring the characteristics of excellence together: combining esthetics and function in a way that lasts in time without falling into stridency or into short-lived fashions.

From these pages, we take up this challenge.

INNOVATION ET AVANT-GARDE
Du métal, des créations risquées et de nouveaux matériaux

Ressentez-vous un frisson d'émotion lorsque vous contemplez quelque chose de nouveau, une forme surprenante, une solution intelligente à un besoin quotidien, une création d'une simplicité choquante, une surface aux reflets métalliques, une démonstration de créativité servant à une condition de fonctionnalité ? Si la réponse est affirmative, vous êtes le bienvenu dans le groupe de l'innovation et de l'avant-garde.

Innover, cela signifie introduire des nouveautés, changer, découvrir, explorer, inventer. Cela signifie, en définitive, être original, aller au-delà des normes établies et des conventions. C'est oser essayer tout ce qui est nouveau.

Ce sont les personnes innovatrices (depuis le premier homme qui osa utiliser le feu) qui ont contribué à l'évolution et à la transformation de l'environnement dans lequel nous vivons.

De cette façon, le créateur industriel, tel un magicien capable d'inventer de nouvelles formes, joue un rôle d'une importance essentielle dans ce type de contextes. La plupart des objets ont un prénom et un nom, celui de leur créateur. Il n'existe qu'une limite : celle de l'imagination du créateur qui devra s'adapter à un objectif et à des conditions techniques qui, cependant, se résolvent de plus en plus rapidement.

Il s'agit donc de contextes dans lesquels la technologie joue elle aussi un rôle important. La tendance qui consiste à créer des espaces dans une atmosphère technologique, aux réminiscences industrielles, apparaît dans les années 70, au moment de la naissance du style "high-tech". Son principal héritage est l'introduction dans les espaces ménagers de matériaux comme les métaux et les éléments synthétiques industriels, dont les reflets et les éclats offrent d'intéressants contrastes avec tous les types de couleurs.

Les personnes habitant dans cette sorte d'environnement sont celles qui ressentent une attraction spéciale pour les tendances les plus avancées du moment, celles qui défient les conventions. Ceci ne signifie pas qu'elles se consacrent à suivre la mode, mais plutôt à la devancer. C'est de là que vient le terme "Avant-garde", pour désigner ce qui, de par son audace, se trouve en avance sur son temps.

Même s'il est courant de penser qu'il s'agit d'une minorité, les adeptes de la conception d'avant-garde sont de plus en plus nombreux. Actuellement, ceci se reflète dans le grand nombre d'entreprises se consacrant au développement de ce type de mobilier, misant sur la créativité à l'état pur, sur les contours aux formes lib-

res, donnant une impulsion à la recherche et à l'introduction de nouveaux matériaux et en offrant leur soutien aux jeunes créateurs.

Le défi réside dans la découverte des inventions qui réunissent toutes les caractéristiques de l'excellence : allier une esthétique et une fonctionnalité résistante au temps sans tomber dans l'extravagance ou dans les modes passagères.

Dans ces pages, nous relèverons ce défi.

INNOVATE UND AVANTGARDISTISCHE INTERIEURS
Metall, gewagtes Design und neue Materialien

Wenn Sie etwas Neues betrachten, Dinge Sie durch ihre außergewöhnliche Form überraschen, geniale Lösungen für einen alltäglichen Bedarfsgegenstand angeboten werden, ein Design durch seine einfache Formgebung fasziniert, Ihr Blick auf widerspiegelnde Metallflächen fällt oder eine enorme Kreativität selbst bei funktionellen Dingen zum Ausdruck kommt – fühlen Sie dann nicht ganz besondere Emotionen in Ihnen hochkommen? Wenn dem so ist, dann seien Sie willkommen in der Gruppe der Avantgardisten und der nach Innovation Strebenden.

Innovativ zu sein, heißt bestehenden Dingen etwas Neues hinzuzufügen, sie zu verändern, zu untersuchen, zu entdecken. In einem Wort, originell zu sein und über das schon Bestehende, das Konventionelle hinauszugehen und etwas Neues zu wagen.

So sind es dann auch diese von innovativen Ideen besessenen Köpfe, die an unserer ständigen Weiterentwicklung beteiligt waren. Angefangen bei demjenigen, der es zum ersten Mal wagte, mit Feuer umzugehen, bis hin zu all denen, die im Laufe der Evolution dafür gesorgt haben, daß unser Umfeld den ständigen Veränderungen angepasst wird.

Somit kommt dem Industriedesigner, diesem Hervorzauberer von immer wieder neuen Formen, in Zusammenhang mit dieser Art von Interieurs eine ganz besondere Bedeutung zu. Die meisten Objekte sind unter einem bestimmten Namen bekannt, sie tragen den ihres Designers. Grenzen werden dem Designer nur durch seine eigene Phantasie gesetzt. Er hat die Aufgabe, die Funktion der Objekte den technischen Bedingungen anzupassen, die sich in unserer modernen Zeit in zunehmendem Tempo ändern.

Somit handelt es sich hier also um Interieurs, die in erster Linie vom Stand der Technologie beeinflußt

werden. Dieser Trend, Räumen ein gewisses technisches Flair mit Reminiszenzen an den Industriebereich zu verleihen, geht auf den Anfang der siebziger Jahre entstandenen, sogenannten High–Tech–Stil zurück. Mit ihm wurden Metalle und industriell hergestellte Synthetikstoffe in den häuslichen Bereich eingeführt. Die Lichtreflexe und der Glanz dieser neuen Materialien steller einen interessanten Kontrast zu jeglicher Farbe her.

Die Bewohner dieser Räume haben ein ganz besonderes Faible für alle modernen, Fortschritt implizierenden Trends, die eine Herausforderung für alles Konventionelle sind. Das bedeutet aber nicht, dass sie nur gewisse Moden mitmachen, sondern dass sie noch darüber hinausgehen. So lässt sich auch der Begriff "Avantgardist" verstehen, mit dem eine Person beschrieben wird, die ihrer Zeit und allen anderen weit voraus ist.

Es kann zwar den Anschein erwecken, dass wir hier nur von einer als Minorität vertretenen Gruppe reden, aber die Realität sieht so aus, dass sich zunehmend mehr Anhänger dem avantgardistische Design verschreiben. Beweis dafür ist, daß sich Unternehmen in wachsender Zahl für die Entwicklung dieser Art von Möbeln interessieren und auf Kreativität in ihrer reinsten Form setzen. Sie treiben die Forschung auf diesem Gebiet voran, führen neue Materialien ein und setzen sich für die Förderung junger Designer ein.

Als große Herausforderung stellt sich die Aufgabe, ein Design zu finden, das den Anspruch auf Ästhetik und Funktion erfüllt, und das Zeiten überdauert, ohne dabei schrill zu wirken oder Opfer vorübergehender Modeerscheinungen zu werden.

Auf diesen Seiten wollen wir uns dieser Herausforderung stellen.

The latest fashions in living and dining rooms

Sofa "Flap" from Francesco Binfaré for Edra.

Canapé "Flap" de Francesco Binfaré pour Edra.

Das Sofa "Flap", das von Francesco Binfaré für Edra entworfen wurde.

La dernière mode en salons et salles à manger

Aktuelle Trends für Wohn- und Esszimmer

There is a series of furniture

that, even one hundred years after its creation, continues to be contemporary and that fits into any present-day environment perfectly. These pieces of furniture, referred to as design classics, were produced by great maestros such as Le Corbusier, Antonio Gaudí, Mies van der Rohe, Frank Lloyd Wright, Marcel Breuer, Charles & Ray Eames or Arne Jacobsen, among many others, who had the vision necessary to go beyond the limits of their time and who established the bases for present-day industrial design. Innovation, functionality, methodology, beauty, quality and passion are the ingredients of this new art form. Their accomplishments fuse with the aim of creating furniture and complements intended to improve the quality of life and perpetuate in time despite the fact that spaces may change. It is what is referred to as having vision of the future.

Il existe une série de meubles

qui, même cent ans après leur création, restent contemporains et s'adaptent parfaitement à n'importe quel contexte actuel. On les appelle les classiques du design, réalisés par de grands maîtres tels que Le Corbusier, Antonio Gaudí, Mies van der Rohe, Frank Lloyd Wright, Marcel Breuer, Charles & Ray Eames ou Arne Jacobsen, entre autres, dont la vision les a projetés au-delà de leur époque et a établi les bases du design industriel actuel. Innovation, fonctionnalité, méthodologie, beauté, qualité et passion, sont les ingrédients de cet art nouveau dont les talents actuels se combinent dans le but de créer des meubles et des accessoires destinés à augmenter la qualité de vie et à résister au temps, malgré l'évolution des espaces. C'est ce qu'on appelle avoir une vision d'avenir.

Es gibt Möbel, die selbst noch

hundert Jahre nach ihrem Entstehen zeitgemäß sind und sich in jegliches moderne Ambiente nahtlos einfügen lassen. Es handelt sich hier um die sogenannten Klassiker, die von großen Meistern wie Le Corbusier, Antonio Gaudí, Mies van der Rohe, Frank Lloyd Wright, Marcel Breuer, Charles & Ray Eames oder Arne Jacobsen, um nur einige zu nennen, entworfen wurden. Sie hatten schon damals eine Vision, die weit über ihre Zeit hinausging und die Grundlagen für das heutige Industriedesign schafften. Die zeitgenössischen Designer haben sich Innovation, Funktionalität, Methodologie, Schönheit, Qualität und Passion auf die Fahnen geschrieben und entwerfen Möbel und komplementäre Objekte, die zur Erhöhung der Lebensqualität beitragen sollen und Zeit und Modeerscheinungen überleben, selbst wenn sich die für sie bestimmten Räume ändern. Damit beweisen auch sie Zukunftsvision.

Mirror with light "LLM"
from Nanda Vigo for Glas.

Miroir avec éclairage "LLM"
de Nanda Vigo pour Glas.

Beleuchteter Spiegel "LLM",
von Nanda Vigo für Glas entworfen.

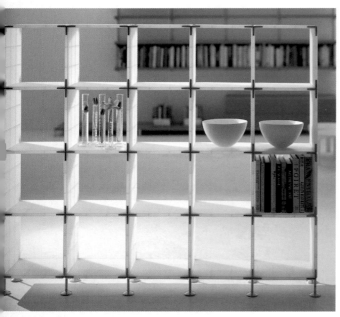

Bookcase "Endless Plastic"
from Werner Aisslinger for Porro.

Bibliothèque "Endless Plastic"
de Werner Aisslinger pour Porro.

Das von Werner Aisslinger für Porro
entworfene Regal "Endless Plastic".

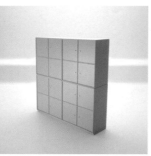

On the left, seat "Bubble".
Design from Eero Aarnio. Produced
by Adelta. On the right,
container furniture from Montana.

À gauche, siège "Bubble"
création de Eero Aarnio. Fabrication
Adelta. À droite, rangement de
Montana.

Links das Sitzmöbel "Bubble",
ein Design von Eero Aarnio und
hergestellt von. Adelta. Rechts ein
Containermöbel von Montana.

Sofa "Gem" with Perspex sides.
From Lodovico Acerbis for Acerbis
International.

Canapé "Gem" avec structure en
métacrylique. De Lodovico Acerbis
pour Acerbis International.

Sofa "Gem" mit Seitenteilen aus
Methacrylat von Lodovico Acerbis
für Acerbis. International.

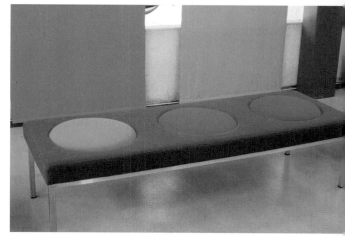

Bench "Spot"
from Mobili by Fredericia.

Banc "Spot"
de Mobili by Fredericia.

Bank "Spot"
von Mobili by Fredericia.

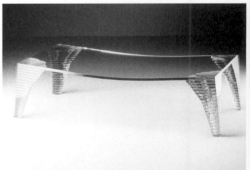

Top, sofa «2100» from Georg Appeltshauser for Rolf Benz.
On the left, modular sofa "Rooby" from Leolux.
On the right, table "Atlas" from P. Starck for Fiam Italia.

En haut, canapé «2100» de Georg Appeltshauser pour Rolf Benz.
À gauche, canapé convertible "Rooby" de Leolux.
À droite, table "Atlas" de P. Starck pour Fiam Italia.

Oben das Sofa «2100», von Georg Appeltshauser für Rolf Benz entworfen.
Links das Modulsofa "Rooby" von Leolux.
Rechts der Tisch "Atlas", von P. Starck für Fiam Italia entworfen.

Top, sofa "Esse" from F. Binfaré for Edra. On the left, seating set from
the collection «6700», from G. Appeltshauser for Rolf Benz.
On the right, mirror "Aula" from R. Dalisi for G as.

En haut, canapé "Esse" de F. Binfaré pour Edra. À gauche, ensemble
de sièges de la collection «6700», de G. Appeltshauser pour Rolf Benz.
À droite, miroir "Aula" de R. Dalisi pour Glas.

Oben das Sofa "Esse", von F. Binfaré für Edra entworfen. Links eine Sitzgruppe
aus der Modellreihe «6700», die von G. Appeltshauser für Rolf Benz
entworfen wurde. Rechts der Spiegel "Aula", Design von R. Dalisi für Glas.

Dining room set "Eclipse" and "Alfa" from Gijs Papavoine for Montis.

Ensemble de salle à manger "Eclipse" et "Alfa" de Gijs Papavoine pour Montis.

Die Esszimmergruppen "Eclipse" und "Alfa" von Gijs Papavoine für Montis.

Stefano Giovannoni is the author of the design "Big Bombo" from Magis.

Stefano Giovannoni signe la création de "Big Bombo" de Magis.

Stefano Giovannoni zeichnet für das Design von "Big Bombo" von Magis.

Model "Omega" from Gijs Papavoine for Montis.

Modèle "Omega" de Gijs Papavoine pour Montis.

Modell "Omega" von Gijs Papavoine für Montis.

Easy chair "Helical Basic" from Leolux.

Fauteuil "Helical Basic" de Leolux.

Sessel "Helical Basic" von Leolux.

Chair designed by Mies van der
Rohe. Produced by Tecta.

Chaise créée par Mies van der
Rohe. Fabrication Tecta.

Ein von Mies van der Rohe
entworfener Stuhl, hergestellt
von Tecta.

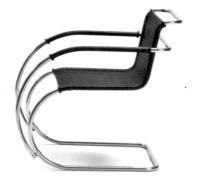

This chaise-longue is an original
design from 1932, created by
Mies van der Rohe. Produced by Tecta.

Cette chaise-longue est une création
originale de 1932, créée par
Mies van der Rohe. Fabriquée par Tecta.

Diese Chaiselongue ist ein im Jahre 1932
vor Mies van der Rohe erstelltes Design.
Hergestellt wird sie von Tecta.

Top image and bottom left image, two compositions from "Life". Design from Roberto Monsani for Acerbis International. Bottom right, composition from the program "Landare" from Nueva Línea.

Image du haut et image du bas à gauche, deux compositions de la gamme "Life", création de Roberto Monsani pour Acerbis International. En bas à droite, composition de la gamme "Landare" de Nueva Línea.

Oben und unten links: Zwei Zusammenstellungen aus der Modellreihe "Life", Design von Roberto Monsani für Acerbis International. Unten rechts: Zusammenstellung aus der Modellreihe "Landare" von Nueva Línea.

From left to right: sofa "Nestor" from J. M. Gady for Liv' It; seat "Titu'" from J. Armgardt for Bonaldo; massage chair "Concept" from Keyton; easy chair "Ata" from S. Micheli for Adrenalina.

De gauche à droite : canapé "Nestor" de J. M. Gady pour Liv' It ; fauteuil "Titu'" de J. Armgardt pour Ronaldo ; fauteuil de massage "Concept" de Keyton ; fauteuil "Ata" de S. Micheli pour Adrenalina.

Von links nach rechts: Das Sofa "Nestor" von J. M. Gady für Liv' It; der von J. Armgardt für Bonaldo entworfene Sessel "Titu'"; der Ruhesessel "Concept" von Keyton; Sessel "Ata", von S. Micheli für Adrenalina entworfen.

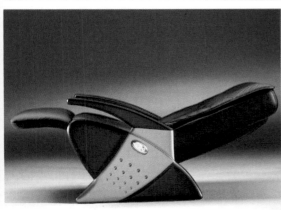

Composition from the program "Contin" from Misura Emme.

Composition de la gamme "Contin" de Misura Emme.

Zusammenstellung aus der Modellreihe "Contin" von Misura Emme.

Container furniture "Magrab" from Innovation.

Rangement "Magrab" de Innovation.

Containermöbel "Magrab" von Innovation.

Composition proposal
by Tissetanta.

Composition proposée
par Tissetanta.

Eine von Tissetanta
angebotene Lösung.

Chair "Bahbar" from G. Bardet for Liv' It. On the right, chairs "Pause-Café" from P. Mourgue for Artelano.

Chaise "Bahbar" de G. Bardet pour Liv' It. À droite, chaises "Pause-Café" de P. Mourgue pour Artelano.

Der Stuhl "Bahbar", Design von G. Bardet für Liv' It. Rechts die Stühle "Pause-Café", die von P. Mourgue für Artelano entworfen wurden.

Below, on the left, table "Alto". Design from Arquirivolto for Bonaldo. In the center, chair "Gas" from J. Gasca for Stua. On the right, center table "Hubble" from Leolux.

En bas à gauche, table "Alto", création de Arquirivolto pour Bonaldo. Au centre, chaise "Gas" de J. Gasca pour Stua. À droite, table basse "Hubble" de Leolux.

Unten links der Tisch "Alto", Design von Arquirivolto für Bonaldo. In der Mitte der Stuhl "Gas" von J. Gasca für Stua. Rechts Couchtisch "Hubble" von Leolux.

Container system "Intu". Design from Niels Bendtsen for Montis.

Rangement "Intu", création de Niels Bendtsen pour Montis.

Containersystem "Intu", Design von Niels Bendtsen für Montis.

Chair from Vibiemme and center table "Rooby" from Leolux.

Chaise de Vibiemme et table basse "Rooby" de Leolux.

Stuhl von Vibiemme und Tisch "Rooby" von Leolux.

These tables, created in 1925-26 by Marcel Breuer are classics of contemporary design. Produced by Tecta.

Ces tables, créées en 1925-26 par Marcel Breuer sont des classiques de la création contemporaine. Fabriquées par Tecta.

Diese 1925-26 von Marcel Breuer entworfenen Tische sind zu Klassikern des modernen Designs geworden. Hergestellt werden sie von Tecta.

Composition for the living room from Nueva Línea.

Composition pour salon de Nueva Línea.

Zusammenstellung für das Wohnzimmer von Nueva Línea.

On the left, dining room set from Maisa. On the right, the shelving program "Delta". A design from Enzo Mari for Robots.

À gauche, ensemble de salle à manger de Maisa. À droite, la gamme d'étagères "Delta" est une création de Enzo Mari pour Robots.

Links eine Esszimmergruppe von Maisa. Rechts das Regalsystem "Delta" mit einem Design von Enzo Mari für Robots.

Table "Link". Design from Hannes Wettstein for Desalto.

Table "Link" création de Hannes Wettstein pour Desalto.

Der von Hannes Wettstein für Desalto entworfene Tisch "Link".

The easy chair "LC1" was designed in 1928 by Le Corbusier, P. Jeanneret and C. Perriand. Produced by Cassina.

Le fauteuil "LC1" a été créé en 1928 par Le Corbusier, P. Jeanneret et C. Perriand. Fabrication Cassina.

Der Sessel "LC1" wurde 1928 von Le Corbusier, P. Jeanneret und C. Perriand entworfen. Hergestellt wird er heute von Cassina.

Sofa "Mr. Koala" and auxiliary tables "Camaleo"
from Giorgetti following the design by Nicola Adami.

Canapé "Mr. Koala" et tables basses "Camaleo"
de Giorgetti, d'après une création de Nicola Adami.

Sofa "Mr. Koala" und Beistelltische "Camaleo"
von Giorgetti, nach einem Design von Nicola Adami.

The easy chair "D-80" was created by Jean Prouvé in 1930. Produced by Tecta.

Le fauteuil "D-80" a été créé par Jean Prouvé en 1930. Fabriqué par Tecta.

Der Sessel "D-80" wurde 1930 von Jean Prouvé entworfen. Hergestellt wird er von Tecta.

Composition from the program "3D Giorno" from Zanette. On the right, shelving from the system "Trieste" from Enzo Mari for Robots.

Composition de la gamme "3D Giorno" de Zanette. À droite, étagère "Trieste" de Enzo Mari pour Robots.

Zusammenstellung aus der Modellreihe "3D Giorno" von Zanette. Rechts: Regale aus der Modellreihe "Trieste" von Enzo Mari für Robots.

Bookcase "New Secret". Design from P. Galloti
and R. Bello Dias for Galloti & Radice.

Bibliothèque "New Secret", création de P. Galloti
et R. Bello Dias pour Galloti & Radice.

Das Regal "New Secret", ein Design von P. Galloti
und R. Bello Dias für Galloti & Radice.

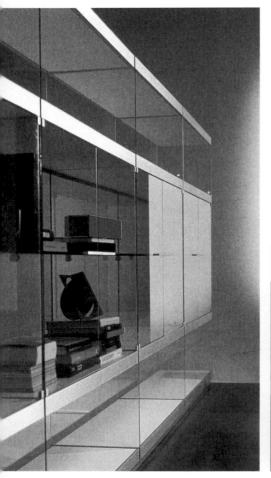

Sofa bed "Speedking" from Innovation.

Canapé-lit "Speedking" de Innovation.

Schlafsofa "Speedking" von Innovation.

Program modular "Pentag" from Misura Emme.

Gamme convertible "Pentag" de Misura Emme.

Modulserie "Pentag" von Misura Emme.

Container furniture for television and audio "Mast"
from P. Cazzaniga for Liv' It.

Support pour matériel audiovisuel "Mast",
de P. Cazzaniga pour Liv' It.

Containermöbel für Fernseh- und Videogeräte "Mast",
von P. Cazzaniga für Liv' It entworfen.

Easy chair "Kira" from J. Broente for Bonaldo.

Fauteuil "Kira", de J. Broente pour Bonaldo.

Der von J. Broente für Bonaldo entworfene Sessel "Kira".

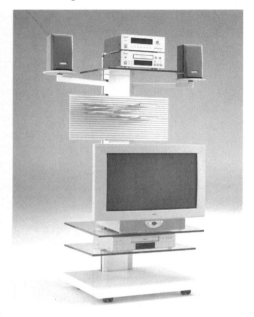

To the left, easy chair "Ekstrem"
from Terje Ekstrøm for Stokke. On
the right, sideboard from Maisa.

A gauche, fauteuil "Ekstrem"
de Terje Ekstrøm pour Stokke.
À droite, buffet de Maisa.

Auf der vorangehenden Seite links
der Sessel "Ekstrem", der von Terje
Ekstrøm für Stokke entworfen
wurde. Rechts eine Anrichte von
Maisa.

Table "8930" and chairs "7200" from Rolf Benz.

Table "8930" et chaises "7200" de Rolf Benz.

Tisch "8930" und Stühle "7200" von Rolf Benz.

On the left, table "Konx" from Ron Arad. On the right,
table "Grillo" from V. Livi. From Fiam Italia.

À gauche, table "Konx" de Ron Arad. À droite, table
"Grillo" de V. Livi. De Fiam Italia.

Links: "Konx" von Ron Arad. Hergestellt. Rechts der
Tisch "Grillo" von V. Livi. Von Fiam Italia.

Bottom left, dining room table
"Golf One" from Galloti & Radice.
On the right, table "8520" from
Hans Karuga for Rolf Benz.

En bas à gauche, table de salle
à manger "Golf One" de Galloti
& Radice. À droite, table "8520"
de Hans Karuga pour Rolf Benz.

Links der Esszimmertisch "Golf
One" von Galloti & Radice.
Rechts der von Hans Karuga für
Rolf Benz entworfene Tisch "8520".

Massimo Iosa Ghini is the author of the design
of the seating set "Chicago" from Roche Bobois.

Massimo Iosa Ghini signe la création de l'ensemble
de sièges "Chicago" de Roche Bobois.

Massimo Iosa Ghini zeichnet für das Design
der Sitzgruppe "Chicago" von Roche Bobois.

Sofa "Circum" and easy chair "Circo". Design from Peter Maly for Cor.

Canapé "Circum" et fauteuil "Circo", création de Peter Maly pour Cor.

Das Sofa "Circum" und der Sessel "Circo", Design von Peter Maly für Cor.

Shelving "You" from Viccarbe.

Bibliothèque "You" de Viccarbe.

Das Regal "You" von Viccarbe.

Sofa "F40" designed by Marcel
Breuer in 1931. Produced by Tecta.

Canapé "F40" créé par Marcel
Breuer en 1931. Fabriqué par Tecta.

Das im Jahre 1931 von Marcel
Breuer entworfene und von Tecta
hergestellte Sofa "F40".

Chaise-longue "Onda" designed
by J. Kressel and I. Shelle for Cor.
On the right, sofa "Nautilus"
from Kagan New York Collection.

Chaise-longue "Onda" créée par
J. Kressel et I. Shelle pour Cor.
À droite, canapé "Nautilus"
de Kagan New York Collection.

Chaiselongue "Onda". ein Design
von J. Kressel und I. Shelle für Cor.
Rechts das Sofa "Nautilus"
von Kagan New York Collection.

Table "Artico" and chairs "Duna". Design from Jorge Pensi for Cassina (photo: Andrea Ferrari).

Table "Artico" et chaises "Duna", création de Jorge Pensi pour Cassina (photo : Andrea Ferrari).

Tisch "Artico" und Stühle "Duna", Design von Jorge Pensi für Cassina (Foto: Andrea Ferrari).

Dining room group "Hopla' System" from Rizza Design & Complementi.

Ensemble de salle à manger "Hopla' System" de Rizza Desig & Complementi.

Die Esszimmergruppe "Hopla' System" von Rizza Design & Complementi.

Chaise-longue "Agua"
from Diego Fortunato for Perobell.

Chaise-longue "Agua"
de Diego Fortunato pour Perobell.

Chaiselongue "Agua"
von Diego Fortunato für Perobell.

Easy chair "Wing-Chair" from Kagan New York
Collection. On the right, chair "Lógica"
from Josep Lluscà for Enea.

Fauteuil "Wing-Chair" de Kagan New York Collection.
À droite, chaise "Lógica" de Josep Lluscà pour Enea.

Sessel "Wing-Chair" von Kagan New York Collection.
Rechts der Stuhl "Lógica" von Josep Lluscà für
Enea entworfen.

Left image, chair "Trienn".
On the right, easy chair "Wibber". All from Leolux.

À gauche, chaise "Trienn".
À droite, fauteuil "Wibber". Ensemble de Leolux.

Links der Stuhl "Trienn" und rechts der Sessel
"Wibber", hergestellt von Leolux.

Bottom left image, table "Verner" from Viccarbe.
On the right, chair "Poltro" from Misura Emme.

Image du bas à gauche, table "Verner" de Viccarbe.
À droite, chaise "Poltro" de Misura Emme.

Unten links der Tisch "Verner" von Viccarbe.
Rechts der Stuhl "Poltro" von Misura Emme.

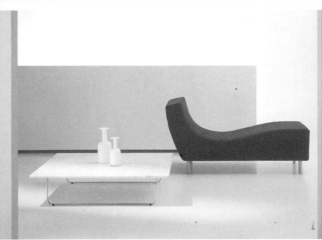

Sofa "LWS" from Philippe Starck and easy chair "LC1" from Le Corbusier, P. Jeanneret and C. Perriand. From Cassina (photo: Andrea Ferrari).

Canapé "LWS" de Philippe Starck et fauteuil "LC1" de Le Corbusier, P. Jeanneret et C. Perriand. De Cassina (photo : Andrea Ferrari).

Sofa "LWS" von Philippe Starck und Sessel "LC1" von Le Corbusier, P. Jeanneret und C. Perriand, von Cassina (Foto: Andrea Ferrari).

Two images from the program "Net" from Lago.

Deux images de la gamme "Net" de Lago.

Zwei Beispiele aus der Modellreihe "Net" von Lago.

Easy chair "Peel"
designed by Olav Eldøy for Stokke.

Fauteuil "Peel",
créé par Olav Eldøy pour Stokke.

Der von Olav Eldøy
für Stokke entworfene Sessel "Peel".

Table "Sirare" from Viccarbe.
Table "Sirare" de Viccarbe.
Der Tisch "Sirare" von Viccarbe.

Shelving from the series "Revers"
from P. Salvadé for Porada.

Étagères de la série "Revers"
de P. Salvadé pour Porada.

Regale aus der Modellreihe "Revers",
von P. Salvadé für Porada entworfen.

Composition from the program
"Palco" from M. Marconato and
T. Zappa for Porada.

Composition de la gamme "Palco"
de M. Marconato et T. Zappa pour
Porada.

Eine Zusammenstellung aus der von
M. Marconato und T. Zappa für Porada.
entworfenen Modellreihe "Palco".

Top image, bookcase "Wall Book" from M. Marconato and T. Zappa for Porada. Bottom left, easy chair from Bodema. In the center, container furniture "Ubiqua" from T. Colzani for Porada. On the right, chair "Lia" from R. Barbieri for Zanotta (photo A&C).

Image du haut, bibliothèque "Wall Book" de M. Marconato et T. Zappa pour Porada. En bas à gauche, fauteuil de Bodema. Au centre, rangement "Ubiqua" de T. Colzani pour Porada. À droite, chaise "Lia" de R. Barbieri pour Zanotta (photo A&C).

Oben das Regal "Wall Book", Design von M. Marconato und T. Zappa für Porada. Unten links ein Sessel von Bodema. In der Mitte das von T. Colzani für Porada entworfene Containermöbel "Ubiqua". Rechts der Stuhl "Lia" von R. Barbieri für Zanotta (Foto A&C).

Easy chairs "Jetsons" from
Guglielmo Berchicci for Giovannetti.

Fauteuils "Jetsons" de Guglielmo
Berchicci pour Giovannetti.

Die Sessel "Jetsons",
die von Guglielmo Berchicci für
Giovannetti entworfen wurden.

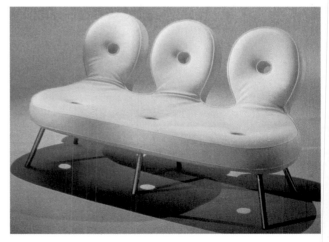

Sofa "Olo". Design from
Simone Micheli for Adrenalina.

Canapé "Olo", création de
Simone Micheli pour Adrenalina.

Sofa "Olo", Design von
Simone Micheli für Adrenalina.

Metallic kitchens

Clock "Tempi Duri" designed by
Marcello Ziliani. Produced by Progetti.

Horloge "Tempi Duri" créée par
Marcello Ziliani. Fabriquée par Progetti.

Uhr "Tempi Duri", Design von Marcello
Ziliani. Hergestellt wird sie von Progetti.

| Des cuisines métalliques

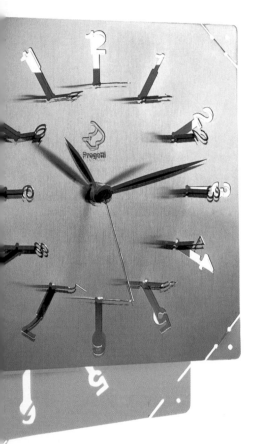

| Küchen aus Stahl

Avant-garde kitchens are like a flash of light, as their metallic surfaces of steel or aluminum give off luminous reflections, filling the space with vitality. Their esthetics reminds us of large industrial kitchens, although their forms adapt to domestic surroundings. Their great facilities for cleanliness and maintenance, along with technical innovations and the highly ergonomic and functional design of the furniture that facilitate the carrying out of different tasks are their main signs of identity. Kitchens of this nature are not exclusive to avant-garde environments as they have the facility to adapt to homes where the general decoration responds to a more traditional taste. Perhaps, this neutral style, although impressive, is one of the keys of their great success.

Die avantgardistischen Küchen wirken wie Lichtblitze, ihre Oberflächen aus Stahl oder Aluminium werfen Lichtstrahlen zurück und geben diesem Raum Leben. Zwar sind ihre Maße auf Privathaushalte zugeschnitten, aber dennoch erinnert ihre Ästhetik an industrielle Großküchen. Sie zeichnen sich in erster Linie dadurch aus, dass sie leicht sauber zu halten sind, technisch auf neustem Stand und ihre Möbel ausgesprochen ergonomisch und so funktional sind, dass hier die verschiedensten Arbeiten erledigt werden können. Diese Art Küche ist jedoch nicht ausschließlich den avantgardistischen Interieurs vorbehalten, sondern sie wird auch in Wohnungen integriert, die sonst in einem etwas tradtionelleren Stil eingerichtet sind. Vielleicht ist gerade diese neutrale, aber dennoch wirkungsvolle Ästhetik der Schlüssel zu ihrem großen Erfolg.

Les cuisines d'avant-garde sont un éclair de lumière, avec leurs surfaces métalliques d'acier ou d'aluminium projetant des reflets lumineux et remplissant la pièce de vitalité. Leur esthétique rappelle les grandes cuisines industrielles, même si leurs formes s'adaptent à l'environnement domestique. Le nettoyage et l'entretien extrêmement simple de ces cuisines, ainsi que les innovations techniques et le design totalement ergonomique et fonctionnel du mobilier, facilitant la réalisation d'un grand nombre de tâches, sont leurs principales marques d'identité. Ce type de cuisines n'est pas réservé aux contextes d'avant-garde, car il peut s'adapter aux demeures dont la décoration générale répond à un goût plus traditionnel. Il se peut que cette esthétique neutre - ce qui ne l'empêche pas d'avoir de l'impact -, soit une des clefs de son grand succès.

Model "Dimension 75" from Poggenphol in maple.

Modèle "Dimension 75" de Poggenphol, en bois d'érable.

Modell "Dimension 75" von Poggenpohl, Ausführung in Ahorn.

Composition from the series "Flavia" from Nobilia.

Composition de la série "Flavia" de Nobilia.

Zusammenstellung aus der Modellreihe "Flavia" von Nobilia.

Kitchen from the series "Tec" from Alno.

Cuisine de la série "Tec" de Alno.

Küche der Modellreihe "Tec" von Alno.

This composition from the series "Monia" from Nobilia combines stainless steel with touches of color.

Cette composition de la série "Monia" de Nobilia, combine l'acier inoxydable et les petites touches de couleurs.

Bei dieser Zusammenstellung aus der Modellreihe "Monia" von Nobilia werden rostfreier Stahl und farbige Elemente miteinander kombiniert.

Cupboards with siding doors from Alno.

Armoires à portes coulissantes de Alno.

Schränke mit Schiebetüren von Alno.

Detail from the model "Ontario Line" from Leicht.

Détail du modèle "Ontario Line" de Leicht.

Detail des Modells "Ontario Line" von Leicht.

Model "Vega" from Scavolini.

Modèle "Vega" de Scavolini.

Das Modell "Vega" von Scavolini.

Model "Grafics" from Leicht.
Modèle "Grafics" de Leicht.
Modell "Grafics" von Leicht.

Composition from the program "Vela". Design from Luca Meda for Dada.

Composition de la gamme "Vela", création de Luca Meda pour Dada.

Eine Zusammenstellung aus der Modellreihe "Vela", Design von Luca Meda für Dada.

Proposal from Bis Bis Imports Boston.

Proposition de Bis Bis Imports Boston.

Ein Vorschlag von Bis Bis Imports Boston.

Composition "Opal" from Nobilia. Below, on the left and center, two possible combinations from the program "Cinqueterre" from Schiffini. On the right, series "Aluminio" from Alno.

Composition "Opal" de Nobilia. En bas à gauche et au centre, deux combinaisons possibles de la gamme "Cinqueterre" de Schiffini. À droite, série "Aluminio" de Alno.

Eine Zusammenstellung aus der Modellreihe "Opal" von Nobilia. Unten links und Mitte zwei Möglichkeiten, Stücke aus der Modellreihe "Cinqueterre" von Schiffini miteinander zu kombinieren. Rechts die Modellreihe "Aluminio" von Alno.

Proposal from the program "Vela"
from Dada. Design from Luca Meda.

Proposition de la gamme "Vela"
de Dada, création de Luca Meda.

Ein Vorschlag aus der
Modellreihe "Vela" von Dada.
Design von Luca Meda.

On the left, model "Fiona" from
Nobilia. In the center, model "Vela"
from Dada. On the right, model
"Melville" from Scavolini.

À gauche, modèle "Fiona"
de Nobilia. Au centre, modèle
"Vela" de Dada. À droite, modèle
"Melville" de Scavolini.

Links das Modell "Fiona"
von Nobilia. In der Mitte das Modell
"Vela" von Dada. Rechts
das Modell "Melville" von Scavolini.

Elegant composition from
the "Sistema 25" from Bulthaup.

Élégante composition de
"Sistema 25" de Bulthaup.

Eine elegante Zusammenstellung
aus dem "Sistema 25"
von Bulthaup.

Model "Astra" from Scavolini, laminated in cherry.
Modèle "Astra" de Scavolini, en bois de cerisier laminé.
Modell "Astra", kirschbaumfurniert, von Scavolini.

Proposal for integrated dining room from Bulthaup.
Proposition de salle à manger intégrée de Bulthaup.
Ein Vorschlag von Bulthaup für ein integriertes Esszimmer.

Top image, model "Sally". Design from Phoem for Febal. Below, on the left, composition from the program "Banco". Design from Luca Meda for Dada. On the right, model "Trend" from Nobilia.

Image du haut, modèle "Sally", création de Phoem pour Febal. En bas à gauche, composition de la gamme "Banco" création de Luca Meda pour Dada. À droite, modèle "Trend" de Nobilia.

Oben das von Phoem für Febal entworfene Modell "Sally". Unten links eine Zusammenstellung aus der Modellreihe "Banco", Design von de Luca Meda für Dada. Rechts das Modell "Trend" von Nobilia.

Composition from the program "System 20" from Bulthaup.

Composition de la gamme "Sistema 20" de Bulthaup.

Zusammenstellung aus der Modellreihe "Sistema 20" von Bulthaup.

Zengiaro Associati are the authors of this design from the program "Evergreen" from Febal.

Zengiaro Associati signe la création de la gamme "Evergreen" de Febal.

Zengiaro Associati zeichnet für das Design der Modellreihe "Evergreen" von Febal.

Program "Star Pro" from Alno.

Gamme "Star Pro" de Alno.

Modellreihe "Star Pro" von Alno.

Possible combination from the program "Largo FG" from Leicht.

Une des combinaisons possibles ce la gamme "Largo FG" de Leicht.

Mögliche Zusammenstellung aus der Modellreihe "Largo FG" von Leicht.

Composition from the system "Flipper" from Zengiaro Associati for Febal.

Composition de la gamme "Flipper" de Zengiaro Associati pour Febal.

Eine Zusammenstellung aus der Modellreihe "Flipper", von Zengiaro Associati für Febal entworfen.

Model "Joy" from Alno.

Modèle "Joy" de Alno.

Das Modell "Joy" von Alno.

Modular composition from the "Sistema 20" from Bulthaup.

Composition convertible de "Sistema 20" de Bulthaup.

Eine Zusammenstellung aus dem Modulsystem "Sistema 20" von Bulthaup.

Model "Tec Pro" from Alno.

Modèle "Tec Pro" de Alno.

Modell "Tec Pro" de Alno.

Composition from the "Sistema 25" from Bulthaup. Below, on the left,
model "Tec" from Alno. On the right, program "Zelig" from Luca Meda for Dada.

Composition de "Sistema 25" de Bulthaup. En bas à gauche,
modèle "Tec" de Alno. À droite, gamme "Zelig" de Luca Meda pour Dada.

Zusammenstellung aus dem Modulsystem "Sistema 25" von Bulthaup. Unten links
das Modell "Tec" von Alno. Rechts die Modellreihe "Zelig" von Luca Meda für Dada.

One of the possible combinations
allowed by the "Sistema 25" from
Bulthaup.

Une combinaison possible avec le
"Sistema 25" de Bulthaup.

Eine der möglichen
Zusammenstellungen aus der
Modellreihe "Sistema 25" von
Bulthaup.

Proposal from the program
"Banko".

Proposition de la gamme
"Banko".

Vorschlag aus der Modellreihe
"Banko".

| Bathroom design

"Box" by Bruna Rapisarda for Regia.

"Box" de Bruna Rapisarda pour Regia.

"Box" von Bruna Rapisarda für Regia.

| Des salles de bain design

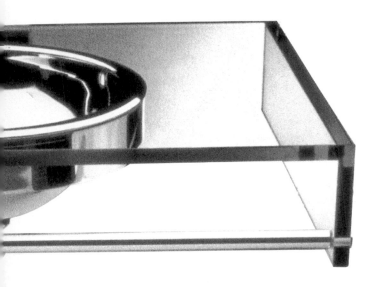

| Designerbadezimmer

We present the new culture of the bathroom. The bathroom understood as a center of technical perfection and formal purity. Bathrooms to be shown off with pride. To be enjoyed slowly, never with haste. To be fallen in love with because of their well-resolved design: the creation of unconventional forms that respond to the necessities of always, but adapt themselves to the new era. They evolve along side new forms of life, looking for new materials and challenges that give answers to esthetic and functional worries that until very few years ago had been ignored. The act of cleanliness will now no longer be something routine, because the bathroom becomes a kind of oasis in the middle of chaos, where not only is the body purified, but, also, the spirit.

Voici une nouvelle façon de concevoir des salles de bain. La salle de bain perçue comme le centre de la perfection technique et de la pureté formelle et conçue pour être exhibée avec fierté ; pour être utilisée tranquillement, sans hâte. Pour tomber amoureux du design bien pensé : la création de formes non conventionnelles, répondant aux besoins de toujours mais s'adaptant aux temps modernes. Elle évolue suivant les nouvelles formes de vie, à la recherche de nouveaux matériaux et de nouveaux défis, répondant aux inquiétudes esthétiques et fonctionnelles qui, il n'y a pas si longtemps, étaient encore totalement ignorées. L'utilisation de la salle de bain ne sera définitivement plus un acte routinier, cette pièce s'étant transformée en une oasis au milieu du chaos où non seulement le corps, mais aussi l'esprit, se purifient.

Hinsichtlich der Badezimmer ist eine neue Kultur entstanden, die wir hier vorstellen möchten. Sie werden als Raum verstanden, in dem Technik und Formgebung ihren höchsten Grad an Perfektion erreichen. Es entstehen Badezimmer, die mit Stolz vorgezeigt werden. Sie wollen in aller Ruhe genossen werden, Hast und Eile sind aus ihnen verbannt. Ihr gut verstandenes Design ist zum Verlieben: Herkömmliche werden durch moderne Formen ersetzt, mit denen die von jeher an das Bad gestellten Ansprüche erfüllt werden, jedoch unter Anpassung an die Erfordernisse der modernen Zeit. Die Badezimmer passen sich den neuen Lebensformen an. Die Suche nach neuen Materialien und Formen wird zur Herausforderung, um so eine Lösung für die modernen Konzepte der Ästhetik und Funktionalität zu finden, denen man bis vor Kurzem keine besondere Bedeutung beigemessen hatte. Der Moment, den wir der Körperpflege widmen, wird ab jetzt nicht mehr zur Routine werden, denn unser Badezimmer ist zu einer Oase mitten in dem uns umgebenden Chaos geworden, in der nicht nur der Körper einer Reinigung unterzogen wird, sondern auch die Seele Ruhe und Entspannung erfährt.

Column from bathroom "Solitude" from Dornbracht.

Colonne de salle de bain "Solitude" de Dornbracht.

Multifunktionssäule "Solitude" von Dornbracht.

Cinzia Ruggeri is the author of the design of the collection "Cinzia's Family" from Nito.

Cinzia Ruggeri signe la création de la collection "Cinzia's Family" de Nito.

Cinzia Ruggeri zeichnet für das Design der Modellreihe "Cinzia's Family" von Nito.

Furniture from the series "Limit" and washbasin "Bol" from Roca.

Mobilier de la série "Limit" et lavabo "Bol" de Roca.

Möbelstücke aus der Modellreihe "Limit" und Waschbecken "Bol" von Roca.

On the left, washbasin "Pamplona" from Capilla &
Viejo: screen "Ima" and bath "Carezza Lake"
from Peter Büchele. All from Rapsel. On the right,
composition "Versilia" from Toscoquattro.
Below on the left, "Pure Basic" from Villeroy & Boch.

À gauche, lavabo "Pamplona" de Capilla & Viejo ;
paravent "Ima" et baignoire "Carezza Lake"
de Peter Büchele. Ensemble de Rapsel. À droite,
composition "Versilia" de Toscoquattro.
En bas à gauche, "Pure Basic" de Villeroy & Boch.

Links das Waschbecken "Pamplona" von Capilla &
Viejo; Duschwand "Ima" und Badewanne "Carezza
Lake" von Peter Büchele. Alles von Rapsel.
Rechts Zusammenstellung "Versilia" von Toscoquattro.
Unten links "Pure Basic" von Villeroy & Boch.

Bath "Lavasca" from Matteo Thun and washbasin "Bouro 1" from E. Souto de Moura. From Rapsel.

Baignoire "Lavasca" de Matteo Thun et lavabo "Bouro 1" de E. Souto de Moura. De Rapsel.

Die Badewanne "Lavasca" von Matteo Thun und das Waschbecken "Bouro 1" von E. Souto de Moura. Hergestellt von Rapsel.

Bathroom furniture from the series "Arizona" from Gama-Decor.

Mobilier de salle de bain de la série "Arizona" de Gama-Decor.

Badezimmermöbel aus der Modellreihe "Arizona" von Gama-Decor.

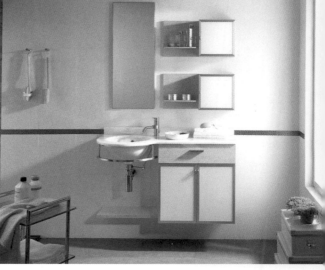

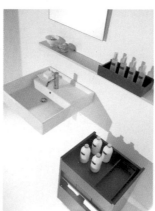

Composition "3002" from Axia. Right: Program "Container" from Industrias Cosmic.

Composition "3002" de Axia. À droite: Gamme "Container" de Industrias Cosmic.

Zusammenstellung "3002" von Axia. Rechts: Die Modellreihe "Container" von Industrias Cosmic.

Sieger Design has developed
this series of bathroom faucets
"Meta Tec" from Dornbracht.

Sieger Design a créé cette série
de robinet pour salle de bain
"Meta Tec", de Dornbracht.

Sieger Design hat die Armaturen
für das Bad "Meta Tec"
für Dornbracht entworfen.

Collection "New Look"
from Industrias Cosmic.

Collection "New Look"
de Industrias Cosmic.

Modellreihe "New Look"
von Industrias Cosmic.

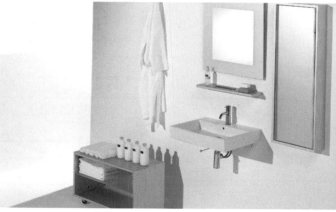

On the left, container furniture "Multibox" from Sieger Design for Duravit.
Top right image, model "Soho NY" from Villeroy & Boch.
Bottom right, program "Metropolis" from Toscoquattro.

À gauche, rangement "Multibox" de Sieger Design pour Duravit.
Image du haut à droite, modèle "Soho NY" de Villeroy & Boch.
En bas à droite, gamme "Metropolis" de Toscoquattro.

Links die Containermöbel "Multibox" von Sieger, Design für Duravit. Oben
rechts das Modell "Soho NY" von Villeroy & Boch.
Unten rechts die Modellreihe "Metropolis" von Toscoquattro.

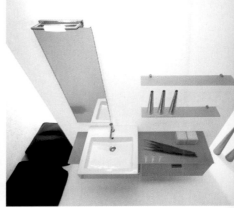

On the right, washbasin "Vero" from Duravit. Below, composition "1018" from Axia.

À droite, lavabo "Vero" de Duravit. En bas, composition "1018" de Axia.

Rechts das Waschbecken "Vero" von Duravit. Unten Modellreihe "1018" von Axia.

Composition "2014" from Axia.

Composition "2014" de Axia.

Modellreihe "2014" von Axia.

Cupboard "Bipop" from Cozza and Mascheroni for Desalto. On the right, composition "1003" from Axia.

Placard "Bipop" de Cozza y Mascheroni pour Desalto. À droite, composition "1003" de Axia.

Der von Cozza und Mascheroni für Desalto entworfene Schrank "Bipop". Rechts die Modellreihe "1003" von Axia.

Composition "3003" from Axia. On the right, washbasin "Gotta" with porcelain surface. From Altro.

Composition "3003" de Axia. À droite, lavabo "Gotta" en porcelaine, de Altro.

Model reihe "3003" von Axia. Rechts das Waschbecken "Gotta" mit Porzellandeckplatte, von Altro.

Shower "Pluvia" designed by Matteo Thun from Rapsel. On the right, composition "3001" from Axia.

Douche "Pluvia" créée par Matteo Thun, de Rapsel. À droite, composition "3001" de Axia.

Die Dusche "Pluvia", Design von Matteo Thun für Rapsel. Rechts die Modellreihe "3001" von Axia.

The avant-garde in the bedroom

Antonio Citterio has developed
the program "Apta" from Maxalto.

Antonio Citterio a créé la gamme
"Apta" de Maxalto.

Von Antonio Citterio ist die Modellreihe
"Apta" von Maxalto entwickelt worden.

Un style d'avant-garde pour la chambre

Avantgardistische
Interieurs für Schlafzimmer

On many occasions, avant-garde esthetics is associated with cold, soulless spaces. Evidently, it depends on what each one of us understands by cold – and what we understand by soul. In general, bedrooms of this sort are decorated with few very well selected elements that follow current tendencies: low beds or beds with metal legs; bed-heads of unusual proportions that sometimes extend to form bedsides tables, chests of draws or a sitting area; closets with smooth, generally metallic, surfaces. The results are unobstructed spaces of a generally austere appearance void of superfluous ornamentation, where night and day, day and night, follow their eternal cycle, intertwining themselves without interruption and allowing the warmth of sleep to invade us and regenerate our souls.

On associe souvent l'esthétique d'avant-garde avec les espaces froids et sans âme. Évidemment, cela dépend de ce qu'on entend par froid – et de ce qu'on entend par âme -. Généralement, la décoration de ce type de chambre est composée de peu d'éléments choisis scrupuleusement et suivant les tendances actuelles : des lits bas ou avec des pieds de métal ; des têtes de lits aux proportions inhabituelles comprenant parfois des tables de nuit, des meubles à tiroirs ou un espace pour s'asseoir ; des armoires aux surfaces lisses et, généralement, métalliques. On peut alors contempler des pièces spacieuses, d'aspect généralement austère sans ornementation superflue où le jour et la nuit, la nuit et le jour, suivent leur cycle éternel, se succédant sans interruption et font en sorte que la chaleur du sommeil nous envahisse et régénère notre âme.

Sehr oft wird die avantgardistische Ästhetk mit kalten, seelenlosen Räumen assoziiert. Hier müsste natürlich zunächst einmal definiert werden, was unter "kalt" und "seelenlos" zu verstehen ist. Generell werden diese Art von Schlafzimmern mit sehr wenigen, unter Berücksichtigung der aktuellen Trends sorgfältig ausgewählten Dingen ausgestattet: Niedrige Betten oder Betten mit Stahlfüßen, außergewöhnlich große Kopfteile, die zuweilen weitergeführt werden und Nachttische, Schubladen oder Sitzflächen aufnehmen, Schränke mit glatten, generell aus Metall hergestellten Oberflächen. Das Ergebnis sind geräumige, nüchtern wirkende Zimmer, in denen auf oberflächliches, schmückendes Beiwerk verzichtet worden ist. Hier wechseln sich Tag und Nacht in ihrem ewigen Zyklus ohne Unterbrechung ab und sorgen dafür, daß uns der Schlaf gefangennimmt und sich die Seele erholen kann.

Bedroom from the collection "Solid & Basic" from Club 8 Company.

Chambre de la collection "Solid & Basic" de Club 8 Company.

Schlafzimmer aus der Modellreihe "Solid & Basic" von Club 8 Company.

Model "New Bed" from Domus.

Modèle "New Bed" de Domus.

Modell "New Bed" von Domus.

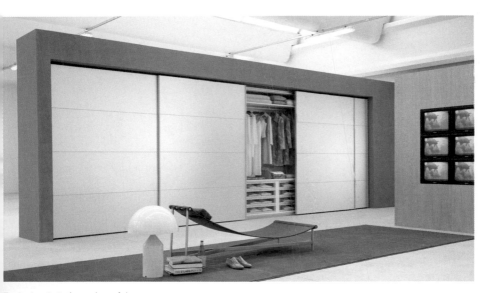

Ennio Arosio is the author of the wardrobe "King" from Mobileffe.

Enr.io Arosio signe la création de l'armoire "King" de Mobileffe.

Ennio Arosio zeichnet für das Design des Schrankes "King" von Mobileffe.

Wardrobe from Mobili by Fredericia.

Armoire de Mobili by Fredericia.

Schrank für Mobili von Fredericia.

Cupboard "Sax" from Misura Emme.

Armoire "Sax" de Misura Emme.

Der Schrank "Sax" von Misura Emme.

On the left, model "Astrid" from Misura Emme.
On the right, image from the collection "Occa"
from Club 8 Company.

À gauche, modèle "Astrid" de Misura Emme. À droite,
image de la collection "Occa" de Club 8 Company.

Links das Modell "Astrid" von Misura Emme.
Rechts die Modellreihe "Occa" von Club 8 Company.

Cassina presents the bed "Sleepy Working Bed" from Philippe Starck (photo: Miro Zagnoli).

Cassina présente le lit "Sleepy Working Bed" de Philippe Starck (photo : Miro Zagnoli).

Cassina präsentiert das Bett "Sleepy Working Bed" von Philippe Starck (Foto: Miro Zagnoli).

Cupboard "Rex" from Misura Emme.

Armoire "Rex" de Misura Emme.

Der Schrank "Rex" von Misura Emme.

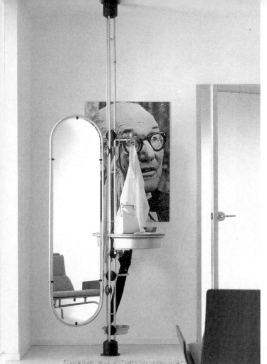

Auxiliary furniture of great versatility. This is the model "Cuccagna" from T. Colzani for Porada.

Meuble d'appoint. Il s'agit du modèle "Cuccagna" de T. Colzani pour Porada.

Äußerst vielseitiges Beistellmöbel. Hier wird das Modell "Cuccagna" gezeigt, das von T. Colzani für Porada entworfen wurde.

On the left, composition from the program "Diva". Design from Ennio Arosio for Verardo. On the right, the chair "Ancella". Design from M. Lovi for Giovannetti. It also fulfils the function of night gallant.

À gauche, composition de la gamme "Diva", création de Ennio Arosio pour Verardo. À droite, la chaise "Ancella", est une création de M. Lovi pour Giovannetti elle peut également remplir la fonction de table de nuit.

Links eine Zusammenstellung aus der Modellreihe "Diva", das Design wurde von Ennio Arosio für Verardo erstellt. Rechts der Stuhl "Ancella", der von M. Lovi für Giovannetti, entworfen wurde und auch als stummer Diener verwandt werden kann.

he model "Lodge" is a design from Rodolfo Dordoni for Molteni & C.

Le modèle "Lodge" est une création de Rodolfo Dordoni pour Molteni & C.

Das Modell "Lodge" ist ein von Rodolfo Dordoni für Molteni & C. erstelltes Design.

lass container furniture "Onda art" from Ron Arad for Fiam Italia.)n the right, bedroom from the rogram "Hopla' System" from izza Design & Complementi.

angements en verre "Onda Kart", e Ron Arad pour Fiam Italia. droite, chambre de la gamme Hopla' System" de Rizza)esign & Complementi.

ontainermöbel aus Glas 'Onda Kart", von Ron Arad ir Fiam Italia entworfen. echts ein Schlafzimmer aus der Modellreihe "Hopla' System" on Rizza Design & Complementi.

Mirror from the program "Pi" from Juventa.

Miroir de la gamme "Pi" de Juventa.

Spiegel aus der Modellreihe "Pi" von Juventa.

Wardrobe proposed by Misura Emm

Armoire proposée par Misura Emm

Von Misura Emme wird dieser Schrank vorgeschlage

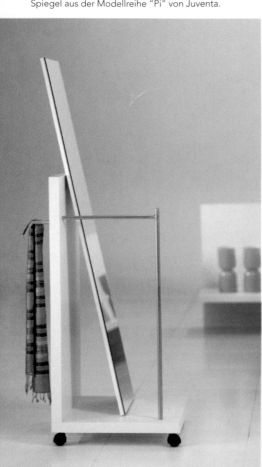

Model "Triplo" from the collection TM Line, from Domus.

Modèle "Triplo" de la collection TM Line, de Domus.

Das Modell "Triplo" aus der Model reihe TM Line von Domus.

Another proposal from the collection "Openside" from Matteograssi
Bottom image, wardrobe "York" from Misura Emme

Une des créations de la collection "Openside", de Matteograssi
Image du bas, armoire "York" de Misura Emme

Ein Vorschlag aus der Modellreihe "Openside" von Matteograssi
Unten der Schrank "York" von Misura Emme

Model "Vanity" from Innovation. In the center, bed from the collection "Inzoni" from Club 8 Company.

Modèle "Vanity" de Innovation. Au centre, lit de la collection "Inzoni" de Club 8 Company.

Modell "Vanity" von Innovation. In der Mitte ein Bett aus der Modellreihe "Inzoni" von Club 8 Company.

One of the possible designs with the collection "Openside" from Matteograssi.

Une autre proposition de la collection "Openside" de Matteograssi.

Eine weiteres Angebot aus der Modellreihe "Openside" von Matteograssi.

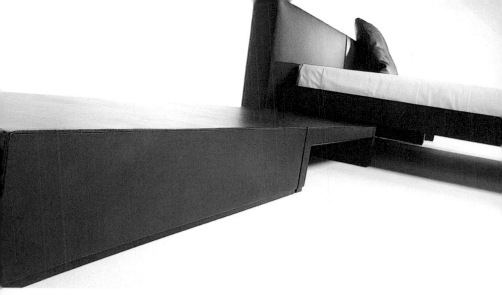

| Creative illumination

The lamp "Saturno" is a re-edition
from Florian Borkenhagen. Produced by Tecta.

La lampe "Saturno" est une nouvelle édition
de Florian Borkenhagen. Fabriquée par Tecta.

Die Lampe "Saturno" ist eine Neuauflage von
Florian Borkenhagen. Hergestellt wird sie von Tecta.

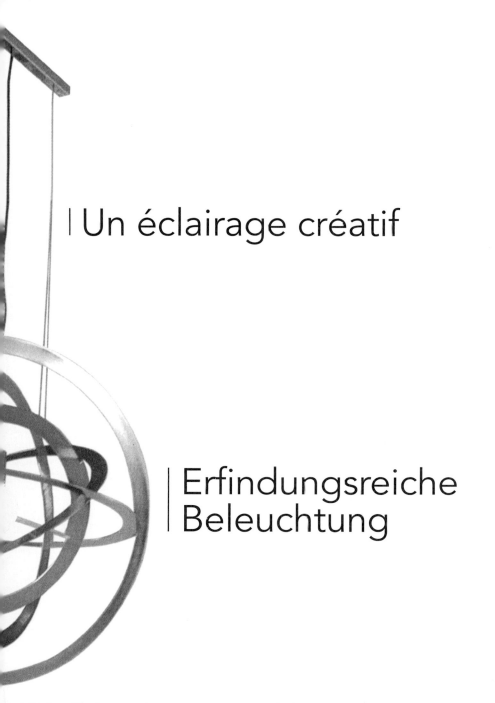

Un éclairage créatif

Erfindungsreiche
Beleuchtung

With a little imagination, a lot of mastery and the necessary tools, you can make a lamp with practically anything: from a plastic detergent bottle, from a strainer to some feathers. A limitless blank page for your creativity. On the other hand, artificial light has an important technical component that must be dominated to obtain the greatest benefit from its multiple aspects. Technical innovations constantly arise (from halogenous light to fiber optics) that give a turn to the incandescent panorama opening new paths to obtain the desired effect with the maximum economy in energy. The "creators of light" do not cease to investigate into new materials and forms and draw, without tiring, new designs on this blank page.

Avec un peu d'imagination, beaucoup de virtuosité et les instruments nécessaires, on peut fabriquer une lampe avec n'importe quel objet : que ce soit une bouteille de détergent en plastique, une passoire ou des plumes. Une infinité de pages restées blanches pour laisser libre cours à la créativité. Par ailleurs, la lumière artificielle comporte un élément technique important qu'il est impératif de dominer afin de tirer le plus grand parti de ses multiples facettes. Des innovations techniques surgissent constamment (de la lumière halogène à la fibre optique), changeant radicalement le panorama lumineux et ouvrant de nouveaux chemins dans le but d'obtenir l'effet recherché en utilisant le moins d'énergie possible. Les "créateurs de lumière" ne cessent de rechercher de nouveaux matériaux et de nouvelles formes, pour faire apparaître sur cette page blanche de nouveaux concepts design.

Es sind lediglich etwas Phantasie, viel Geschicklichkeit und das geeignete Handwerkszeug erforderlich, um aus fast jeglichem Gegenstand eine Lampe entstehen zu lassen: Angefangen bei einer Waschmittelbox aus Kunststoff bis hin zu einem Sieb oder ein paar Federn. Hier werden der Kreativität keine Grenzen gesetzt. Bei Kunstlicht ist andererseits der technische Aspekt nicht zu vergessen, denn man muss schon über die entsprechenden Kenntnisse verfügen, um die vielfältigen Möglichkeiten nutzen zu können. Ständig kommen technische Neuheiten auf den Markt (vom Halogenlicht bis hin zur faseroptischen Energie), die dem Beleuchungssektor neue Aspekte geben und neue Wege aufzeigen, mit denen die gewünschten Lichteffekte mit maximaler Energieersparnis erzielt werden. Die "Lichtdesigner" probieren weiterhin ständig neue Materialien und Formen aus, die sie dann in Form neuer Designs vorstellen.

"Llum" is a design from Pau Durán for Dab
"Llum" est une création de Pau Durán pour Dab
"Llum" ist ein Design von Pau Durán für Dab

The suspended lamp "Ierace" from
Matali Crasset for Artemide.

Plafonnier "Ierace" de Matali Crasset
pour Artemide.

Hängelampe "Ierace", von Matali Crasset
für Artemide entworfen.

On the following page, standard lamp "Marc".
Design from David Abad for Dab. On the right,
the lamp "L40" was designed in 1920
by Gerrit Rietveld. Produced by Tecta.

Sur la page suivante, lampadaire "Marc", création de
David Abad pour Dab. À droite, la lampe "L40" a été
créée en 1920 par Gerrit Rietveld. Fabriquée par Tecta.

Auf der folgenden Seite die Stehlampe "Marc",
Design von David Abad für Dab. Rechts die Lampe
"L40", die 1920 von Gerrit Rietveld entworfen wurde.
Hergestellt werden die Lampen von Tecta.

On the left, model "Viena" from Domus.
On the right, spotlights "Flash" from Carpyen.

À gauche, modèle "Viena" de Domus.
À droite, spots "Flash" de Carpyen.

Links das Modell "Viena" von Domus.
Rechts die Strahler "Flash" von Carpyen.

On the following page, system "Ya Ya Ho"
from Ingo Maurer. Bottom left image, model "Ala".
On the right, variation from "Ala"
with a gray felt shade. From Diemo Alfons.

Sur la page suivante, modèle "Ya Ya Ho"
de Ingo Maurer. Image du bas à gauche, modèle "Ala".
À droite, variation de "Ala" recouvert de feutre gris.
De Diemo Alfons.

Auf der folgenden Seite das System "Ya Ya Ho"
von Ingo Maurer. Unten links das Modell "Ala".
Rechts eine Variante von "Ala" mit einem Schirm
aus grauem Filz. Von Diemo Alfons

On the left, model "Elisabeth Glase" from Domus.
On the right, suspended lamp "Birds, Birds, Birds"
from Ingo Maurer.

À gauche, modèle "Elisabeth Glase" de Domus. À
droite, plafonnier "Birds, Birds, Birds" de Ingo Maurer.

Links das Modell "Elisabeth Glase" von Domus. Rechts
die Hängelampe "Birds, Birds, Birds" von Ingo Maurer.

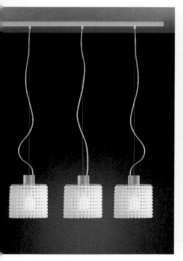

The lamp "Te" is 1,90 m high. From Lievore, Altherr and Molina for Vibia.

La lampe "Te" mesure 1,90 m de haut. De Lievore, Altherr et Molina pour Vibia.

Die Lampe "Te" ist 1,90 m hoch. Von Lievore, Altherr und Molina für Vibia.

"Alhambra" in its standard lamp version with diffuser in transparent polypropylene. Design from Ray Power for Luzifer.

Lampe "Alhambra" en version lampadaire, avec diffuseur en polypropylène transparent. Création de Ray Power pour Luzifer.

"Alhambra" als Stehlampe mit Diffusor aus durchsichtigem Polypropylen. Design von Ray Power für Luzifer.

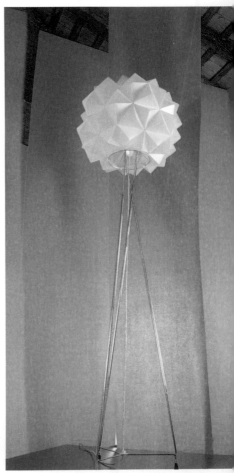

M. A. Ciganda is the author of this design from "Axo".
Produced by Grupo B. Lux.

M. A. Ciganda signe la création de "Axo".
Fabriqué par Grupo B. Lux.

M. A. Ciganda zeichnet für das Design von "Axo".
Hergestellt wird die Lampe von Grupo B. Lux.

Model "Escala" from Cristina Figarola for Dab.

Modèle "Escala" de Cristina Figarola pour Dab.

Modell "Escala", von Cristina Figarola für Dab entworfen.

The "Huevo de Colón" is a design
from G. Ordeig for Santa & Cole (photo: C. Masiá).

Le "Huevo de Colón" est une création de
G. Ordeig pour Santa & Cole (photo : C. Masiá).

Das "Huevo de Colón" ist ein Design von G. Ordeig
für Santa & Cole (Foto: C. Masiá)

Model "Lucellino" in its wall version.
From Ingo Maurer.

Modèle "Lucellino" version applique.
De Ingo Maurer.

Modell "Lucellino" als Wandlampe
von Ingo Maurer.

On the left, appliance "Ilde" from David Abad for Dab. On the right, table lamp "Lucera" from Viccarbe.

À gauche, applique "Ilde" de David Abad pour Dab. À droite, lampe-table "Lucera" de Viccarbe.

Links die Wandlampe "Ilde" von David Abad für Dab. Rechts die Nachttischlampe "Lucera" von Viccarbe.

Standard lamp "Mr. Levi"
from Viccarbe.

Lampadaire "Mr. Levi"
de Viccarbe.

Stehlampe "Mr. Levi"
von Viccarbe.

Lamps from Prealpi.

Lampes de Prealpi.

Lampen von Prealpi.

Standard lamp "Ilia" from Mauro
Bertoldini for Classicon.

Lampadaires "Ilia" de Mauro
Bertoldini pour Classicon.

Die Stehlampe "Ilia", von Mauro
Bertoldini für Classicon entworfen.

Model "System Logico". Design
from Michele de Lucchi and
Gerhard Reichert for Artemide.

Modèle "Sistema Logico",
création de Michele de Lucchi
e Gerhard Reichert pour Artemide.

Modell aus der Modellreihe
"Sistema Logico",
Design von Michele de Lucchi
und Gerhard Reichert für Artemide.

Another version of
"System Logico". On the right,
table lamp "Kaio" from Ernesto
Gismondi. All from Artemide.

Une autre version de
"Sistema Logico". À droite, lampe
de bureau "Kaio" de Ernesto
Gismondi. Ensemble de Artemide.

Eine andere Ausführung von
"Sistema Logico". Rechts die
Tischlampe "Kaio" von Ernesto
Gismondi. Alle Lampen werden
von Artemide angeboten.

Two versions from "Lucera" from Viccarbe.

Deux versions de "Lucera" de Viccarbe.

Zwei Ausführungen von "Lucera" von Viccarbe.

On the left, "Flip Flap" from P. Christian; in the center, "Son from Fontana Arte. On the right, system "Stardust" from Ingo Maurer.

À gauche, "Flip Flap" de P. Christian ; au centre, "Son" de Fontana Arte. À droite, modèle "Stardust" de Ingo Maurer.

Links "Flip Flap" von P. Christian; in der Mitte "Son" von Fontana Arte. Rechts das System "Stardust" von Ingo Maurer.

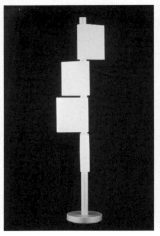

Suspended lamp "Project X"
from Tobias Grau.

Plafonnier "Project X"
de Tobias Grau.

Hängelampe "Project X"
von Tobias Grau.

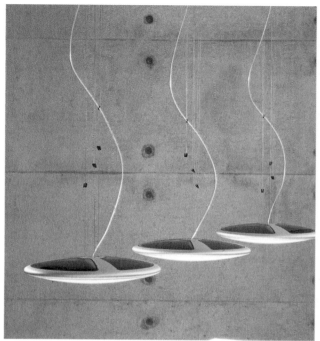

Table lamp "Sui" from Carlotta
from Bevilacqua for Artemide.

Lampe de bureau "Sui" de Carlotta
de Bevilacqua pour Artemide.

Die von Carlotta de Bevilacqua
für Artemide entworfene
Tischlampe "Sui".

Table version of "Rem"
from David Abad for Dab.

Lampe de bureau de "Rem",
de David Abad pour Dab.

Das Modell "Rem" als
Tischlampe, Design von David
Abad für Dab.

Left: "Duck Light" from Ernesto
Gismondi for Artemide. In the
center, appliance "Pailla". Design
from Eileen Gray and produced
by Classicon. Right: Suspended
lamp "Oh Mei Ma Kabir"
from Ingo Maurer.

À gauche: "Duck Light"
de Ernesto Gismondi pour
Artemide. Au centre, applique
"Pailla", création de Eileen Gray
et fabriquée par Classicon.
À droite: plafonnier "Oh Mei Ma
Kabir" de Ingo Maurer.

Links: "Duck Light" von Ernesto
Gismondi für Artemide.
In der Mitte Wandlampe "Pailla",
Design von Eileen Gray,
hergestellt von Classicon.Rechts:
Hängelampe "Oh Mei Ma Kabir"
von Ingo Maurer.

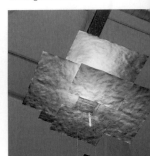

On the left, model "One-Two" from James Irvine for Artemide. On the right, "Gatpac" from Josep Torres Clavé for Santa & Cole (photo: C. Masiá)

À gauche, modèle "One-Two" de James Irvine pour Artemide. À droite, "Gatpac" de Josep Torres Clavé pour Santa & Cole (photo : C. Masiá).

Links das Modell "One-Two" von James Irvine für Artemide. Rechts "Gatpac" von Josep Torres Clavé für Santa & Cole (Foto: C. Masiá).

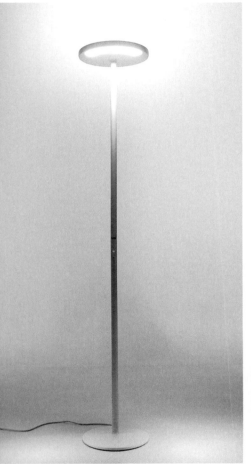

Detail from the sistema "Ya Ya Ho" which offers numerous posibilites. From Ingo Maurer.

Détail de l'ensemble "Ya Ya Ho", offrant de nombreuses possibilités. De Ingo Maurer.

Ein Detail des Systems "Ya Ya Ho", das verschiedenste Kombinationsmöglichkeiten bietet. Von Ingo Maurer.

On the left, lamp "Tesa" from Mauro Marzollo for Itre. In the center, "Tam Tam" from M. Mazzer for Itre. On the right, halogen lamp "Tria" from Carpyen.

À gauche, lampe "Tesa" de Mauro Marzollo pour Itre. Au centre, "Tam Tam" de M. Mazzer pour Itre. À droite, lampe allogène "Tria" de Carpyen.

Links die Lampe "Tesa", die von Mauro Marzollo für Itre entworfen wurde. In der Mitte "Tam Tam" von M. Mazzer für Itre. Rechts die Halogenlampe "Tria" von Carpyen.

Suspended lamp "Porca Miseria" from Ingo Maurer.

Plafonnier "Porca Miseria" de Ingo Maurer.

Die Hängelampe "Porca Miseria" von Ingo Maurer.

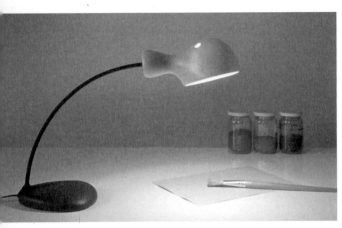

Writing desk lamp "Pipa" from Joan Augé for Taller Uno.

Lampe de bureau "Pipa", de Joan Augé pour Taller Uno.

Die Schreibtischlampe "Pipa", von Joan Augé für Taller Uno entworfen.

On the left, model "Samba" from Helena Poch. On the right, table lamp "Reflexión". Design from Nancy Robbins. From Taller Uno.

À gauche, modèle "Samba" de Helena Poch. À droite, lampe de bureau "Reflexión", création de Nancy Robbins. De Taller Uno.

Links das Modell "Samba" von Helena Poch. Rechts die Tischlampe "Reflexión", Design von Nancy Robbins. Hergestellt von Taller Uno.

On the right, model "Alhambra" from Ray Power in a suspended version. From Luzifer. Below, T. Arola is the author of the design "Badlamp" from Santa & Cole (photo: C. Masiá).

À droite, modèle "Alhambra" de Ray Power, version plafonnier. De Luzifer. En bas, T. Arola signe la création de "Badlamp", de Santa & Cole (photo : C. Masiá).

Rechts das Modell "Alhambra" von Ray Power als Hängelampe. Von Luzifer. Unten: T. Arola zeichnet für das Design von "Badlamp" von Santa & Cole (Foto: C. Masiá).

THE TRADITIONAL AND NOSTALGIC
Homely spaces, with an air between rustic and romantic

On the opposite side of the coin to innovative environments, where nothing reminds us of the past, atmospheres are found where a nostalgic and traditional zest prevails. They are those places where decoration evolves far from the latest stylistic tendencies, barely suffering from the passing of time, or doing so with the introduction of the subtlest of changes.

They are environments that emerge from traditions and memories, taking furniture and objects that remind us of other times as a foundation. Based upon references already acknowledged, these types of surroundings have the ability to transmit security and protection to the people that inhabit them, who feel nostalgia for the furniture and decorative objects of long ago.

Objects crafted by hand will be, therefore, the most appreciated by the defenders of this style. Antiquities also occupy a predominant place in the diverse areas, whether they have been inherited or recuperated from some street market or specialized store. In addition to bringing airs of other times, they also pay tribute to the artistic past of a particular zone. An antique piece combined with furniture of a more current design can offer remarkable results, the uniting of past and present in the same space.

The preference for rustic furniture, of rural reminiscence, is another of the characteristics of these types of interiors. The typical image of a house in the country, with its earthen floors, its majestic wooden beams, its wooden furniture that, in spite of its simplicity, can present from time to time laborious carvings – and that tends to be passed down through the generations —, its joyful floral patterns and its beautiful practicality tend to be the example to follow for those who wish to achieve a certain rural air in the heart of the city.

Later, all that remains to be added are a few touches of light romanticism: some light and airy linen curtains, a bed with a canopy that reminds us of the ones that were used of old, a decoration based on tones of white with a few floral brushstrokes or pastel shades, a small side table finished in such a way that it possesses an aged appearance, a wall painted with natural pigments... and, to round it all off, any personal detail that offers a touch of mystery or of hidden meaning to the eyes of visitors.

Also, into this classification fits classical furniture with a renovated aspect (for example, a Queen Anne chair with present-day upholstery), contributing to a certain elegance to the surroundings, without unnecessarily overloading it.

Comfort and warmth are the great allies of this type of decoration. Inevitably, this kind of furniture provides an aura of rest and well being that gives rise to a pleasant sensation, which is popularly known as "being comfortable".

NOSTALGIQUES ET TRADITIONNELLES
Des espaces accueillants, entre rustiques et romantiques

Sur la face opposée des ambiances novatrices, là où rien ne nous renvoie dans le passé, on trouve des atmosphères où dominent la tradition et la nostalgie. Ce sont des endroits où la décoration n'a rien à voir avec les dernières tendances stylistiques, ne souffre pas du passage du temps ou, dans le cas contraire, évolue en introduisant des changements subtiles.

Ce sont des ambiances qui surgissent de la tradition et du souvenir, qui prennent comme point de référence les meubles et les objets qui nous rappellent d'autres époques. À partir de ces références déjà connues, ce type d'environnement peut transmettre la sécurité et la protection à ceux qui y vivent et qui ressentent une certaine nostalgie pour les meubles et les objets décoratifs d'autrefois.

Les objets artisanaux seront donc les plus appréciés par les défenseurs de ce style. Les antiquités occupent elles aussi une grande place dans les différentes pièces. Qu'elles aient été héritées, trouvées sur les étalages d'un marché aux puces ou dans une boutique spécialisée, elles apportent le souffle d'une autre époque et sont un tribut au passé artistique d'une zone déterminée. Si on met côte à côte une antiquité et un mobilier de style plus actuel on peut obtenir des résultats étonnants car cela nous permet d'unir le passé et le présent dans un même espace.

Une certaine préférence pour le mobilier rustique aux réminiscences champêtres est une autre caractéristique de ce type de décoration d'intérieurs. L'image typique d'une maison de campagne avec des sols en terre, des poutres, des meubles en bois qui, malgré leur simplicité, peuvent parfois être travaillés —et qui sont souvent hérités de père en fils—, des imprimés floraux et une certaine commodité, sont souvent un exemple à suivre pour tous ceux qui veulent obtenir un petit air rustique au milieu de la ville.

Il suffira ensuite d'ajouter de petites touches d'un léger romantisme : des rideaux de dentelle vaporeux, un lit à baldaquin identifique à ceux que l'on utilisait autrefois, une décoration basée sur des tons de blancs et quelques imprimés floraux ou de légers tons pastels, une table de nuit à l'aspect vieilli, un mur peint avec des couleurs naturelles… et, pour couronner le tout, le petit détail personnel apportant une touche de mystère ou une signification incompréhensible aux yeux des v siteurs.

On peut également ajouter à cet éventail les meubles classiques à restaurés (par exemp e, un fauteuil à accoudoirs recouvert d'un tissu de style actuel) qui cortribueront à former un ensemble d'une certaine élégarce sans pour autant charger l'ambiance.

Le confort et la chaleur sont les grands alliés de ce type de décoration car il s'en dégagera inévitablement un halo de bien-être et de repos, une agréable sensation rappelant l'expression populaire "être à l'aise".

INTERIEURS IM NOSTALGISCHEN UND TRADITIONELLEN STIL
Gemütliche Räume im rustikalen oder romantischen Stil

Das Gegenteil der innovativen Interieurs, bei denen nichts mehr an die Vergangenheit erinnert, sind die Räume, die in einem traditionelleren, nostalgischem Stil gehalten sind. Es handelt sich hierbei um Räume, bei deren Ausstattung die Trends der modernen Innenarchitektur in keiner Weise berücksichtigt worden sind; hier scheint die Zeit stehengeblieben zu sein, man hat auf jegliche Änderungen verzichtet.

Es sind Räume, bei deren Ausstattung Tradition und Erinnerung als die wichtigsten Kriterien angesehen werden. Es werden Möbel und Gegenstände ausgewählt, die uns an vergangene Zeiten erinnern. Diese Räume zeichnen sich aufgrund ihrer Eigenschaften dadurch aus, daß sie den in ihnen lebenden Personen ein Gefühl der Sicherheit und Schutz geben. Hinzu kommt, dass die Bewohner Nostalgie für Möbel und dekorative Elemente aus vergangenen Zeiten empfinden.

Aus diesem Grund haben die Anhänger dieser Stilrichtung ein besonderes Faible für handwerklich hergestellte Dinge entwickelt.. Aber auch den antiken Möbelstücken wird in den verschiedenen Räumen ein privilegierter Platz zugewiesen. Sie können ererbt oder auf einem Trödelmarkt oder bei einem Antiquitätenhändler erworben worden sein und bringen nicht nur ein Flair vergangener Zeiten in die Wohnung, sondern s nd auch als Tribut an die künstlerische Vergangenheit einer bestimmten Region zu werten. Ein antikes Stück mit Designermöbeln zu kombinieren kann durch das Nebeneinander von Vergangenheit und Modernität eine erstaunliche Wirkung hervorrufen.

Bei dieser Art von Interieurs werden auch gerne rustikale Möbel mit klarer Reminiszenz auf ländliches Ambiente verwandt. Vor unserem geistigen Auge erscheint das typische Bauernhaus mit Lehmboden, stabilen Deckenträgern aus Holz und eingerichtet mit Holzmöbeln, die trotz ihrer Einfachheit manchmal kunstvolle Schnitzarbeiten aufweisen und oft von Generation auf Generation vererbt werden. Polster mit lustigen Blumenmustern, schön und praktisch. Alles zusammen bekommt für alle diejenigen Modellcharakter, die sich mitten in der Stadt ein Ambiente mit gewissem ländlichen Flair schaffen wollen.

Das Ganze muß dann nur noch mit ein paar romantischen Details ausgeschmückt werden: duftige Leinengardir en, ein Himmelbett, das an vergangene Zeiten erinnert. Die Innenausstattung wird vorwiegend in Weiß gehalten, eventuell mit e n paar zarten Blumenmustern oder mit einigen Farbtupfern in Pastelltönen. Ein kleiner Nachttisch, dem durch eine entsprechende Behandlung Patina verliehen w rd, eine mit Naturpigmentfarben gestrichene Wand ... gehören ebenfalls dazu. Abgerundet wird das Ganze mit einem ganz persönlichen Detail, von dem etwas Mysteriöses ausgeht und dessen Sinn für den fremden Betrachter nicht zu enträtseln ist.

In diese Kategorie gehören auch die Möbel klassischen St ls, denen ein neues Aussehen verliehen worden ist (z.B. ein alter Ohrensessel mit einem modernen Bezugsstoff), und die dem Interieur eine gewisse Eleganz geben, ohne es jedoch zu sehr zu überladen.

Komfort und Gemütlichkeit sind die beiden Dinge, auf die bei dieser Art von Innendekoration besonders viel Wert gelegt wird. . Die dazugehörenden Möbel müssen somit ein Gefühl des Wohlbefindens und der Entspannung vermitteln und dazu beitragen, daß wir uns in unseren vier Wänden "pudelwohl" fühlen.

Living and dining rooms with retro atmospheres

Sofa "Aries" from Léon Krier for Giorgetti.

Canapé "Aries" de Léon Krier pour Giorgetti.

Sofa "Aries", das von Léon Krier für Giorgetti entworfen wurde.

Des salons et des salles à manger avec des airs rétro

Wohn- und Esszimmer mit dem Flair aus vergangenen Zeiten

Without necessarily falling into excesses or classical forms, an atmosphere reminiscent of something, we have already known, can be attained. An atmosphere that takes us back to old conversations held next to the heat of burning embers, to readings wrapped up in the comfort of a soft Queen Anne chair and to bookcases full of books, to family meals at splendid wooden tables, to afternoon naps on sofas upholstered in sumptuous fabrics... These are atmospheres that enfold us in their warmth and memories, protecting us from the coldness of the exterior world. An habitual resource for young defenders of these atmospheres is the introduction of restored classical elements into the decoration. While retaining their evocative capacity, they connect, at the same time, with the present.

Sans tomber dans l'excès, ni dans les formes classiques, on peut obtenir une atmosphère nous rappelant de vieilles conversations autour du feu, des heures de lecture assis sur un fauteuil douillet et dans une bibliothèque remplie de bons livres, des repas familiaux sur de grandes tables en bois, des siestes sur des canapés recouverts de tissus somptueux… Ce sont des environnements qui nous enveloppent de chaleur et de souvenirs, et nous protègent de la froideur du monde extérieur. Les défenseurs de ce type de contextes font souvent appel aux classiques restaurés qui permettent de garder une certaine force évocatrice se connectant avec le présent.

Man muss Räume weder mit nostalgischen Dingen überladen noch auf klassische Formen zurückgreifen, um ein Ambiente herzustellen, das uns an Vergangenes erinnert, an Gespräche vor dem Kamin, an Stunden der Lektüre in einem komfortablen, weichen Ohrensessel und an bis oben gefüllte Bücherregale, an Mahlzeiten, die an prächtigen Holztischen im Kreise der Familie eingenommen wurden, an Siestas auf mit edlen Stoffen bezogenen Sofas... Wir lassen uns von der von diesem Ambiente ausgehenden Wärme und den mit ihm verbundenen Erinnerungen gefangennehmen, hier fühlen wir uns vor der Kälte und Unpersönlichkeit unserer Umwelt geschützt. Junge Leute, die eine Vorliebe für diese Art von Interieurs entwickelt haben, integrieren in ihr Ambiente gerne einen sogenannten Klassiker, der, in neuer Auflage, seinen Charme aus vergangenen Zeiten erhalten hat, aber gleichzeitig auch zu modernen Einrichtungen passt.

Clothes stand "Dimitri" from Nils Holger Moorman.
Porte-manteau "Dimitri" de Nils Holger Moorman.
Garderobe "Dimitri" von Nils Holger Moorman.

Table "Capotavola" and chairs "Risiedo" from Luca Meda for Molteni & C.

Table "Capotavola" et chaises "Risiedo" de Luca Meda pour Molteni & C.

Tisch "Capotavola" und Stühle "Risiedo", von Luca meda für Molteni & C. entworfen.

On the left, container furniture "Elysee" from Selva Style International. On the right, sofa "Primafila" and auxiliary table "Poggio" from Luca Meda for Molteni & C.

À gauche, rangements "Elysee" de Selva Style International. À droite, canapé "Primafila" et table "Poggio" de Luca Meda pour Molteni & C.

Links Containermöbel "Elysee" von Selva Style International. Rechts das Sofa "Primafila" und der Tisch "Poggio" von Luca Meda für Molteni & C. entworfen.

Dining room group "Empire" from the series
Selva Art Collection from Selva Style International.

Ensemble de salle à manger "Empire" de la série
Selva Art Collection de Selva Style International.

Esszimmergruppe "Empire" aus der Modellreihe
Selva Art Collection von Selva Style International.

The table "Alum" is a design from
A. Lucatelle for Cattelan Italia.

La table "Alum" est une création
de A. Lucatelle pour Cattelan Italia.

Der Tisch "Alum" ist ein Design
von A. Lucatelle für Cattelan Italia.

Elegant sofa upholstered in leather "Blondos" from Vincent Sheppard.

Élégant canapé en cuir "Blondos" de Vincent Sheppard.

Das elegante Ledersofa "Blondos" von Vincent Sheppard.

On the left, living room "Louis Philippe" from the series Selva Classic Style from Selva Style International. On the right, easy chair "James" from Vincent Sheppard.

À gauche, salon "Louis Philippe" de la série Selva Classic Style de Selva Style International. À droite, fauteuil "James" de Vincent Sheppard.

Links das Wohnzimmer "Louis Philippe" aus der Modellreihe Selva Classic Style von Selva Style International.Rechts der Sessel "James" von Vincent Sheppard.

Dining room, with a light rustic air, from the collection "Mayflower". From Zenia House.

Salle à manger de la collection "Mayflower" avec un léger ton rustique, de Zenia House.

Esszimmer mit einem leicht rustikalen Flair aus der Modellreihe "Mayflower" von Zenia House.

Dining room set in cherry
from Annibale Colombo.

Banc en bois de cerisier
de Annibale Colombo.

Eßzimmergruppe aus Kirschbaum
von Annibale Colombo.

Bench in cherry from Annibale
Colombo.

Ensemble de salle à manger en bois
de cerisier de Annibale Colombo.

Eine Bank aus Kirschbaum
von Annibale Colombo.

Writing desk with complements from Inthai.

Ensemble de meubles de bureau accessoires de Inthai.

Schreibtischgruppe und Accessoires von Inthai.

Display cabinet "Mita". Design from A. and T. Scarpa for Molteni & C. On the right, Table "Platón" designed by J.L. Pérez Ortega for Muebles Do+Ce.

Vitrine "Mita", création de A. et T. Scarpa pour Molteni & C. À droite, table "Platón" créée par J.L. Pérez Ortega pour Muebles Do+Ce.

Die Vitrine "Mita", Design von A. und T. Scarpa für Molteni & C Rechts: Der Tisch "Platón" ist ein Design von J.L. Pérez Ortega für Muebles Do+Ce.

From left to right: different models with backrests
in wickerwork or leather from Fredericia Furniture.

De gauche à droite : différents modèles avec dossier
quadrillé ou en cuir de Fredericia Furniture.

Von links nach rechts: Verschiedene Modelle mit
Rückenlehne aus Rohrgeflecht oder mit Lederpolster
von Fredericia Furniture.

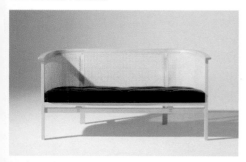

Dining room from the collection "Loomtime" from Roche Bobois.

Salle à manger de la collection "Loomtime" de Roche Bobois.

Ein Esszimmer aus der Modellreihe "Loomtime" von Roche Bobois.

Bookcase "Egal"
from Nils Holger Moorman.

Bibliothèque "Egal"
de Nils Holger Moorman.

Regal "Egal"
von Nils Holger Moorman.

Sofa "Cleopatra" from Biccapa
Italia. Right, "Gondola" set from
Vincent Sheppard.

Canapé "Cleopatra" de Biccapa
Italia. À droite, ensembles
"Gondola" de Vincent Sheppard.

Sofa "Cleopatra" von Biccapa Italia.
Rechts die Gruppe "Gondola"
von Vincent Sheppard.

Table "Pey". Design from J. M. Massana
and J.M. Tremoleda for Mobles 114.

Table "Pey" création de J. M Massana
et J.M. Tremoleda pour Mobles 114.

Der Tisch "Pey" ist ein Design
von J.M Massana und J. M. Tremoleda Mobles 114.

Easy chairs "Pissolino" from Giacomo Passal
for Andreu World.

Fauteuils "Pissolino" de Giacomo Passal
pour Andreu World.

Die von Giacomo Passal für Andreu World
entworfenen Sessel "Pissolino".

Group "Tonelle" from the collection Los Provinciales in French pine. From Roche Bobois.

Ensemble "Tonelle" de la collection Los Provinciales. De Roche Bobois.

Gruppe "Tonelle" aus der Modellreihe Los Provinciales, Ausführung in französischer Pinie. Von Roche Bobois.

Living room "Valmaison", in cherry, from the collection Los Provinciales from Roche Bobois.

Salle à manger "Valmaison" en bois de cerisier, de la collection Los Provinciales de Roche Bobois.

Esszimmer "Valmaison" aus Kirsch aus der Modellreihe Los Provicniales von Roche Bobois.

Table "Edo" and chairs "Aro"
designed by Chi Wing Lo for Giorgetti.

Table "Edo" et chaises "Aro",
créées par Chi Wing Lo pour Giorgetti.

Tisch "Edo" und Stühle "Aro",
Design von Chi Wing Lo für Giorgetti.

Below, on the left, table "Valentin" from E. Zenere
for Cattelan Italia. On the right, collection
"Elvira Madigan" from Trip Trap Denmark.

En bas à gauche, table "Valentin" de E. Zenere
pour Cattelan Italia. À droite, collection
"Elvira Madigan" de Trip Trap Denmark.

Unten links der Tisch "Valentin" von E. Zenere
für Cattelan Italia entworfen. Rechts die Modellreihe
"Elvira Madigan" von Trip Trap Denmark.

On the left, sofa "Conseta" from F. W. Möller for Cor.
On the right, Easy chair "Giulia Club" from Fendi.

À gauche, canapé "Conseta" de F. W. Möller pour Cor.
À droite, fauteuil "Giulia Club" de Fendi.

Links das Sofa "Conseta" von F. W. Möller für Cor.
Rechts der Sessel "Giulia Club" von Fendi.

Different composition of
"Conseta" from F. W. Möller for Cor.

Autre composition
"Conseta" de F. W. Möller pour Cor.

Eine weitere Zusammenstellung
aus "Conseta", Design von F. W.
Möller für Cor.

Composition "Paradiso"
from the collection Los Provinciales
from Roche Bobois.

Composition "Paradiso"
de la collection Los Provinciales
de Roche Bobois.

Zusammenstellung "Paradiso"
aus der Modellreihe Los Provinciales
von Roche Bobois.

Model "Greenwich"
from the collection Los Viajeros
from Roche Bobois.

Modèle "Greenwich"
de Roche Bobois.

Modell "Greenwich"
aus der Modellreihe Los Viajeros
von Roche Bobois.

Table "Sagredo" and chair "Celestia"
from Massimo Scolari for Giorgetti.

Table "Sagredo" et chaise "Celestia"
de Massimo Scolari pour Giorgetti.

Der Tisch "Sagredo" und der Stuhl "Celestia",
Design von Massimo Scolari für Giorgetti.

Top image, living room "Empire"
from Selva Style International.
Below, on the left, model "Europa"
from Bonestil. On the right, table
"La vita" from Studio Kronos for
Cattelan Italia.

Image du haut, salon "Empire"
de Selva Style International. En bas
à gauche, modèle "Europa" de
Bonestil. À droite, table "La vita" de
Studio Kronos pour Cattelan Italia.

Oben das Wohnzimmer "Empire"
von Selva Style International. Unten
links das Modell "Europa"
von Bonestil. Rechts der Tisch
"La vita", von Studio Kronos
für Cattelan Italia entworfen.

Dining room set designed
by Léon Krier. From Giorgetti.

Ensemble de salle à manger
créé par Léon Krier. De Giorgetti.

Von Léon Krier.
für Giorgetti. Conjunto
entworfenes Esszimmer

Bookcase "Jupiter" from Massimo Scolari for Giorgetti.

Bibliothèque "Jupiter" de Massimo Scolari pour Giorgetti.

Von Massimo Scolari für Giorgetti entworfenes Regal "Jupiter".

On the left, detail from the collection "Mayflower" from Zenia House.

À gauche, détail de la collection "Mayflower" de Zenia House.

Links ein Detail aus der Modellreihe "Mayflower" von Zenia House.

From left to right: two wing chairs in leather, designed
by Peter Mogensen for Fredericia Furniture. Two easy
chairs from the collection "Progetti Cuoio" designed
by Umberto Asnago for Giorgetti. Auxiliary table from
the collection "Mayflower" from Zenia House.

De gauche à droite : deux fauteuils avec accoudoirs en
cuir, créés par Peter Mogensen pour Fredericia
Furniture. Deux modèles de fauteuils de la collection
"Progetti Cuoio", créés par Umberto Asnago pour
Giorgetti. Table d'appoint de la collection "Mayflower"
de Zenia House.

Von links nach rechts: Zwei Ohrensessel aus Leder, von
Peter Mogensen für Fredericia Furniture entworfen.
Zwei Sessel aus der Modellreihe "Progetti Cuoio", von
Umberto Asnago für Giorgetti entworfen. Beistelltisch
aus der Modellreihe "Mayflower" von Zenia House.

| Des cuisines rustiques

| Rustic kitchens

| Rustikale Küchen

Furniture from the collection
"Natura" from Nobilia.

Meubles de la collection
"Natura" de Nobilia.

Möbel aus der Modellreihe
"Natura" von Nobilia.

Kitchens hold the most popu lar rustic esthetics intact, almost without introducing variations with respect to old standards. Although they include the most advanced household appliances, these are camouflaged in such a way that they do not detract from a magical reminiscence of the country. Space permitting, these kitchens include a breakfast area that reinforces their function as a meeting place for the family. The most contemporary versions incorporate wickerwork drawers, a material alternated with wood, and work posts set in the center of the room that give a present-day air without losing any traditional essence. Also, a recent introduction has been to paint wooden cupboard doors in light pastel shades, mainly blue, green, yellow and white, although, of course, they are finished to give an aged appearance.

Les cuisines gardent intacte l'esthétique rustique la plus populaire, et n'y introduisent que quelques variations par rapport aux anciens modèles. La présence des appareils électroménagers les plus modernes n'altère n'altèrent en aucune façon la magie de la réminiscence champêtre. Dans la mesure du possible, ces cuisines comprennent un espace repas renforçant leur fonction de pièce idéale pour les moments partagés en famille. Les versions les plus modernes comportent des tiroirs en osier faisant jeu avec le bois, et des plans de travail situés au centre de la pièce apportant une certaine touche contemporaine sans jamais en laisser perdre l'essence traditionnelle. La nouveauté réside également dans une finition donnant un style vieilli à des armoires dont les portes peuvent être peintes en tons pastels, principalement bleu, vert, jaune ou blanc.

Bei Konzipieren dieser Küchen sind im Vergleich zu den alten Modellen keine großen Veränderungen vorgenommen worden, und so haben diese Art Küchen über die Jahre hin ihren rustikalen, volkstümlichen Stil beibehalten. Natürlich sind sie heute auch mit modernsten Elektroküchengeräten ausgestattet, diese aber werden geschickt getarnt, damit sie nicht die magische Wirkung beeinträchtigen, die durch die Reminiszenz an das ländliche Ambiente erzeugt wird. Wenn genug Platz zur Verfügung steht, werden diese Küchen durch ein Office erweitert und erfüllen somit noch im verstärkten Maße ihre Funktion als Familientreffpunkt. Bei den in einem etwas moderneren Stil gehaltenen Küchen wird für Schubladen gerne Weidengeflecht verwandt, und der Arbeitstisch als Block in der Mitte angeordnet. Sie bekommen dadurch ein modernes Flair, ohne dabei ihren ursprünglichen Stil zu verlieren. Neuerdings ist auch die Tendenz zu beobachten, die Holztüren der Schränke in leichten Pastelltönen zu streichen – vorzugsweise werden dazu Blau, Grün, Gelb und Weiß verwandt. Anschließend wird dann allerdings dafür gesorgt, daß sie durch entsprechende Behandlung die richtige Patina bekommen.

Proposal with a marked rural style from Alno.
Proposition de style rustique de Alno.
Vorschlag im ausgeprägten Landhausstil von Alno.

Model "Alhambra" from Febal. Designed by Effe Tierre.

Modèle "Alhambra" de Febal, créé par Effe Tierre.

Das Modell "Alhambra" von Febal, Design von Effe Tierre

Detail from a composition
from Alno.

Détail d'une composition de Alno.

Detail aus einer Zusammenstellung
von Alno.

Buffet from the series "Country" from Nobilia.

Buffet de la série "Country" de Nobilia.

Buffet aus der Modellreihe "Country" von Nobilia.

Proposal from Alno.

Proposition de Alno.

Ein Vorschlag von Alno.

Composition from the series
"Castello" from Nobilia.

Composition de la série
"Castello" de Nobilia.

Zusammenstellung aus der
Modellreihe "Castello" von Nobilia.

Proposal with a romantic air from
Nils Holger Moorman.

Proposition aux notes romantiques
de Nils Holger Moorman.

Ein Vorschlag mit romantischem
Flair von Nils Holger Moorman .

Composition from the series
"Alhambra", from Effe Tierre
for Febal.

Composition de la série
"Alhambra", de Effe Tierre
pour Febal.

Eine Zusammenstellung
aus der Modellreihe "Alhambra",
von Effe Tierre für Febal..

Model "Casale", from Effe Tierre
for Febal.

Modèle "Casale", création de Effe
Tierre pour Febal.

Das Modell "Casale",.
von Effe Tierre für Febal.

Composition from the program "Ranch" from Alno.

Composition de la gamme "Ranch" de Alno.

Zusammenstellung aus der Modellreihe "Ranch" von Alno.

Detail of the old style scullery from "Ranch" from Alno.

Détail de l'évier de style ancien de "Ranch", de Alno.

Detail des im alten Stil gehaltenen Spülbeckens "Ranch" von Alno.

Kitchen from the program "Lugano" from Nobilia.

Cuisine de la gamme "Lugano" de Nobilia.

Eine Küche aus der Modellserie "Lugano" von Nobilia.

Compositior from the series
"Skan" from Alno.

Composition de la série "Skan"
de Alno.

Eine Zusammenstellung aus der
Modellreihe 'Skan" von Alno.

Kitchen "Country" from Nobilia.

Cuisine "Country" de Nobilia.

Die Küche "Country" von Nobilia. gezeigt

On the right, model "York" from Alno. Below, on the left, program "Boheme", from Febal. Below, on the right, detail from the program "Skan" from Alno.

À droite, modèle "York" de Alno. En bas à gauche, gamme "Boheme", de Febal. En bas à droite, détail de la gamme "Skan" de Alno.

Rechts das Modell "York" von Alno. Links unten die Modellreihe "Boheme" von Febal. Unten rechts ein Detail aus der Modellreihe "Skan" von Alno.

Composition in a rustic style with a central working area. From Leicht.

Composition de style rustique avec installation centrale, de Leicht.

Eine im rustikalen Stil gehaltene Zusammenstellung mit einer zentral angeordneten Einheit von Leicht.

Composition from the firm Oster.

Composition signée Oster.

Zusammenstellung von der Firma Oster.

Detail of the scullery from the composition from Leicht.

Détail de l'évier de la composition de Leicht.

Detail der Spüle aus der Modellreihe von Leicht..

Image from the program "Contea" from Febal.

Image de la gamme "Contea" de Febal.

Modellreihe "Contea" von Febal.

Model "Sinfonía 2000" from Febal.

Modèle "Sinfonía 2000" de Febal.

Modell "Sinfonia 2000" von Febal.

Zengiaro Associati are the authors of the design "Flora", from Febal.

Zengiaro Associati signe la création de "Flora", de Febal.

Zengiaro Associati zeichnet für das Design von "Flora", hergestellt von Febal.

Composition from the series "Frame" from Alno.

Composition de la série "Frame" de Alno.

Eine Zusammenstellung aus der Modellreihe "Frame" von Alno.

Composition "Port" from Alno.

Composition "Port" de Alno.

Zusammenstellung "Port" von Alno.

Modelo "Cambridge" de Oster.

Modèle "Cambridge" de Oster.

Modell "Cambridge" von Oster.

Kitchen from the program "Elysée"
from Veneta Cucine.

Cuisine de la gamme "Elysée"
de Veneta Cucine.

Eine Küche aus der Modellreihe
"Elysée" von Veneta Cucine.

Program "Rosatea".
Design from Interni Due for Febal.

Gamme "Rosatea",
création de Interni Due pour Febal.

Die von Interni Due für Febal
entworfene Modellreihe "Rosatea".

On the left, model "Reno" from Nobilia.
On the right, program "Medea",
designed by Studio Phoem for Febal.

À gauche, modèle "Reno" de Nobilia. À droite,
gamme "Medea", créée par Studio Phoem pour Febal.

Links das Modell "Reno" von Nobilia.
Rechts die Modellreihe "Medea",
Design von Studio Phoem für Febal.

Composition from the program
"Plus" from Alno.

Composition de la gamme
"Plus" de Alno.

Zusammenstellung aus der
Modellreihe "Plus" von Alno.

Program "Maya" from Febal.
On the right, model "Morena"
from Nobilia.

Gamme "Maya" de Febal. À droite,
modèle "Morena" de Nobilia.

Modellreihe "Maya" von Febal.
Rechts das Modell "Morena"
von Nobilia.

Bathrooms with a style from the past

Proposal from Bis Bis Imports Boston.

Proposition de Bis Bis Imports Boston.

Ein Vorschlag von Bis Bis Imports Boston.

Des salles de bain à l'ancienne

Badezimmer mit einem Flair aus vergangenen Zeiten

A certain aura of romanticism
tends to be the predominant note
in bathrooms of this style. It is as if fragrances of fresh flowers and lavender had
been introduced into the atmosphere. As if
upon opening the window, we could catch a
glimpse of a piece of the English countryside.
Classical bathroom design has lasted throughout
time without ceasing to maintain an attracti-
veness to an important part of the population.
White, porcelain washbasins of rounded or friv-
olous forms; furniture with worked, wooden
fronts or with lattice doors; mirrors in thick
wooden frames; charming, oval bathtubs with
cast iron legs; delicate ceramic accessories,
...seem to be the indispensable guests of these
bathrooms that have universal and timeless esthetics and that blend tradition with elegance
and present-day comfort.

Une certaine pointe de roman-
tisme est souvent la note prédomi-
nante de ce type de salles de bain.
C'est un peu comme si on y introduisait des arômes de fleurs fraîches et de lavande ou comme si
on ouvrait la fenêtre sur un fragment de campagne
anglaise. Les créations classiques dans le domaine de la salle de bain ne se sont jamais perdues et
continuent à exercer une grande fascination sur
une bonne partie de la population. Des lavabos en
porcelaine blanche aux formes arrondies ou capri-
cieuses, des meubles en bois sculpté ou aux portes cannées, des miroirs décorés d'épais cadres en
bois, d'intimes baignoires ovales aux pieds en fer
forgé, des accessoires délicats en céramique, ...
tous ces éléments semblent devenir les hôtes in-
dispensables de ces salles de bain d'une esthétique universelle et intemporelle mélangeant la tradition, l'élégance et le confort les plus actuels.

Charakteristisch für diese Ba-
dezimmer ist der Hauch von Roman-
tik, von dem sie umgeben sind. Die Luft
duftet nach frischen Blumen und Lavendel,
und wir können uns vorstellen, dass sich beim
Öffnen des Fensters vor unseren Augen eine
englische Landschaft ausbreitet. Im Laufe der
Jahre ist das klassische Design für Badezimmer ausgereifter geworden, ohne dabei an
Faszination zu verlieren, die viele noch für diese Art Badezimmer empfinden. Waschbecken
aus weißem Porzellan mit abgerundeten oder
ausgefallenen Formen, Möbel mit ausgearbei-
teten Vorderfronten oder mit Gittertüren,
Spiegel mit breiten Holzrahmen, liebenswerte,
ovale Badewannen mit gußeisernen Füßen,
feine Accessoires aus Keramik ... sind die uner-
lässlichen Details, von der die Ästhetik dieser
universellen und zeitlosen Bäder geprägt wird
und bei denen traditionelle Werte mit dem
heutigen Anspruch nach Eleganz und Komfort in Einklang gebracht werden.

Composition from the program
"Badjournal" from Keramag.

Composition de la gamme
"Badjournal" de Keramag.

Zusammenstellung aus der Modellreihe
"Badjournal" von Keramag.

Washroom group from the series
"Badjournal" from Keramag.

Ensemble de lavabos de la série
"Badjournal" de Keramag.

Badezimmerausstattung aus der
Modellreihe "Badjournal"
von Keramag.

On the left, the series "1930" from Duravit entails
re-edition of designs from the 30's. On the right,
the series "America" from Roca is a reinterpretation
of classical design.

À gauche, la série "1930" de Duravit suppose une
nouvelle édition des créations des années 30.
À droite, la série "America" de Roca est une nouvelle
interprétation du design classique.

Links die Modellreihe "1930" von Duravit,
eine Neuauflage des Designs aus den 30-er Jahren.
Rechts die Modellreihe "America" von Roca,
eine neue Interpretation des klassischen Designs.

Left: Bath "Circle". Bottom: bathroom fittings from the collection "Hommage". All from Villeroy and Boch.

À gauche: baignoire "Circle". En bas: sanitaires de la collection "Hommage". Ensemble de Villeroy y Boch.

Links Badewanne "Circle". In der Mitte Sanitärmodule aus der Modellreihe "Hommage". Alle Artikel von Villeroy und Boch.

Baths from Bis Bis Imports Boston.

Baignoire de Bis Bis Imports Boston.

Badewannen von Bis Bis Imports Boston.

On the following page, the top and bottom right images show two possibilities from the program "Hommage" from Villeroy & Boch. Bottom left, faucets "Madison" from Dornbracht.

Sur la page suivante, l'image du haut et celle du bas montrent deux possibilités proposées par la gamme "Hommage" de Villeroy & Boch. En bas à gauche, robinet "Madison" de Dornbracht.

Auf der folgenden Seite werden oben und unten rechts zwei Zusammenstellungen aus der Modellreihe "Hommage" von Villeroy & Boch gezeigt. Unten links Armaturen "Madison" von Dornbracht.

On the following page,
composition from the program "Cotta" from Keramag.

Sur la page suivante,
composition de la gamme "Cotta" de Keramag.

Auf der nachfolgenden Seite eine Zusammenstellung
aus der Modellreihe "Cotta" von Keramag.

The washroom "Orchidee"
from Duravit reproduces floral forms.

Le lavabo "Orchidee"
de Duravit reproduit des formes florales.

Bei dem Design des Waschbeckens "Orchidee"
von Duravit hat man sich von Blumenformen
inspirieren lassen.

On the left, composition from the program
"Hommage" from Villeroy & Boch. On the right,
proposal from Bis Bis Imports Boston.

À gauche, composition de la gamme "Hommage"
de Villeroy & Boch. À droite, proposition
de Bis Bis Imports Boston.

Links eine Zusammenstellung aus der Modellreihe
"Hommage" von Villeroy & Boch. Rechts ein Vorschlag
von Bis Bis Imports Boston.

Model "Derby" from Gama-Decor.

Modèle "Derby" de Gama-Decor.

Das Modell "Derby" von Gama-Decor.

Sieger Design have been inspired by the old English tradition in their design for "New Country" from Duravit.

Sieger Design s'est inspiré de la vieille tradition anglaise pour la création de "New Country" de Duravit.

Sieger Design bei dem Entwurf von "New Country" für Duravit von der alten englischen Tradition inspirieren lassen.

On the left, model "Riviere" from Gama-Decor. On the right, oval bath "Newcast" in cast-iron from Roca.

À gauche, modèle "Riviere" de Gama-Decor. À droite, baignoire ovale en fer fondu "Newcast" de Roca.

Links das Modell "Riviere" von Gama-Decor. Rechts die ovale Badewanne "Newcast" aus Gusseisen von Roca.

Model "Times" and model "Viena",
with twin cavities, from Gama-Decor.

Modèle "Times" et modèle "Viena",
de Gama-Decor.

Modell "Times" und Modell "Viena"
mit zwei Waschbecken von Gama-Decor.

Model "Ottocento"
from Gama-Decor.

Modèle "Ottocento"
de Gama-Decor.

Modell "Ottocento"
von Gama-Decor.

Faucets "Madison" inspired in classical
design, from Dornbracht.

Robinet "Madison" inspiré
du design classique, de Dornbracht.

Vom klassischen Design inspirierte Armaturen
"Madison" von Dornbracht.

Beds with canopies and more romanticism

Model "Bes", from Massimo Scolari
for Giorgetti.

Modèle "Bes", de Massimo Scolari
pour Giorgetti.

Das Modell "Bes", von Massimo Scolari
für Giorgetti entworfen.

Des lits à baldaquin et du romantisme

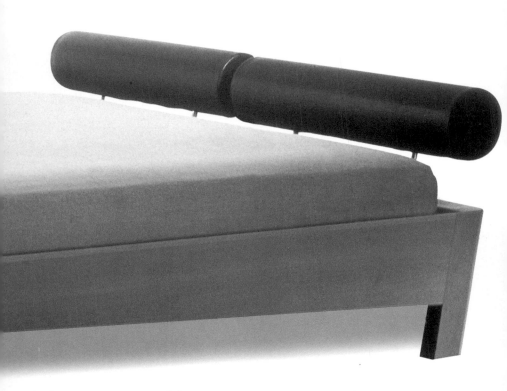

Himmelbetten und andere romantische Details

These bedrooms seem to be aimed at recreating a rural lifestyle.

Evasion as an excuse to transform a small piece of the city into our own particular vision of nature and which allows us to enjoy eternal vacations in our homes. To awake engulfed in light, airy linen that hangs from above, to walk barefoot over a wooden dais, to keep your clothes in a wardrobe that has been carved with the greatest of skill, etc., these are some of the luxuries to which we can succumb in these surroundings so full of classical touches. In this form of decoration, a feminine touch tends to be more evident than in other styles as everything seems to be impregnated with a light romanticism that sweetens our dreams.

Recréer le style de vie caractéristique de la campagne ou de la montagne semble être le but recherché.

L'évasion est une excuse pour transformer un petit morceau de ville en une vision particulière de la nature, nous permettant ainsi de profiter de vacances éternelles dans notre propre maison, de vacances éternelles. Se réveiller enveloppé du voile vaporeux d'un lit à baldaquin, marcher pieds nus sur un parquet, ranger ses vêtements dans une penderie chaleureuse délicatement dessinée, … voici quelques luxes auxquels nous pourrions succomber dans ce contexte classique. Dans ce type de décoration, la touche féminine est souvent plus évidente que dans n'importe quel autre style car tout semble imprégné d'un léger romantisme.

Mit diesen Schlafzimmern will man sich ein Stück Leben auf dem Lande oder in den Bergen in die Wohnung holen.

Stadtflucht ist der Grund, der dazu treibt, sich mitten in der Stadt Natur auf eine kleine Fläche zu projizieren, um so im eigenen Heim immerwährende Ferien genießen zu können. Unter dem duftigen Schleier eines Himmelbetts zu erwachen, barfuß über Holzdielen zu laufen, Kleidung in einem wunderschön geschnitzten Schrank aufzubewahren etc., das sind nur einige der Privilegien, die wir in diesem klassisch angehauchten Ambiente genießen können. Bei dieser Innendekoration ist stärker als bei anderen die weibliche Hand zu spüren, denn ihr Stil ist von dieser leichten Romantik geprägt, von der uns süße Träume beschert werden.

Bed with canopy from the collection "Mayflower" from Zenia House.

Lit à baldaquin de la collection "Mayflower" de Zenia House.

Himmelbett aus der Modellreihe "Mayflower" von Zenia House.

Bedroom from the program "Solid & Basic"
from Club 8 Company.

Chambre de la gamme "Solid & Basic"
de Club 8 Company.

Schlafzimmer aus der Modellreihe "Solid & Basic"
von Club 8 Company.

On the right, model "Blondos" from Vincent Sheppard.
Below, on the left, composition "Solid & Basic"
from Club 8 Company. On the right, proposal
from Bis Bis Imports Boston.

À droite, modèle "Blondos" de Vincent Sheppard. En bas
à gauche, composition "Solid & Basic" de Club 8
Company. À droite, proposition de Bis Bis Imports Boston.

Rechts das Modell "Blondos" von Vincent Sheppard.
Unten links eine Zusammenstellung aus
"Solid & Basic" von Club 8 Company.
Rechts ein Vorschlag von Bis Bis Imports Boston.

Top image on following page, bed "Claudiano", from Massimo Scolari for Giorgetti. Below, two compositions from Bis Bis Imports Boston.

Image du haut page suivante, lit "Claudiano", de Massimo Scolari pour Giorgetti. En bas, deux compositions de Bis Bis Imports Boston.

Auf der nachfolgenden Seite oben: Das von Massimo Scolari für Giorgetti entworfene Bett "Claudiano". Unten Zusammenstellungen von Bis Bis Imports Boston.

Model "Iron Line" from Domus.

Modèle "Iron Line" de Domus.

Modell "Iron Line" von Domus.

Bed "Juliet" from Ciacci.

Lit "Juliet" de Ciacci.

Bett "Juliet" von Ciacci

On the left, model "Claudiano" from Massimo Scolari for Giorgetti. Below, on the left, composition from Bis Bis Imports Boston. On the right, writing desk "Epi" and chair "Aro" from Chi Wing Lo for Giorgetti.

À gauche, modèle "Claudiano" de Massimo Scolari pour Giorgetti. En bas à gauche, composition de Bis Bis Imports Boston. À droite, bureau "Epi" et chaise "Aro" de Chi Wing Lo pour Giorgetti.

Links das von Massimo Scolari für Giorgetti entworfene Modell "Claudiano". Unten links eine Zusammenstellung von Bis Bis Imports Boston. Rechts der Schreibtisch "Epi" und der Stuhl "Aro" von Chi Wing Lo für Giorgetti entworfen.

Composition "Carla" in solid cherry, from the collection Los Provinciales from Roche Bobois.

Composition "Carla" en bois de cerisier massif, de la collection Los Provinciales de Roche Bobois.

Zusammenstellung "Carla" in massivem Kirschbaum aus der Modellreihe Los Provinciales von Roche Bobois

Bed "Ginevra" from Ciacci.
Lit "Ginevra" de Ciacci.
Das Bett "Ginevra" von Ciacci.

Bedroom from Prealpi.
Chambre de Prealpi.
Schlafzimmer von Prealpi.

Bedroom from the collection "Basic" from Club 8 Company.
Chambre de la collection "Basic" de Club 8 Company.
Schlafzimmer aus der Modellreihe "Basic" von Club 8 Company.

Proposal from Prealpi.

Proposition de Prealpi.

Ein Vorschlag von Prealpi.

Philippe Starck is the author of the design "Sleepy Working Bed" from Cassina (Photo: Miro Zagnoli).

Philippe Starck signe la création de "Sleepy Working Bed" de Cassina (photo : Miro Zagnoli).

Philippe Starck zeichnet für das Design von "Sleepy Working Bed" von Cassina (Foto: Miro Zagnoli).

Bed and complements from the collection "Mayflower" from Zenia House.

Lit et accessoires de la collection "Mayflower" de Zenia House.

Bett und Accessoires aus der Modellreihe "Mayflower" von Zenia House.

On the left, chest of drawers "Chiave di violino" from B. Reichlin and G. Geronzi for Molteni & C. On the right, model "Bes" from Massimo Scolari for Giorgetti.

À gauche, meuble à tiroirs "Chiave di violino", de B. Reichlin et G. Geronzi pour Molteni & C. À droite, modèle "Bes", de Massimo Scolari pour Giorgetti.

Links die Kommode "Chiave di violino", Design von B. Reichlin und G. Geronzi für Molteni & C. Rechts das Modell "Bes", von Massimo Scolari für Giorgetti entworfen.

On the right, "Témenos" from Léon Krier for Giorgetti. Below, on the left, chest of drawers from Zenia House. On the right, "Nottetempo", from B. Reichlin and G. Geronzi for Molteni & C.

À droite, "Témenos" de Léon Krier pour Giorgetti. En bas à gauche, meuble à tiroirs de Zenia House. À droite, "Nottetempo", de B. Reichlin et G. Geronzi pour Molteni & C.

Rechts "Témenos", von Léon Krier für Giorgetti entworfen. Unten links eine Kommode von Zenia House. Rechts "Nottetempo", Design von B. Reichlin und G. Geronzi für Molteni & C.

| Cozy lighting

Suspened lamp "Kumi"
from A. Moya for Dab.

Plafonnier "Kumi"
de A. Moya pour Dab.

Hängelampe "Kumi",
Design von A. Moya für Dab.

| Un éclairage accueillant

| Gemütliches Licht

There are concepts that come back time and time again or that, simply, never leave us, although they continually change their appearance so as not to be caught as stragglers in the race against time. This is the case of a good number of lamps of classical design whose presence has not only given light to the lives of our forefathers, but continue, in the present, to illuminate our lives as well. They can change the materials. They can change the technology. They can slightly modify the forms. The generations or the decor may change. But the concept remains the same: they are table lamps, standard lamps, suspended or wall appliances that give a warm, intimate illumination and introduce their old splendor into our present-day homes. New evidence that good design is everlasting.

Il existe certains concepts qui reviennent régulièrement ou qui, simplement, ne disparaissent jamais, même s'ils évoluent suffisamment pour ne pas rester en arrière dans la course contre le temps. C'est le cas d'un bon nombre de créations classiques de lampes dont la présence a éclairé la vie de nos arrière-grands-parents et continue à éclairer la nôtre. Les matériaux peuvent changer. La technologie peut évoluer. Les formes peuvent être légèrement modifiées. Les générations ou les décors peuvent être différents. Mais le concept reste toujours le même : il s'agit de lampes de bureau, de lampadaires ou d'appliques fournissant un éclairage chaleureux et intime et laissant la marque de leur splendeur traditionnelle dans les demeures de notre époque. Nous constatons à nouveau que les créations de qualité sont immortelles.

Es gibt Konzeptionen, die immer und immer wiederkehren, oder, besser gesagt, die eigentlich nie ganz in Vergessenheit geraten, wenngleich auch die Aufmachung der Objekte verändert wird, damit sie mit der modernen Zeit mithalten können. Dieses trifft auch für eine große Anzahl der klassischen Lampendesigns zu; diese Beleuchtungskörper brachten schon Licht in das Leben unserer Urgroßeltern und werden auch das unsrige erhellen. Materialien können sich ändern, ebenso wie Technologien es tun. Die Formen können sich leicht verändern. Die Generationen oder die Einrichtung können sich ändern. Aber das Konzept bleibt: Es handelt sich um Tisch– oder Stehlampen, Hänge– oder Wandlampen, die ein warmes, gemütliches Licht geben und mit ihrem alten Glanz Einzug in unsere modernen Wohnungen halten. Wiederum ein Beweis dafür, dass gutes Design unvergänglich ist.

Reading lamp "Melanpo Terra".
Design from Adrien Gardère for Artemide.

Liseuse "Melanpo Terra",
création de Adrien Gardère pour Artemide.

Leselampe "Melanpo Terra",
Design von Adrien Gardère für Artemide.

"Ginger e Fred" in a suspended version,
from Fontana Arte.

"Ginger e Fred" plafonnier,
de Fontana Arte.

"Ginger e Fred" als Hängelampe,
von Fontana Arte.

"Rosi Lamp" from Nils Holger Moorman.

"Rosi Lamp" de Nils Holger Moorman.

"Rosi Lamp" von Nils Holger Moorman.

Melanpo Terra" combines classical forms with modern materials. From Adrien Gardère for Artemide.

"Melanpo Terra" combine les formes classiques et les matériaux modernes. De Adrien Gardère pour Artemide.

"Melanpo Terra" werden klassische Formen mit modernen Materialien kombiniert. Design von Adrien Gardère für Artemide.

On the left, "Claudia", table version, from A. Moya for Dab. In the center, "Roattino" is a design from Eileen Gray produced by Classicon. On the right, "Claudia" in its suspended version, from Dab.

À gauche, "Claudia" de bureau de A. Moya pour Dab. Au centre, "Roattino" est une création de Eileen Gray fabriquée par Classicon. À droite, "Claudia" plafonnier, de Dab.

Links die Tischlampe "Claudia", von A. Moya für Dab entworfen. In der Mitte "Roattino", ein von Classicon hergestelltes Design. Rechts "Claudia" als Hängelampe, von Dab.

On the left, "Ritz" is a design from Joan Augé for Taller Uno. On the right, the lamp "TMM" is a design classic from M. Milá produced by Santa & Cole.

À gauche, "Ritz" est une création de Joan Augé pour Taller Uno. À droite, la lampe "TMM" est un classique du design de M. Milá, fabriquée par Santa & Cole.

Links wird "Ritz" gezeigt, ein für Taller Uno von Joan Augé angefertigtes Design. Rechts die Lampe "TMM", ein klassisches Design von M. Milá, hergestellt von Santa & Cole.

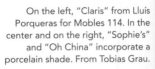

On the left, "Claris" from Lluís Porqueras for Mobles 114. In the center and on the right, "Sophie's" and "Oh China" incorporate a porcelain shade. From Tobias Grau.

À gauche, "Claris" de Lluís Porqueras pour Mobles 114. Au centre et à droite, "Sophie's" et "Oh China" introduisent un diffuseur en porcelaine de chine, de Tobias Grau.

Links die Lampe "Claris", von Lluís Porqueras für Mobles 114 entworfen. In der Mitte und rechts "Sophie's" und "Oh China" mit Diffusoren aus chinesischem Porzellan. Von Tobias Grau.

On the left, modelo "Tria-XL" from Carpyen.
On the right, lamp "Marilyn" from Vibia.

À gauche, « Tria-XL » de Carpyen. À droite,
modèle " Marilyn " de Vibia.

Links Modell "Tria-XL" von Carpyen.
Rechts Modell "Marilyn" von Vibia.

On the left, proposal from Inthai. In
the center, "Palmus" from Léon
Krier for Giorgetti. On the right,
model "Gran" from Joan Augé for
Taller Uno.

À gauche, proposition de Inthai. Au
centre, "Palmus" de Léon Krier pour
Giorgetti. À droite, modèle "Gran"
de Joan Augé pour Taller Uno.

Links ein Vorschlag von Inthai. In der
Mitte "Palmus", von Léon Krier für
Giorgetti entworfen. Rechts das
Modell "Gran" von Joan Augé für
Taller Uno entworfen.

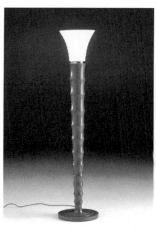

Articulated appliance "Break" from Ramón Isern for Tramo. On the right, "Tulip" from Lievore, Altherr and Molina for Vibia.

Applique articulée "Break" de Ramón Isern pour Tramo. À droite, "Tulip" de Lievore, Altherr et Molina pour Vibia.

Wandlampe mit Gelenk "Break", von Ramón Isern für Tramo entworfen. Rechts "Tulip", von Lievore, Altherr und Molina für Vibia entworfen.

Jaume Sans designed "Pie de Salón" in 1963. Produced by Santa & Cole (photo: C. Masiá).

Jaume Sans a créé "Pie de Salón" en 1963. Fabrication Santa & Cole (photo : C. Masiá).

Jaume Sans entwarf 1963 "Pie de Salón". Hergestellt wird sie von Santa & Cole (Foto: C. Masiá).

On the left, "Clip" from J. A. Blanc and P. J. Vidal for Tramo. On the right, "Diana" from A. Milá, F. Correa and M. Milá for Santa & Cole (photo: C. Masiá).

À gauche, "Clip" de J. A. Blanc et P. J. Vidal pour Tramo. À droite, "Diana" de A. Milá, F. Correa et M. Milá pour Santa & Cole (photo : C. Masiá).

Links "Clip", Design von J. A. Blanc und P. J. Vidal für Tramo. Rechts "Diana", von A. Milá, F. Correa und M. Milá für Santa & Cole entworfen (Foto: C. Masiá).

MINIMALISTS AND THE ESSENTIAL
Searching for essence and purity

What does living in a minimalist and essential environment imply? It implies, firstly, being able to do away with all that is not indispensable, to create atmospheres constructed from what each of us considers to be important. On the other hand, it means loving forms and essential colors, pure, free from superfluous ornamentation and artifice. The underlying idea would be to eliminate the noise that surrounds us, understanding as noise all that obstructs our vision, all that which has neither sense nor place in the space we inhabit. The objective, therefore, is to attain a silence favorable for relaxation, tranquility, which enables us to center on our own interiors and on all that is minimal, in the details that form the nuclei of objects.

Straight lines, which give rise to simple primary geometric forms, come to life in very basic elements, which are born from the attempt at catching the essential.

There is a sentence that summarizes the spirit of minimalist art and that can also be applied to the decoration of interiors: get as much tension as possible by using the minimum of means.

Because of this, the materials employed take on a special importance, as much in the furniture as in the surfaces of floors and walls. As a recommendation, they should be made of noble materials, which have a capacity to stand out by themselves and are visually pure, such as wood or steel.

Due to the characteristic scarcity of furniture and the practical absence of decorative complements inherent in this style, in a minimalist space, the position of particular elements with regard to that of others has great importance. The composition should make the individuality of each one of them stand out, at the same time that it transmits a general impression of the whole that should be harmonious and balanced. In environments of this kind, natural light is given a leading role, as it provokes its impact on particular spaces or objects, achieving dramatic effects, greatly theatrical, that alter the appearance of the interior at the pace that the sun changes position in the sky. Similar effects can also be achieved with a rational use of artificial light.

Minimalism is generally associated with the omnipresence of whiteness and with a kind of praise of emptiness. Although it is actually a great deal more than this. Taking as reference the artistic movement known as "minimal art" that arose in the United States in the 60's, and that generates forms which have their own meanings and which are directed to the mind of the observer, minimalism in interior design is based on a process of reduction, that rotates around the basic concepts of space, light and form. Thus, it is not a case of creating empty spaces, but of achieving restrained spaces, full of purity, where we can live surrounded by a beautiful silence.

MINIMALISTES ET ESSENTIELLES
À la recherche d'essence et de pureté

Que signifie vivre dans une ambiance minimaliste et essentielle? Cela veut dire, tout d'abord, être capable de se défaire de tout ce qui n'est pas indispensable et de créer des atmosphères à partir de ce qui a de l'importance. Cela veut dire, d'autre part, aimer les couleurs et les formes essentielles, pures, libres d'ornements superflus et d'artifices. L'idée sous-jacente serait l'élimination du bruit qui nous entoure, c'est-à-dire le bruit de tout ce qui dérange notre vue, de tout ce qui n'a pas de sens ni de place dans l'espace dans lequel nous vivons. L'objectif est donc d'obtenir un silence propice à la relaxation, à la tranquillité, nous permettant de centrer notre regard sur nous-mêmes et sur les détails formant le noyau des objets.

Les lignes droites donnant naissance à des formes géométriques, simples et primaires prennent vie au travers d'éléments de base capables d'attraper l'essentiel des objets.

Il existe une phrase résumant l'esprit de l'art minimaliste et qui peut également s'appliquer à la décoration d'intérieurs : obtenir la tension maximum en utilisant le minimum de moyens.

C'est pour cette raison que les matériaux utilisés ont une très grande importance, tant pour le mobilier que pour les surfaces des sols et des murs. Il est conseillé de choisir des matériaux nobles, capables de se révéler par eux-mêmes et visuellement purs, comme le bois ou l'acier.

De par l'absence de mobilier et d'accessoires décoratifs caractéristiques de ce style, la position des éléments les uns par rapport aux autres est très importante dans une pièce minimaliste. La composition doit mettre en valeur l'individualité de chacun d'entre eux et en même temps, transmettre une impression générale d'ensemble harmonieux et équilibré. Dans ce type d'ambiance, la lumière est le protagoniste car elle joue un rôle sur l'espace et les objets en obtenant des effets dramatiques, d'une grande théâtralité, et ou en changeant l'aspect d'un intérieur suivant la position du soleil. On peut obtenir des effets similaires en faisant un bon usage de la lumière artificielle.

Généralement, on associe le minimalisme à l'omniprésence de la couleur blanche et à une sorte de culte du vide. Mais, en réalité, cela va bien plus loin. Si on prend comme référence le mouvement artistique connu sous le nom de "minimal art" apparu aux Etats-Unis dans les années 60 et générant des formes qui agissent directement sur l'esprit de l'observateur, le minimalisme dans la décoration d'intérieurs est fondé sur une procédure de réduction et sur les concepts de base de l'espace, de la lumière et des formes.

Il ne s'agit donc pas de créer des espaces vides, mais plutôt d'obtenir des espaces sobres, purs, où il sera possible de vivre entouré de silence.

MINIMALISTISCHE IINTERIEURS
Auf der Suche nach dem Wesentlichen und reinen Formen

Was bedeutet es, in einem minimalistischen und auf das Wesentliche beschränkten Ambiente zu leben? In erster Linie bedeutet es, sich von allem nicht unbedingt Notwendigem zu trennen und sich einen Wohnbereich zu schaffen, der nur mit Dingen ausgestattet wird, die man für wichtig und unerläßlich hält. Außerdem drückt man auf diese Weise seine Vorliebe für pure Farben und Formen aus, für Gegenstände ohne überflüssige Ornamente, frei jeglicher künstlich wirkender Elemente. Der nächste, sich daraus ergebende Schritt, wäre das Ausschalten aller uns umgebender Geräusche, wobei wir als Geräusche in diesem Zusammenhang alles das verstehen, was wir nicht gerne ansehen, d.h., alles das, was nicht in den von uns bewohnten Raum passt. Unser Ziel ist es deshalb, eine Ruhe herzustellen, die wir zur Entspannung brauchen, eine Ruhe, die es uns erlaubt, unseren Blick nach innen und auf die minimalistischen Dinge zu richten und uns auf die Essenz der Dinge zu konzentrieren.

Aus geraden Linien entstehen einfache, geometrische, ursprüngliche Formen, die in elementare Elemente umgesetzt werden, bei denen versucht wird, sie auf das Wesentliche zu beschränken.

Der Grundgedanke der minimalistischen Kunst läßt sich mit einem Satz zusammenfassen, der auch für Inneneinrichtungen Gültigkeit hat: Höchste Spannung ist mit minimalem Aufwand zu erzielen.

Somit bekommen die sowohl für die Möbel als auch für Böden und Wände verwandten Materialien einen hohen Stellenwert. Es sind vorzugsweise edle Materialien zu verwenden, die nur schon allein durch ihre Eigenschaften wirken und ein unverfälschtes Bild vermitteln – wie zum Beispiel Holz oder Stahl.

Da sich ein minimalistisch ausgestatteter Raum durch wenige Möbel und das Fehlen jeglicher, mit diesem Stil nicht in Einklang zu bringenden dekorativer Elemente auszeichnet, gewinnt die Anordnung der einzelnen Möbelstücke zueinander größte Bedeutung. In dem Gesamtbild muß der Solitärcharakter eines jeden Objektes herausgestellt werden und gleichzeitig ein Gefühl der Zusammengehörigkeit übermittelt werden. Insgesamt muß alles harmonisch und ausgewogen wirken.

Bei dieser Art von Interieurs spielt das Tageslicht eine wichtige Rolle. Es wird auf bestimmte Räume oder Objekte gelenkt, wobei dramatische Effekte hergestellt werden, die einer gewissen Theatralik nicht entbehren, und dem Ambiente je nach Sonneneinfall einen anderen Charakter verleihen. Gleiche Effekte können mit dem geschickten Einsatz von Kunstlicht hergestellt werden.

Generell wird Minimalismus mit der Allgegenwärtigkeit der Farbe Weiß und einer Art Kult hinsichtlich des leeren Raums assoziiert. Aber in Wirklichkeit geht es um viel mehr, als nur um dieses. Unter Berufung auf die in den sechziger Jahren in den Vereinigten Staaten entstandene Kunstrichtung, aus der Formen hervorgegangen sind, die aus sich selbst heraus verständlich waren und von dem Betrachter auf direktem Wege aufgenommen werden konnten, handelt es sich bei dem auf die Innendekoration angewandten Minimalismus um einen Prozess des Reduzierens, der sich in die Grundkonzeption von Raum, Licht und Form integriert.

Es geht also nicht darum, leere Räume zu kreieren, sondern es werden vielmehr sparsam ausgestatte Bereiche geschaffen, die sich durch ihre reinen Linien und Formen auszeichnen, und in denen man von einer wunderbaren Ruhe umgeben leben kann.

The basics in living and dining rooms

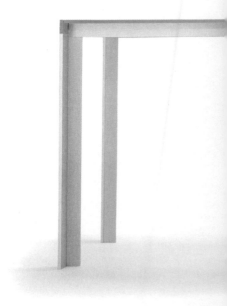

Table "Deneb" and chair
"Gas" by Jesús Gasca for Stua.

Table "Deneb" et chaise
"Gas" de Jesús Gasca pour Stua.

Tisch "Deneb" und Stuhl "Gas",
von Jesús Gasca für Stua.

L'essentiel en salons et salles à manger

Grundelemente für Wohn- und Esszimmer

Peacefulness and a feeling of well being are the sensations that predominate in these places where the void is worshipped. A good dose of equilibrium is crucial when it comes to choosing the small number of elements that will come to form part of this universe, as these will be responsible for endowing meaning to the emptiness. It is as important to bear in mind their design, which should be essentially geometric, as the materials they are made of given that quality is especially relevant in these spaces. It is a question of creating the maximum amount of expressiveness and emotion possible with a minimum of elements so that air, light and purity are able to circulate unhindered in their flight.

La tranquillité et le bien-être sont les sensations qui dominent dans ces endroits où le vide fait l'objet d'une sorte de vénération. Ce qui est fondamental, c'est une grande dose d'équilibre au moment de choisir les quelques éléments qui feront partie de cet univers et qui seront chargés de donner une signification à ce vide. Il est indispensable de prendre en compte à la fois le design, dont les lignes devront être essentiellement géométriques, et les matériaux, dont la qualité est d'une grande importance dans ces contextes. Il s'agit de créer, avec le moins d'éléments possible, une ambiance pleine d'expression et d'émotion pour que l'air, la lumière et la pureté puissent circuler librement.

Ruhe und Wohlbefinden sind die Maxime für diese Räume, in denen Leere zum Kult erhoben wird. Die wenigen Objekte oder Elemente, die in dieses Universum integriert werden sollen, müssen mit äußerster Umsicht ausgesucht werden, da sie es sind, von denen in dem leeren Raum die Akzente gesetzt werden. Design spielt hier eine sehr wichtige Rolle – die Gegenstände sollten vorzugsweise geometrische Formen aufweisen – ebenso wie die verwandten Materialien, denn in diesen Interieurs kommt der Qualität eine besonders wichtige Rolle zu. Mit so wenigen Elementen wie nur eben möglich soll ein hoher Grad an Expressivität erzielt und starke Gefühle hervorgerufen werden; Licht, Luft und reine Linienführung dürfen durch nichts eingeschränkt werden.

Composition "Spacio Next" from Pianca.
Composition "Spacio Next" de Pianca.
Zusammenstellung "Spacio Next" von Pianca.

Easy chairs "Colubi" from Viccarbe. Below, chair "Cone"
from Humberto and Fernando Campana for Edra.

Fauteuils "Colubi" de Viccarbe. En bas, chaise "Cone"
de Humberto et Fernando Campana pour Edra.

Die Sessel "Colubi" von Viccarbe. Unten der von Humberto
und Fernando Campana für Edra entworfene Stuhl "Cone".

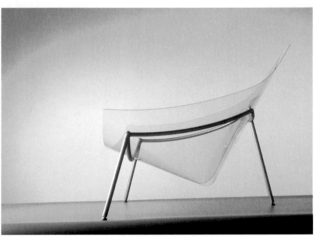

Georg Appeltshauser is the author of the design
of the sofa "6700" from Rolf Benz.

Georg Appeltshauser signe la création du canapé
"6700" de Rolf Benz.

Von Georg Appeltshauser für Rolf Benz
entworfene Sofa "6700".

Bench from the program "Do It" from Viccarbe. Below, on the left, leather sofa "Openside" from Matteograssi. On the right, table "Ponte" from e15.

Banc de la gamme "Do It" de Viccarbe. En bas à gauche, canapé en cuir "Openside" de Matteograssi. À droite, table "Ponte" de e15.

Bank aus der Modellreihe "Do It" von Viccarbe. Unten links das Ledersofa "Openside" von Matteograssi. Rechts der Tisch "Ponte" von e15.

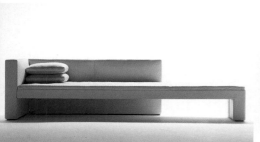

On the right, composition from the collection "Basic" from Club 8 Company. Below, on the left, proposal for a dining room from Porro. On the right, table "Gac" from Rafemar.

À droite, composition de la collection "Basic" de Club 8 Company. En bas à gauche, proposition de salle à manger de Porro. À droite, table "Gac" de Rafemar.

Rechts eine Zusammenstellung aus der Modellre he "Basic" von Club 8 Company. Unten links ein Vorschlag für das Esszimmer von Porro. Rechts der Tisch "Gac" von Rafemar.

Top image, leather chairs "Derby" from Matteograssi. On the left, table "Bigfoot" and chairs "Hans" from e15. On the right, chairs from dining room "April" from Matteograssi.

Image du haut, chaises en cuir "Derby" de Matteograssi. À gauche, table "bigfoot" et chaises "Hans" de e15. A gauche, chaises de salle à manger "April" de Matteograssi.

Oben die Lederstühle "Derby" von Matteograssi. Links der Tisch "bigfoot" und die Stühle "Hans" von e15. Rechts Esszimmerstühle "April" von Matteograssi.

On the right, leather sofa "Double" from Matteograssi. Top, proposal from Cattelan Italia. On the left, table "Tau" from Rafemar.

À droite, canapé en cuir "Double" de Matteograssi. En haut, proposition de Cattelan Italia. En bas à gauche, table "Tau" de Rafemar.

Rechts das Ledersofa "Double" von Matteograssi. Oben ein Vorschlag von Cattelan Italia. Links der Tisch "Tau" von Rafemar.

Sofa "Aire" designed by Diego Fortunato for Perobell.

Canapé "Aire" créé par Diego Fortunato pour Perobell.

Das Sofa "Aire" wurde von Diego Fortunato für Perobell entworfen.

Modular composition "Sintesi" from Poliform.

Composition convertible "Sintesi" de Poliform.

Zusammenstellung aus dem Modulsystem "Sintesi" von Poliform.

On the left, bookcase "Giro" from Rafemar. On the right, composition from Bis Bis Imports Boston.

À gauche, bibliothèque "Giro" de Rafemar. À droite, composition de Bis Bis Imports Boston.

Links das Regal "Giro" von Rafemar. Rechts eine Zusammenstellung von Bis Bis Imports Boston.

Mirror "Gray", table "Balzona"
(design from Opera) and chair
"Ida" (design from R. Lazzeroni)
from Casamilano.

Miroir "Gray", table "Balzona"
(création de Opera) et chaise "Ida"
(création de R. Lazzeroni), de
Casamilano.

Spiegel "Gray", Tisch "Balzona"
(Design von Opera) und Stuhl "Ida"
(Design von R. Lazzeroni);
hergestellt von Casamilano.

Table "Ferro" from Piero L ssoni for Porro.

Table "Ferro" de Piero Lissoni pour Porro.

Der Tisch "Ferro", Design von Piero Lissoni für Porro.

On the left, table "Minosse" from Misura Emme. On the right, modular program "Net" from Lago.

À gauche, table "Minosse" de Misura Emme. À droite, gamme convertible "Net" de Lago.

Links der Tisch "Minosse" von Misura Emme. Rechts die Modul-Modellreihe "Net" von Lago.

Table "Motion" and chairs "Form" from Calligaris. Below, on the left, sofa "Ginger" from Jorge Pensi for Perobell. On the right, container furniture "Hey–Gi" from Misura Emme.

Table "Motion" et chaises "Form" de Calligaris. En bas à gauche, canapé "Ginger" de Jorge Pensi pour Perobell. À droite, rangement "Hey-Gi" de Misura Emme.

Der Tisch "Motion" und die Stühle "Form" von Calligaris. Unten links das Sofa "Ginger", das von Jorge Pensi für Perobell entworfen wurde. Rechts das Containermöbel "Hey-Gi" von Misura Emme.

Table for dining room "Top" from Rafemar.

Table de salle à manger "Top" de Rafemar.

Der Esszimmertisch "Top" von Rafemar.

On the left, composition from the program "Life" from Roberto Monsani for Acerbis International. On the right, bookcase from the program "Evolution" from Rolf Benz.

À gauche, composition de la gamme "Life" de Roberto Monsani pour Acerbis International. À droite, bibliothèque de la gamme "Evolution" de Rolf Benz.

Links eine Zusammenstellung aus der Modellreihe "Life", von Roberto Monsani für Acerbis International entworfen. Rechts ein Regal aus der Modellreihe "Evolution" von Rolf Benz.

On the right, sofa "Arthe" from W. Scheider & Partners for Cor. Below, on the left, sideboard "Madison" from Cattelan Italia. On the right, table "Fabian" and sideboard "Farah" from e15.

À droite, canapés "Arthe" de W. Scheider & Partners pour Cor. En bas à gauche, buffet "Madison" de Cattelan Italia. À droite, table "Fabian" et buffet "Farah" de e15.

Rechts die Sofas "Arthe" , Design von W. Scheider & Partners für Cor. Unten links die Anrichte "Madison" von Cattelan Italia. Rechts der Tisch "Fabian" und die Anrichte "Farah" von e15.

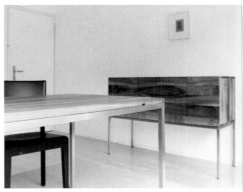

Chaise–longues "Virginia". Design
from Antonello Mosca for Giorgetti.

Chaise-longues "Virginia", création
de Antonello Mosca pour Giorgetti.

Die von Antonello Mosca für
Giorgetti. entworfene Chaiselongue
"Virginia".

Composition from Thonet
(photo: Markus Tollhopf).

Composition de Thonet
(photo : Markus Tollhopf).

Zusammenstellung mit Möbeln
von Thonet (Foto: Markus Tollhopf).

Furniture from the collection "Na Xemena"
from Gandía Blasco.

Mobilier de la collection "Na Xemena"
de Gandía Blasco.

Möbel aus der Modellreihe "Na Xemena"
von Gandía Blasco.

On the left, sofa from Bodema. On the right, the chair
"Casablanca" is a design from C. Pillet for Artelano.

À gauche, canapé de Bodema. À droite,
la chaise "Casablanca" est une création de C. Pillet
pour Artelano.

Links ein Sofa von Bodema. Rechts der Stuhl
"Casablanca" , Design von C. Pillet für Artelano.

On the left, table "Extention" from Ennio Arosio for Glas.
On the right, sideboard "Cartesio" from R. and S. Verardo for Verardo.

À gauche, table "Extention" de Ennio Arosio pour Glas.
À droite, buffet "Cartesio" de R. et S. Verardo pour Verardo.

Links der von Ennio Arosio für Glas entworfene Tisch "Extention". Rechts
die Anrichte "Cartesio", von R. und S. Verardo für Verardo entworfen.

Furniture with wheels "Dry" from
Prospero Rasulo for Glas.

Meubles sur roulettes "Dry" de
Prospero Rasulo pour Glas.

Möbel auf Rädern "Dry" , von
Prospero Rasulo für Glas entworfen.

Table "Aprile" from Lorenzo Arosio for Glas.

Table "Aprile" de Lorenzo Arosio pour Glas.

Der von Lorenzo Arosio für Glas entworfene Tisch "Aprile".

Composition from the modulat
program "Pass" from Luca Meda
for Molteni & C.

Composition de la gamme
convertible "Pass", de Luca Meda
pour Molteni & C.

Zusammenstellung aus der
Modul-Modellreihe "Pass",
die von Luca Meda für Molteni & C.
entworfen wurde.

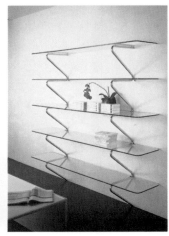

On the left, shelves with lights
"Light Light" from Nanda Vigo
for Glas. On the right, shelving
"Arianna" from Lorenzo Arosio
for Glas.

À gauche, étagères avec éclairage
integré "Light Light" de Nanda
Vigo pour Glas. À droite,
bibliothèque "Arianna"
de Lorenzo Arosio pour Glas.

Links Regal mit Beleuchtung
"Light Light", von Nanda Vigo
für Glas entworfen. Rechts
das Regal "Arianna",
Design von Lorenzo Arosio für Glas.

Sofa "Master" and furniture from the program
"Screen" from Antonello Mosca for Giorgetti.

Canapé "Master" et meubles de la gamme "Screen",
de Antonello Mosca pour Giorgetti.

Das Sofa "Master" und Möbel aus der Modellreihe
"Screen", Design von Antonello Mosca für Giorgetti.

Top left table "Helsinki 484" from Caronni and Bonanomi for Desalto.
On the right, tables "Seventies" from Artelano. Bottom left, "Riviera" from
Pascal Mourgue for Artelano. On the right, sofa "Let–in" from Bodema.

En haut à gauche, table "Helsinki 484" de Caronni et Bonanomi pour
Desalto. À droite, tables "Seventies" de Artelano. En bas à gauche, "Riviera"
de Pascal Mourgue pour Artelano. À droite, canapé "Let-in" de Bodema.

Oben links Tisch "Helsinki 484", Design von Caronni und Bonanomi für
Desalto. Rechts die Tische "Seventies" von Artelano. Unten links "Riviera"
von Pascal Mourgue für Artelano. Rechts das Sofa "Let-in" von Bodema.

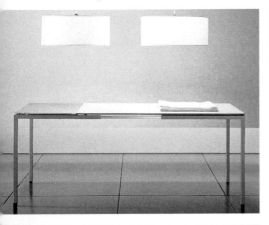

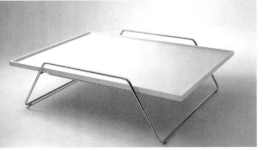

On the left, easy chair Ghost from C. Boeri and T. Katanayaci for Fiam Italia. On the right, mirror "Seif" from Julia Dozsa for Glas.

À gauche, fauteuil Ghost de C. Boeri et T. Katanayagi pour Fiam Italia. À droite, miroir "Seif" de Julia Dozsa pour Glas.

Links der von C. Boeri und T. Katanayagi für Fiam Italia entworfene Sessel "Ghost".Rechts der von Julia Dozsa für Glas entworfene Spiegel "Seif".

Below left, table "Helsinki 485" from Caronni and Bonanomi for Desalto. Center, glass table "Ragno" from Vittorio Livi for Fiam Italia. On the right, CD container "Sgt Pepper" from M. Cazzar for Glas.

En bas à gauche, table "Helsinki 485" de Caronni et Bonanomi pour Desalto. Au centre, table en verre "Ragno" de Vittorio Livi pour Fiam Italia. À droite, rangement à CD's "Sgt Pepper" de M. Cazzar pour Glas.

Unten links der Tisch "Helsinki 485", Design von Caronni und Bonanomi für Desalto. In der Mitte der Glastisch "Ragno", Design von Vittorio Livi für Fiam Italia. Rechts die CD-Box "Sgt Pepper". die von M. Cazzar für Glas entworfen wurde.

| Kitchens in white

Composition from the program "Banco"
from Luca Meda for Dada.

Composition de la gamme "Banco"
de Luca Meda pour Dada.

Eine Zusammenstellung aus der Modellreihe
"Banco", Design von Luca Meda für Dada.

Des cuisines en blanc

Weiße Küchen

The idea of total order, inherent in minimalism, is most clearly demonstrated in the kitchen. Smooth surfaces, predominantly in luminous white, with no form of relief or unnecessary ornamentation, and esthetics based on industrial functionality and where everything is in its place are their identifying marks. Also, glass has a recurrent presence that responds to a search for sum and substance with transparencies and lightness. The simplicity and harshness of these compositions force the essence of the use of these different elements to stand out, fleeing from the ostentatious accumulation of objects and facilitating, at the same time, freedom of movement to enable the carrying out of different tasks.

Le concept d'ordre total inhérent au minimalisme trouve sa plus belle raison d'être dans la cuisine. Des surfaces lisses et d'un blanc lumineux, sans relief ou ornement superflu, d'une esthétique basée sur la fonctionnalité industrielle, et selon laquelle chaque objet doit se trouver à sa place, sont les marques de son identité. La présence du verre joue, elle aussi, un grand rôle et répond à une certaine recherche de l'essence, des transparences et de la légèreté. La simplicité et la rigueur de ces compositions mettent en valeur la fonction de chacun des éléments et évitent l'accumulation d'objets pour facilité la liberté de mouvement dans la réalisation des tâches quotidiennes.

Das dem Minimalismus eigene Konzept der absoluten Ordnung findet in der Küche seine höchste Ausdrucksform. Als Beweis dafür können die glatten, vorzugsweise in leuchtendem Weiß gehaltenen Oberflächen ohne jegliches überflüssige Relief oder Ornament und eine Ästhetik genannt werden, die sich auf eine industrielle Funktionalität beruft, bei der jedes Ding seinen Platz und seine eigene Identität hat. Auch Glas wird gerne verwandt, um somit den Anspruch auf das Wesentliche, Transparenz und Leichtigkeit zu erfüllen. Die Einfachheit und Strenge dieser Einrichtung unterstreicht die reine Funktionalität der einzelnen Elemente, wobei auf das Zurschaustellen von Objekten verzichtet wird und somit gleichzeitig ausreichend Platz geschaffen wird, um sich frei bewegen und ungehindert die verschiedenen Arbeiten verrichten zu können.

Proposal from Bis Bis Imports Boston.

Proposition de Bis Bis Imports Boston.

Ein Vorschlag von Bis Bis Imports Boston.

Program "Banko" from E. Tonucci for Triangolo. Below, on the left, proposal from Minotti Cucine. On the right, composition from "Banco" from L. Meda for Dada.

Gamme "Banko" de E. Tonucci pour Triangolo. En bas à gauche, proposition de Minotti Cucine. À droite, composition de "Banco" de L. Meda pour Dada.

Die von E. Tonucci für Triangolo entworfene Modellreihe "Banko". Unten links ein Vorschlag Minotti Cucine. Rechts eine Zusammenstellung aus "Banko", Design von Meda für Dada.

Top, composition from Minotti Cucine. On the right,
model "Espace" from Veneta Cucine.

En haut, composition de Minotti Cucine. À droite,
modèle "Espace" de Veneta Cucine.

Oben eine Zusammenstellung von Minotti Cucine.
Rechts das Modell "Espace" von Veneta Cucine.

Program "Alu 2000"
from Poggenpohl.

Gamme "Alu 2000"
de Poggenpohl.

Die Modellreihe "Alu 2000"
von Foggenpohl.

Top, model "Tec" from Alno.
On the left, collection "Laminate" from Schiffini.

En haut, modèle "Tec" de Alno.
À gauche, collection "Laminate" de Schiffini.

Oben das Modell "Tec" von Alno.
Links die Modellreihe "Laminate" von Schiffini.

Model "Playa" from Effe Tierre for Febal. Bottom left, proposal from Minotti.

Modèle "Playa" de Effe Tierre pour Febal. En bas à gauche, proposition de Minotti.

Das von Effe Tierre für Febal entworfene Modell "Playa". Unten ein Vorschlag von Minotti.

Bottom right, Program "Banco" from L. Meda for Dada.

En bas à droite, Gamme "Banco" de L. Meda pour Dada.

Unten rechts Die von L. Meda für dada entworfene Modellreihe "Banco".

Model "Perla" from Nobilia.
Below, program "Quadrante" from F. Laviani for Dada.

Modèle "Perla" de Nobilia.
En bas, gamme "Quadrante" de F. Laviani pour Dada.

Das Modell "Perla" von Nobilia. Unten die Modellreihe
"Quadrante", die von F. Laviani für Dada entworfen wurde..

Composition from the "Sistema 25"
from Bulthaup.

Composition du "Sistema 25"
de Bulthaup.

Zusammenstellung aus dem "Sistema 25"
von Bulthaup.

Proposals with essential lines from Minotti Cucine. Below, on the right, program "Banco" from Dada.

Propositions aux lignes essentielles de Minotti Cucine. En bas à droite, gamme "Banco" de Dada.

Vorschläge von Minotti Cucine mit einer sich auf das Wesentliche beschränkenden Linienführung. Unten rechts die Modellreihe "Banco" von Dada.

Proposal from Alno.

Proposition de Alno.

Eir Vorschlag von Alno.

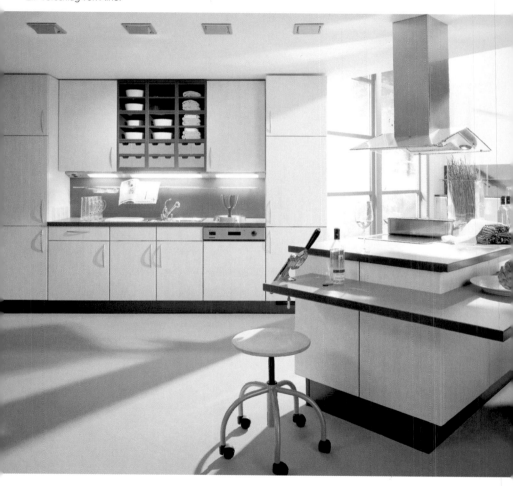

| Transparent bathrooms

Program "Pluvia" from Toscoquattro.

Gamme "Pluvia" de Toscoquattro.

Die Modellreihe "Pluvia" von Toscoquattro.

Des salles de bain diaphanes

diaphanes

Badezimmer
und Transparenz

Bathrooms become a setting where transparencies shine: the flowing of water, the bluish reflections of glass, the beauty of absence. They are crystalline spaces of great visual amplitude, thanks to the use of furniture of a great lightness, which intensifies the sensation of space. Thus, the tendency to reduce perspective in minimalism is translated in washbasins and glass shelves and in bathroom furniture with translucent glass doors that are found suspended in the air, or fixed to the wall, or on metallic legs, contributing to a sensation of weightlessness. It is also possible to create a minimalist bathroom using wood, provided that it is designed in a simple style and that it generates a composition that is rigorously harmonic and simple.

Les salles de bain se sont trans-formées en une scène sur laquelle brillent les transparences : le cours de l'eau, les reflets bleutés du verre, la beauté de l'absence. L'utilisation d'un mobilier léger, intensifiant la sensation d'espace, crée ces pièces diaphanes et d'une grande amplitude visuelle. De cette façon, la perspective réductrice du minimalisme se traduit par des lavabos et des étagères en verre, et par des meubles de salle de bain aux portes en verre translucide suspendus au plafond, accrochés au mur ou sur pieds métalliques, provoquant une impression d'absence de pesanteur. Si la composition est rigoureusement harmonieuse et montre des lignes extrêmement simples, il est également possible d'utiliser le bois pour la création de salles de bain minimalistes

Diese Badezimmer verwandeln sich in von Transparenz geprägte Szenarien, getragen vom Glanz des fließenden Wassers, des vom Glas und Spiegel reflektierten bläulichen Lichts, der Schönheit des Wesentlichen. Die Verwendung von sehr leicht wirkenden Möbeln unterstreicht in diesen hellen übersichtlichen Räumen noch zusätzlich das Gefühl der Weitläufigkeit. Hier wird also der sich auf das Wesentliche beschränkende Minimalismus in Waschbecken und Ablagen aus Glas und Badezimmermöbel mit durchscheinenden Glastüren übersetzt, die in der Luft zu schweben scheinen. Sie sind entweder an der Wand befestigt oder stehen auf Metallfüßen und vermitteln ein Gefühl der Schwerelosigkeit. In einem in minimalistischem Stil gehaltenen Bad findet aber auch Holz seine Anwendung, vorausgesetzt, das Design zeichnet sich durch klare Linien aus und es entstehen insgesamt harmonische, einfache Formen.

Faucets "Tara" from Sieger Design for Dornbracht.

Robinet "Tara" de Sieger Design pour Dornbracht.

Von Sieger Design für Dornbracht entworfene Armaturen "Tara".

Bathroom furniture from Keramag. On the left, washbasin and glass surface "Image" from Altro. In the center, proposal from Bis Bis Imports Boston. On the right, faucets "Belle du Jour" from Sieger Design for Dornbracht.

Meubles de salle de bain de Keramag. À gauche, lavabo et surface en verre "Image' de Altro. Au centre, proposition de Bis Bis Imports Bostor. À droite, robinet "Belle de Jour" de Sieger Design pour Dornbracht.

Badezimmermöbel von Keramag. Links Waschbecken und Deckplatte "Image" aus Glas von Altro. In der Mitte ein Vorschlag von Bis Bis Imports Boston. Rechts Armaturen "Belle de Jour" von Sieger Design für Dornbracht.

Composition "Pluvia" from Toscoquattro.

Composition "Pluvia" de Toscoquattro.

Zusammenstellung "Pluvia" von Toscoquattro.

On the left, proposal from Domus. On the right, washbasin "Gotta" with porcelain surface from Altro.

À gauche, proposition de Domus. À droite, lavabo "Gotta" avec surface en porcelaine, de Altro.

Links ein Vorschlag von Domus. Rechts das Waschbecken "Gotta" mit einer Deckplatte aus Porzellan; von Altro.

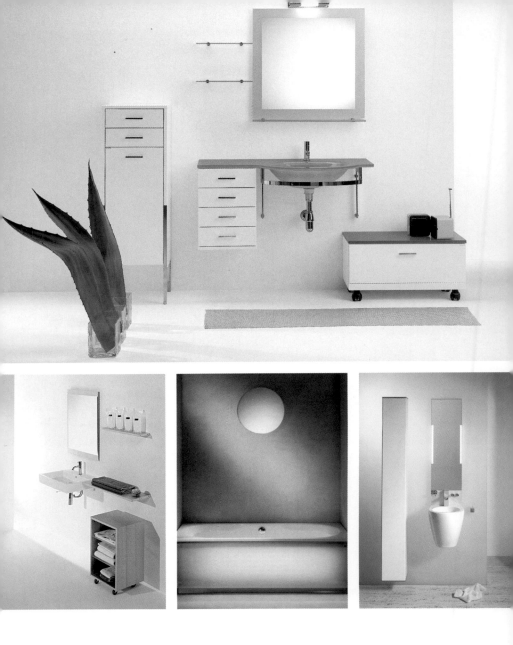

On the Previous page, top image, program "Metropolis" from Toscoquattro. Bottom left, proposal from Domus. In the center, composition from Bis Bis Imports Boston. On the right, furniture from Keramag.

Sur la page précédente, image du haut, gamme "Metropolis" de Toscoquattro. En bas à gauche, proposition de Domus. Au centre, composition de Bis Bis Imports Boston. À droite, mobilier de Keramag.

Auf der vorangehenden Seite oben die Modellreihe "Metropolis" von Toscoquattro. Unten links ein Vorschlag von Domus. In der Mitte eine Zusammenstellung von Bis Bis Imports Boston. Rechts Möbel von Keramag.

Two compositions from the program "Vivano" from Keramag.

Deux compositions de la gamme "Vivano" de Keramag.

Zwei Zusammenstellungen aus der Modellreihe "Vivano" von Keramag.

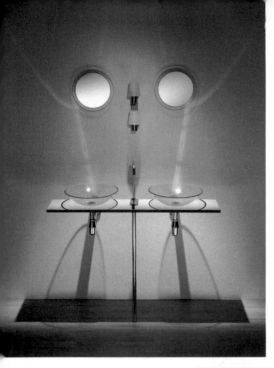

On the left, program "Top System" from Altro. On the right, furniture from the collection "Regata" from Roca.

À gauche, gamme "Top System" de Altro. À droite, mobilier de la collection "Regata" de Roca.

Links die Modellreihe "Top System" von Altro. Möbel aus der Modellreihe "Regata" von Roca.

Composition from the program "Pluvia" from Toscoquattro.

Composition de la gamme "Pluvia" de Toscoquattro.

Eine Zusammenstellung aus der Modellreihe "Pluvia" von Toscoquattro.

Another combination from the program "Pluvia" from Toscoquattro.

Autre combinaison pour la gamme "Pluvia" de Toscoquattro.

Verschiedene Zusammenstellungen aus der Modellreihe "Pluvia" von Toscoquattro.

On the left, trolley "Ambulante" from Glas. Below, from left to right, composition "2016", "2014" and "2021" from Axia.

À gauche, chariot "Ambulante" de Glas. En bas, de gauche à droite, composition "2016", "2014" et "2021" de Axia.

Links der Wagen "Ambulante" von Glas. Unten, von links nach rechts Zusammenstellungen aus "2016", "2014" und "2021" von Axia.

Composition "1030" from Axia.

Composition "1030" de Axia.

Eine Zusammenstellung aus "1030" von Axia.

Composition "3005" from Axia.
On the right, mirror "Cuore
Mio", from R. Dalisi for Glas.

Composition "3005" de Axia. À
droite, miroir "Cuore Mio", de R.
Dalisi pour Glas.

Zusammenstellung aus "3005"
von Axia. Rechts der Spiegel
"Cuore Mio", der von R. Dalisi
für Glas entworfen wurde.

Top image, bathroom fittings and furniture designed by Norman Foster for Duravit. Bottom left, Philippe Starck is the author of the design of "Jelly Cube" from Duravit. On the right, washbasin from the series "Box". Designed by Bruna Rapisarda for Regia.

Image du haut, sanitaires et mobiliers créés par Norman Foster pour Duravit. En bas à gauche, Philippe Starck signe la création de "Jelly Cube" de Duravit. À droite, lavabo de la série "Box", créé par Bruna Rapisarda pour Regia.

Oben die von Norman Foster für Duravit entworfenen Sanitäranlagen und Badezimmermöbel. Unten links das Design "Jelly Cube", das Philippe Starck für Duravit erstellt hat. Rechts ein Waschbecken aus der Modellreihe "Box", Design von Bruna Rapisarda für Regia.

Shower from the series "Logic" from Cesana.

Douche de la série "Logic" de Cesana.

Dusche aus der Modellreihe "Logic" von Cesana.

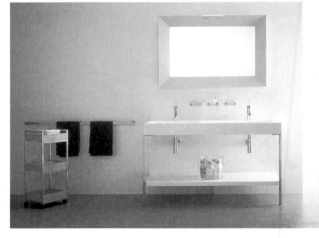

Composition "3005" from Axia.

Composition "3005" de Axia.

Zusammenstellung aus "3005" von Axia.

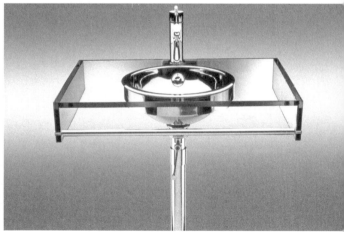

| Compact bedrooms

"Double" from Matteograssi.

"Double" de Matteograssi.

"Double" von Matteograssi.

Des chambres
aux lignes concises

Schlafzimmer mit
konziser Formgebung

Minimalist bedrooms are like a place of retreat, a sacred place of worship, where we can carry out each day, and each night, a regenerating exercise of introspection that permits us to center on ourselves and to listen to our interior voice. Without reaching the asceticism of a monastic cell, they are austere spaces that help us evade the "noise" that constantly enfolds us in the exterior world. The minimalist ideal would be the classical Japanese futon extended upon a tatami in an empty room. Without reaching this extreme, we must bear in mind that silence, understood as the elimination of everything that is superfluous, should be the main guest of the most intimate zone of our home.

Les chambres minimalistes ressemblent à un lieu d'isolement, de culte, un endroit sacré où l'on peut effectuer, jour après jour, nuit après nuit, un exercice d'introspection régénérateur nous permettant de nous concentrer sur nous-mêmes et d'écouter notre voix intérieure. Sans en arriver à l'ascétisme d'une cellule monacale, ces pièces austères nous aident à fuir le bruit du monde extérieur qui nous entoure constamment. L'idéal minimaliste serait un futon japonais classique sur un tatami dans une chambre vide. Sans en arriver à cette extrémité, il faut cependant tenir compte du fait que le silence, considéré comme l'élimination du superflu, doit être l'hôte principal de la pièce la plus intime de notre demeure.

Minimalistische Schlafzimmer sind Orte des Rückzugs, wie heilige Kultstätten, wo jeden Tag und jede Nacht regenerierende Exerzitien zur Selbstfindung getrieben werden können, mit denen wir zu uns selbst zurückfinden und auf unsere innere Stimme hören können. Sie wirken zwar nicht so asketisch wie eine Mönchszelle, sind aber schmucklose Räume, in denen wir Zuflucht vor dem Lärm finden, von dem wir in der Außenwelt ständig umgeben sind. Höchste Ausdrucksform des Minimalismus wäre in diesem Zusammennang ein in einem leeren Raum aufgestelltes klassisches japanisches Futon. Ohne bis zu diesem Extrem zu gehen, sollte aber berücksichtigt werden, daß Ruhe als Verzicht auf alles Oberflächliche zu verstehen ist und für den intimsten und persönlichsten Bereich unserer Wohnung von größter Bedeutung ist.

Furniture from the collection "Do it" from Viccarbe.

Mobilier de la collection "Do it" de Viccarbe.

Möbel aus der Modellreihe "Do it" von Viccarbe.

Proposal for bedroom from Porro.

Proposition pour la chambre
de Porro.

Ein Vorschlag zur
Schlafzimmergestaltung von Porro.

On the left, wardrobe interior
designed by Misura Emme. On the
right, program "Le Notti" from
Claudio Silvestrin for Mobileffe.

À gauche, armoire créée par Misura
Emme. À droite, gamme "Le Notti"
de Claudio Silvestrin pour
Mobileffe.

Links Innenraum des von Misura
Emme entworfenen Schrankes.
Rechts die Modellreihe "Le Notti",
Design von Claudio Silvestrin für
Mobileffe.

Above, model "Alfa" from Emaf
Progetti for Zanotta. On the left,
drawers "Sistem" from Rafemar. On
the right, "Le Notti" from C.
Silvestrin for Mobileffe.

En haut, modèle "Alfa" de Emaf
Progetti pour Zanotta. À gauche,
tiroirs "Sistem" de Rafemar. À
droite, "Le Notti" de C. Silvestrin
pour Mobileffe.

Oben das Modell "Alfa", das Emaf
Progetti für Zanotta entworfen hat.
Links Kommode "Sistem" von
Rafemar. Rechts "Le Notti", Design
von C. Silvestrin für Mobileffe.

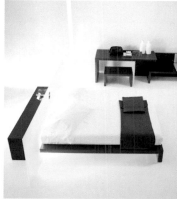

Top images: bedroom "Ando" from Poliform and wardrobe interior
"Varia". Below, bed "Giorgia" and wardrobe "Ki" from Misura Emme.

Images du haut : chambre "Ando" de Poliform et armoire "Varia". En bas,
lit "Giorgia" et armoire "Ki" de Misura Emme.

Oben: Schlafzimmer "Ando" von Poliform und Innenraum des Schrankes
"Varia". Unten das Bett "Giorgia" und der Schrank "Ki" von Misura Emme.

On the left, wardrobe "7 volte 7" from L. Meda for Molteni & C. On the right, "Double" from Matteograssi. Below, wardrobe "Milano" and wardrobe "Yu" from Misura Emme.

À gauche, armoire "7 volte 7" de L. Meda pour Molteni & C. À droite, "Double" de Matteograssi. En bas, armoire "Milano" et armoire "Yu" de Misura Emme.

Links der von L. Meda für Molteni & C A entworfene Schrank "7 volte 7". Rechts "Double" von Matteograssi. Unten die Schränke "Milano" und "Yu" von Misura Emme.

Proposal from the series
"Openside" from Matteograssi.

Proposition de la série "Openside"
de Matteograssi.

Vorschlag aus der Modellreihe
"Openside" von Matteograssi.

On the left, bed "Openside" from
Matteograssi. On the right,
composition "Soho" from Gandía
Blasco.

À gauche, lit "Openside" de
Matteograssi. À droite, composition
"Soho" de Gandía Blasco.

Links das Bett "Openside" von
Matteograssi. Rechts eine
Zusammenstellung aus "Soho" von
Gandía Blasco.

Bed from the program "Openside" from Matteograssi.

Lit de la gamme "Openside" de Matteograssi.

Das Bett aus der Modellreihe "Openside" von Matteograssi.

Bottom images, two possible combinations from the program "Pi" from Juventa.

Images du bas, deux combinaisons possibles pour la gamme "Pi" de Juventa.

Unten zwei Zusammenstellungen aus der Modellreihe "Pi" von Juventa.

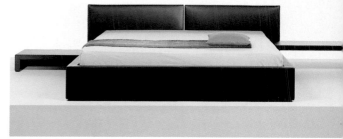

Bed "Noor" with leather bed–head from L. Acerbis for
Acerbis International.

Lit "Noor" avec tête de lit en cuir, de L. Acerbis pour
Acerbis International.

Das Bett "Noor" mit Kopfteil aus Leder, Design von L.
Acerbis für Acerbis International.

Bedroom from the collection "Solid & Basic"
from Club 8 Company.

Chambre de la collection "Solid & Basic" de Club 8
Company.

Ein Schlafzimmer aus der Modellreihe
"Solid & Basic" von Club 8 Company

Bedroom from the program "Plan" from Matteograssi.

Chambre de la gamme "Plan" de Matteograssi.

Ein Schlafzimmer aus der Modellreihe "Plan" von Matteograssi.

Wardrobe interior from the collection "Plan" from Misura Emme.

Armoire de la collection "Plan" de Misura Emme.

Innenraum eines Schrankes aus der Modellreihe "Plan" von Misura Emme.

Lights in search of simplicity

Wall lamp "Marc" from David Abad for Dab.

Applique "Marc" de David Abad pour Dab.

Wandlampe "Marc" , die von David Abad für Dab entworfen wurde.

Un éclairage en quête de simplicité

Durch ihre Einfachheit geprägte Lichtquellen

To create sources of light based on the principles of minimalism requires an effort in restraint and sufficient wisdom to know how to get to the bottom of the luminary process. Once again, we reach basic nature, to extract from her the beauty of formal purity and an expressive strength that only elementary forms can project. On occasions, to get to simplicity is a complex process, but once obtained it is capable of communicating great things. These lamps are able to blend in with their surroundings, in which, provided that it is desired, they can go completely unnoticed. They enhanced the space itself and contribute to an indefinable sensation of warmth to the atmosphere from their discrete position.

Créer des foyers de lumière basés sur les principes du minimalisme demande un gros effort de retenue et de sagesse permettant d'atteindre le fondement du procédé lumineux. Une fois de plus, nous partons à la recherche de l'essence pour extraire la beauté de la pureté formelle et une force expressive ne projetant que des formes élémentaires. Atteindre la simplicité est, parfois, une procédure complexe qui, une fois surpassée, nous permet de communiquer de grandes choses. Ces lampes peuvent s'intégrer à n'importe quel environnement et passer inaperçues chaque fois que vous le souhaitez : elles mettront en valeur une pièce spacieuse et dégageront de façon discrète une atmosphère infiniment chaleureuse.

Es erfordert schon einige Zurückhaltung hinsichtlich der Formgebung und ausreichende Kenntnisse über Beleuchtungstechnik, um Lichtquellen vorzusehen, die den Prinzipien des Minimalismus entsprechen. Wir kommen auch hier wieder auf das Wesentliche zurück, um aus ihm die Schönheit der reinen Form zu schöpfen und zu einer Ausdrucksform zu gelangen, die nur von elementaren Formen projiziert werden kann. Einfachheit herzustellen. kann manchmal zu einem sehr komplexer Prozeß werden. Gelingt das Vorhaben, so wird eine großartige Kommunikation zwischen Objekten und Betrachter hergestellt. Diese Lampen können so in den Raum integriert werden, dass sie bei Bedarf überhaupt nicht in Erscheinung treten, dem Raum selber Bedeutung zuweisen und so eine Atmosphäre herstellen, von der ein unbeschreibliches Gefühl des Wohlbehagens auslöst wird.

Wall lamp "Hook" from David Abad for Dab.

Applique "Hook" de David Abad pour Dab.

Wandlampe "Hook" , die von David Abad für Dab entworfen wurde.

From left to right: "Gles" from R. Giovanetti and "Slice" from C. Tamborini
for Fontana Arte; "Talo suspensión" from N. Poulton for Artemide; "Tram"
from Dab; "Dean" from C. Williams for Fontana Arte; "Atum" from
F. Dedelley for Classicon.

De gauche à droite : "Gles" de R. Giovanetti et "Slice" de C. Tamborini
pour Fontana Arte ; "Talo" plafonnier de N. Poulton pour Artemide ;
"Tram" de Dab ; "Dean" de C. Williams pour Fontana Arte ; "Atum" de
F. Dedelley pour Classicon.

Von links nach rechts: "Gles" von R. Giovanetti und "Slice" von C.
Tamborini für Fontana Arte; "Talo suspensión" von N. Poulton für Artemide;
"Tram" von Dab; "Dean" von C. Williams für Fontana Arte; "Atum" von
F. Dedelley für Classicon.

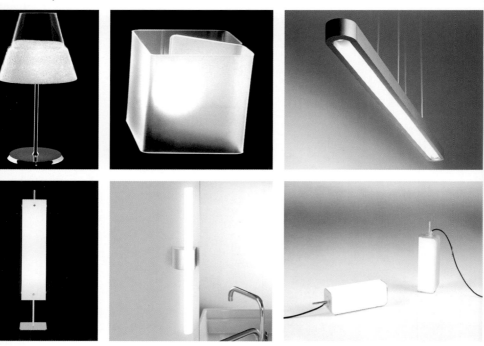

From left to right: "Ilde" suspended; "Ilde" wall lamp; "Deco"; "Marc" suspended and "Centra". Designed by David Abad for Dab.

De gauche à droite : "Ilde" plafonnier ; "Ilde" applique ; "Deco" ; "Marc" plafonnier et "Centra", créations de david Abac pour Dab.

Von links nach rechts: Hängelampe "Ilde"; Wandlampe "Ilde"; "Deco"; Hängelampe "Marc" und "Centra", von David Abad für Dab entworfen.

Suspended lamp "Zettel'z"
from Ingo Maurer.

Plafonnier "Zettel'z"
de Ingo Maurer.

Hängelampe "Zettel'z"
von Ingo Maurer.

On the left, "Spaguetti" from R.
Benedito for Vibia. In the center,
"Bill" from Tobias Grau. On the
right, "Fil" from A. Siza Vieira for
Mobles 114.

À gauche, "Spaguetti" de R.
Benedito pour Vibia. Au centre,
"Bill" de Tobias Grau. À droite, "Fil"
de A. Siza Vieira pour Mobles 114.

Links "Spaguetti", Design von R.
Benedito für Vibia. In der Mitte
"Bill" von Tobias Grau. Rechts "Fil",
von A. Siza Vieira für Mobles 114
entworfen.

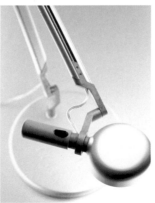

Suspended lamp "Nite", from
Jorge Pensi for B. Lux.

Plafonnier "Nite", de Jorge Pensi
pour B. Lux.

Die von Jorge Pensi für B. Lux
entworfene Hängelampe "Nite".

On the left, "Aran" from D. Abad
for Dab. In the center, "Nulla" from
E. Gismondi for Artemide. On the
right, "Nite" from J. Pensi for
B. Lux.

À gauche, "Aran" de D. Abad pour
Dab. Au centre, "Nulla" de E.
Gismondi pour Artemide. À droite,
"Nite" de J. Pensi pour B. Lux.

Links "Aran" von D. Abad für Dab.
In der Mitte "Nulla" von E.
Gismondi für Artemide. Rechts
"Nite" von J. Pensi für B. Lux.

Table lamps "Q–Bo" from C. Serra and J. A. Herrero for B. Lux.

Lampes de bureau "Q-Bo" de C. Serra et J. A. Herrero pour B. Lux.

Tischlampen "Q-Bo" , Design von C. Serra und J. A. Herrero für B. Lux.

On the left, wall lamp "Dany" from Fabia Foà for I Tre. On the right, "Wo Bist du Edison" from Ingo Maurer.

À gauche, applique "Dany" de Fabia Foà pour I Tre. À droite, "Wo Bist du Edison" de Ingo Maurer.

Links Wandlampe "Dany", Design von Fabia Foà für I Tre. Rechts, "Wo Bist du Edison" von Ingo Maurer.

On the right, "Yin Flu" from C. from Bevilacqua for Artemide. Below, on the left, "Trecentosessantagradi". Center, "Cubi" and right "Obe". All from I Tre.

À droite, "Yin Flu" de C. de Bevilacqua pour Artemide. En bas à gauche, "Trecentosessantagradi". Au centre, "Cubi" et à droite ""Obe". Ensemble de I Tre.

Rechts "Yin Flu", die von C. de Bevilacqua für Artemide entworfen wurde. Unten links "Trecentosessantagradi". In der Mitte "Cubi" und rechts "Obe". Alle Lampen von I Tre.

Travellers and Cross-Cultural Surroundings
The mixture of cultures as a philosophy of life.
Oriental influences, Arabian, African...

To live in surroundings inspired in other ways of understanding life implies, above all, a great cultural wealth. It implies welcoming different ideologies into the heart of our home. It implies knowing other forms of art and craft. It implies, in short, soaking up the diversity of the world without having to move from the comfort of your own home.

Apart from all that we can bring back in our suitcase as an eternal souvenir of our vacations (a wooden sculpture from Africa, a kilim from Turkey, some silk curtains from India, some lamps from Morocco, some embroidered cushions from Nepal, a box with incrustations of marquetry from Iran, a carved table from Tunisia, a piece of linen or batik with colors that come from the African savannah, a Tibetan mandala, and so on), large decorating firms find, on many occasions, their inspiration for the creation of new collections in other cultures, in the same way as happens in the world of fashion.

These days, it is easy to find establishments specialized in exotic furniture in large European cities: from small stores that sell Moroccan craft products to the chains specialized in selling futons and auxiliary furniture from Japan. The Asian carpet stores are also familiar – those that generally sell carpets of great value —, the ones that offer all kinds of oriental articles — especially from India that fill any space, as large as it may be,

with the intense colors and drawings of their fabrics —, others that present sculptures, paintings and craft objects that come from a fascinating Africa, the large stores that proffer all kinds of furniture of the so-called colonial style — from Indonesia or Thailand —, the inestimable Chinese bazaars with all kinds of articles characterized by a certain kitsch air — able to cheer up the most serious of shelves — and, of course, the stores of always, where we can acquire typical Mediterranean craft products.

The combination of all this can evidently turn out to be explosive. The creation of atmospheres that transport us to distant places requires a special ability to avoid falling into responses teeming with soulless souvenirs.

Although nothing can substitute the pleasure of traveling, of discovering, of wandering around the streets, of searching through rambling market stalls to find objects that tell us a story whenever we look at them, at least, we still have the possibility of recreating. That is to say, to introduce exotic details into our small homes that allow us to live, as they stimulate our imagination and memories, in other places.

It is an escape to other cultures for which we feel a special affinity, filling our space with multi-cultural wealth.

Interculturelles et Voyageuses
Le mélange des cultures comme philosophie de vie.
Influences orientales, africaines, arabes…

Vivre dans des contextes inspirés par d'autres façons de voir la vie suppose, avant tout, la présence d'une grande richesse culturelle. Cela suppose également la connaissance d'autres types d'art et d'artisanat. Cela suppose, en définitive, le fait de savoir absorber la diversité du monde entier sans avoir à sortir de chez so.

Mis à part tout ce que l'on peut emporter dans sa valise comme souvenir éternel d'un voyage (une sculpture africaine en bois, un kilim de Turquie, des rideaux en soie rapportés de l'Inde, des lampes du Maroc, des coussins cousus au Népal, une boîte incrustée d'Iran, une table de chevet en bois sculpté de Tunisie, une toile ou batik aux couleurs de la savane africaine, un mandala tibétain, …), les grandes signatures de la décoration trouvent souvent leur inspiration pour la création de nouvelles collections dans d'autres cultures, tout comme dans le monde de la mode.

Actuellement, il est facile de trouver dans les grandes villes européennes, des établissements spécialisés dans le mobilier exotique : depuis les petites boutiques vendant des produits artisanaux du Maroc, jusqu'aux grandes chaînes de magasins consacrées à la vente de futons et de meubles auxiliaires d'origine japonaise. Il existe également les boutiques de tapis asiatiques –généralement de grande valeur –, celles offrant tout type d'articles orientaux – des articles importés spécialement de l'Inde, aux couleurs intenses et aux dessins abondants– celles présentant des sculptures, des tableaux et des objets artisanaux importés de la fascinante Afrique. Les grandes surfaces elles aussi nous proposent tout type de meubles de style colonial – importés d'Indonésie ou de Thaïlande -, les bazars chinois avec leurs articles de toutes sortes caractérisés par un certain style kitsch – capables d'égayer l'étagère la plus mono-tone- et, évidemment, les commerces de toujours où nous pouvons trouver des produits artisanaux typiques de la zone méditerranéenne.

La combinaison de tous ces éléments peut évidemment sembler explosive. La création d'environnements capables de nous transporter vers des pays lointains demande un talent spécial afin d'éviter de tomber dans les répliques pleines de souvenirs sans âme. Même si rien ne peut remplacer le plaisir de voyager, de connaî-tre, de se promener, de fouiller dans des étalages dés-ordonnés, de tomber sur des objets nous racontant une histoire chaque fois que nous les regardons, il nous re-ste au moins la possibilité de recréer ; c'est-à-dire, d'in-troduire dans notre demeure de petites notes exo-tiques qui nous transportent vers des endroits différents et stimulent notre imagination et notre mémoire.

Il s'agit d'une escapade vers d'autres cultures pour lesquelles nous ressentons une affinité spéciale et qui remplissent notre espace d'une richesse multi-culturelle.

Von Verschiedenen Kulturen und Reiseeindrücken Geprägte Interieurs
Die Mischung von Elementen aus verschiedenen Kulturen als Lebensphilosophie; orientalischer, afrikanischer, arabischer Einfluß

In Interieurs zu leben, bei deren Ausstattung man sich von dem Lebensstil fremder Völker hat inspirieren las-sen, stellen in erster Linie eine Bereicherung auf kultu-reller Ebene dar und setzt die Kenntnis und Berücksich-tigung verschiedener Lebensweisen und Ideologien voraus. Außerdem muß man natürlich ein Verständnis für andere Ausdrucksformen der Kunst und des Kunst-handwerks mitbringen. Das bedeutet also, die Mannig-faltigkeit unserer Welt in unseren Wohnbereich zu ho-len, ohne dazu erst auf Reisen gehen zu müssen.

Außer den Dingen, die wir als Souvenir im Koffer mit nach Hause bringen (eine afrikanische Holzfigur, ein Ke-lim aus der Türkei, Seidengardinen aus Indien, marok-kanische Lampen, ein paar bestickte Kissen aus Nepal, ein mit Intarsia geschmücktes Kästchen aus dem Iran, ein mit Schnitzereien verziertes Tischchen aus Tunesien, ein Leinen– oder Batiktuch in den Farben der afrikani-schen Savanne, ein Mandala aus Tibet und noch unzäh-lige andere Dinge) können wir auch zu Hause ähnliche Objekte finden, die von den großen Ausstattungshäu-sern angeboten werden, und bei deren Design man sich von fremden Kulturen hat inspirieren lassen. Der-selbe Trend ist in der Welt der Mode zu beobachten.

Heutzutage ist es leicht, in den europäischen Groß-städten auf exotische Möbel spezialisierte Läden zu fin-den; angefangen bei den kleinen Boutiquen, die Kunst-handwerk aus Marokko anbieten bis hin zu den Ladenketten, die Futons und in Japan hergestellte Bei-stellmöbel in ihrem Verkaufsangebot führen.

Nichts Außergewöhnliches sind auch die Läden mit orientalischen Teppichen – bei denen es sich generell um hochwertige Stücke handelt –oder auch die, in de-nen jegliche Art von aus orientalischen Ländern impor-tierten Produkten zu finden ist. Insbesondere wird hier in Indien hergestellte Ware angeboten, w e zum Bei-spiel die Stoffe, die mit ihren kräftigen Farben und aus-drucksstarken Mustern jeglichen Raum – wie groß er auch immer sein möge – füllen. Andere Geschäfte lok-ken wiederum mit Skulpturen, Bildern und Kunsthand-werk aus dem faszinierenden Afrika; in Großmärkten sind Möbel im sogenannten Kolonialstil zu finden, die aus Indonesien oder Thailand importiert werden; die unzähligen chinesischen Basare sind eine wahre Fund-grube für Objekte jeglicher Art, sicherlich oft e n wenig kitschig, die aber dennoch jedem Regal eine heitere Note verleihen können. Und dann gibt es natürlich noch diese schon von jeher bestehenden Läden, in denen wir die für den Mittelmeerraum typischen, kunsthandwerk-lich hergestellten Artikel finden.

Vermischen wir alle diese Stilrichtungen miteinan-der, kann ein sehr spannungsgeladenes Ambiente ent-stehen. Es erfordert jedoch schon einige Geschicklich-keit, Räume zu schaffen, durch die wir uns in ferne Länder versetzt fühlen, ohne daß es sich dabei nur um eine seelenlose Ansammlung von Souvenirs handelt.

Das Vergnügen zu reisen, Neues kennenzulernen, durch Gassen zu bummeln, in etwas heruntergekomme-nen Lädchen herumzustöbern und Dinge zu finden, die uns, jedesmal, wenn wir sie betrachten, immer wieder eine Geschichte erzählen, kann natürlich durch nichts ersetzt werden, aber immerhin bleibt uns die Möglich-keit der "Rekonstruktion", d.h. wir nehmen in unseren Wohnbereich kleine exotische Details auf, die uns Le-bensfreude vermitteln und die Vorstellung und Erinner-ung an fremde Welten wachhalten.

Es ist wie ein Abstecher in andere Kulturen, für die wir ein besonderes Faible entwickelt haben, und mit dem wir unserem Ambiente eine multi–kulturelle Note verleihen.

Ethnic living and dining rooms

Group "Thomas" from Insa.
Design from E. Arosio and S. Mariani.

Ensemble "Thomas" de Insa,
création de E. Arosio et S. Mariani.

Gruppe "Thomas" von Insa,
Design von E. Arosio und S. Mariani.

Des salons et des salles à manger ethniques

Wohn- und Esszimmer mit ethnischem Flair

To listen to the echoes of other cultures from the comforts of our own home is a formidable experience. Generally, objects and furniture that are from other countries or that have been influenced by symbols from other cultures, mainly those of Asian or African origin, have a great visual strength. Because of this, at times, it is sufficient to include just a few complements that, in combination with western tendencies, create an atmosphere with an ethnic touch without falling into solutions that are too topical or too excessive. Some fabrics, some colors, some icons, some fragrances, some pieces of craftsmanship, some simple cushions or a table set at floor level can transport us with ease to those exotic places that awaken in us our capacity to dream with the same fascination that we had when we were children.

Percevoir les échos venant d'autres cultures depuis notre propre demeure, c'est une expérience formidable. Généralement, les meubles et les objets venant d'autres pays ou subissant l'influence de leurs symboles, principalement ceux d'Asie ou d'Afrique, comportent une grande force visuelle. C'est pour cette raison qu'il suffit parfois d'inclure quelques accessoires qui, combinés avec les tendances occidentales, permettent de créer une ambiance aux notes ethniques, sans tomber dans les répliques trop évidentes ou trop excessives. Des tissus, des couleurs, des icônes, des arômes, des pièces artisanales, de simples coussins ou une table au ras du sol peuvent facilement nous transporter vers ces lieux exotiques et réveiller notre imagination de la même façon que lorsque nous étions enfants.

Es ist schon ein großartiges Gefühl, wenn wir in unserer eigenen Wohnung den Einfluss fremder Kulturen erleben. Die meisten der aus anderen Ländern stammenden Möbel und die von deren Symbolik geprägten Objekte werden vorwiegend aus Asien und Afrika importiert und beeindrucken durch ihre starke visuelle Ausdruckskraft. Deshalb braucht man oft nur wenige Details in die nach westlichem Stil konzipierte Einrichtung aufzunehmen, um dem Interieur eine ethnische Note zu verleihen, ohne dabei auf zu viele banale Repliken zurückzugreifen. Ein paar Stoffe, Farben, Ikone, Aromen, kunsthandwerklich hergestellte Objekte, mehrere einfache Kissen oder ein niedriger Tisch können schon ausreichen, um uns an jene exotischen Orte zu bringen, die in uns Erinnerungen wachrufen, und die von uns mit derselben Faszination erlebt werden, wie wir sie schon als Kinder verspürt haben.

Dining room set "Cesare" from Grupo Tissetanta.

Ensemble de salle à manger "Cesare" du Grupo Tissetanta.

Esszimmergruppe "Cesare" von Grupo Tissetanta.

Cupboard "Magic" from R. and S. Verardo for Verardo.

Armoire "Magic" de R. et S. Verardo pour Verardo.

Der von R. und S. Verardo für Verardo entworfene Schrank "Magic".

Proposal from
Bis Bis Imports Boston.

Proposition de
Bis Bis Imports Boston.

Ein Vorschlag von
Bis Bis Imports Boston.

Sideboard from Bis Bis Imports
Boston. On the right, sofa "Mixer"
from Insa.

Buffet de Bis Bis Imports Boston. À
droite, canapé "Mixer" de Insa.

Anrichte von Bis Bis Imports Boston.
Rechts das Sofa "Mixer" von Insa.

Proposal from Bis Bis Imports Boston.

Proposition de Bis Bis Imports Boston.

Ein Vorschlag von Bis Bis Imports Boston.

Container furniture from the collection "Apta" from A. Citterio for Maxalto.

Meuble de la collection "Apta" de A. Citterio pour Maxalto.

Ein Element aus der Modellreihe "Apta", entworfen von A. Citterio für Maxalto.

The collection "Piccadilly" reminds us of Africa. From the Maison Coloniale.

La collection "Picadilly" a des réminiscences africaines. De La Maison Coloniale.

Die Modellreihe "Picadilly" lässt Erinnerungen an Afrika wach werden; von La Maison Coloniale.

Composition from the collection "Mandalay" from the Maison Coloniale.

Composition de la gamme "Mandalay", de La Maison Coloniale.

Eine Zusammenstellung aus der Modellreihe "Mandalay" von La Maison Coloniale.

Sofa "Lowrider Woody" from Innovation.

Canapé "Lowrider Woody" de Innovation.

Das Sofa "Lowrider Woody" von Innovation.

Sofa bed "Rollo" from Innovation.

Canapé-lit "Rollo" de Innovation.

Schlafsofa "Rollo" von Innovation.

Diverse models of puffs from Innovation.

Différents modèles de poufs de Innovation.

Verschiedene Hockermodelle von Innovation.

Living room "Elixir" from the collection Los Contemporáneos, designed by Hans Hopfer for Roche Bobois.

Salon "Elixir" de la collection Los Contemporáneos, créé par Hans Hopfer pour Roche Bobois.

Wohnzimmer "Elixir" aus der Modellreihe Los Contemporáneos, Design von Hans Hopfer für Roche Bobois.

Easy chairs "D.F. Uno" from Diego Fortunato for Perobell.

Fauteuils "D.F. Uno" de Diego Fortunato pour Perobell.

Die Sessel "D.F. Uno", Design von Diego Fortunato für Perobell.

Table "Senzatempo" and chairs "Style" from Calligaris.

Table "Senzatempo" et chaises "Style" de Calligaris.

Der Tisch "Senzatempo" und die Stühle "Style" von Calligaris.

Easy chair "It" with accessories from R. Lazzeroni and easy chairs "Caleidos" from Studio Opera Work in Progress. From Insa.

Fauteuil "It" avec accessoires, de R. Lazzeroni et fauteuils "Caleidos" de Studio Opera Work in Progress. De Insa.

Der Sessel "It" mit Accessoires von R. Lazzeroni und die Sessel "Caleidos" von Studio Opera Work in Progress; hergestellt von Insa.

Sofa "Marocco", chest of drawers
"Stripe" and textile table "Asmir"
from Paola Navone for Casamilano.

Canapé "Marocco", commode
"Stripe" et table "Asmir", de Paola
Navone pour Casamilano.

Das Sofa "Marocco", die Kommode
"Stripe" und der Tisch "Asmir",
Design von Paola Navone für
Casamilano.

Container furniture "The Box"
from Peteer van Riet for Juventa.

Rangements "The Box"
de Peteer van Riet pour Juventa.

Die von de Peter van Riet für
Juventa entworfenen
Containermöbel "The Box".

A proposal with a colonial air from Inthai.

Teinte coloniale pour cette proposition de Inthai.

Dieser Vorschlag von Inthai weckt Erinnerungen an die Kolonialzeit.

On the left, mirror "Duke" from G. Manzali for Cattelan Italia. On the right, mirror "LLM" from Nanda Vigo for Glas.

À gauche, miroir "Duke" de G. Manzali pour Cattelan Italia. À droite, miroir "LLM" de Nanda Vigo pour Glas.

Links der von G. Manzali für Cattelan Italia entworfene Spiegel "Duke". Rechts der Spiegel "LLM", Design von Nanda Vigo für Glas.

Composition "Kronos" from E. Arosio for Verardo.

Composition "Kronos" de E. Arosio pour Verardo.

Die Zusammenstellung "Kronos" ist von E. Arosio für Verardo entworfen worden.

Extendable table "Foresta Nera" from E. Arosio for Glas.

Table à rallonge "Foresta Nera" de E. Arosio pour Glas.

Der von E. Arosio für Glas entworfene Ausziehtisch "Foresta Nera".

Shelving system "Pontaccio" from Lago.

Ensemble d'étagères "Pontaccio" de Lago.

Das Regalsystem "Pontaccio" von Lago.

Center table "Irupe" from Lievore, Altherr and Molina for Muebles Do+Ce. In the center, tables from Arco Meubel.

Table basse "Irupe" de Lievore, Altherr et Molina pour Muebles Do+Ce. Au centre, tables de Arco Meubel.

Der Tisch "Irupe", von Lievore, Altherr und Molina für Muebles Do+Ce entworfen. In der Mitte Tische von Arco Meubel.

Collection "Bengal" from the Maison Coloniale.

Collection "Bengal" de La Maison Coloniale.

Modellreihe "Bengal" von La Maison Coloniale.

Seating system "Mahjong". Design from Hans Hopfer for Roche Bobois.

Ensemble de sièges "Mahjong", création de Hans Hopfer pour Roche Bobois.

Sitzgruppe "Mahjong", Design von Hans Hopfer für Roche Bobois.

Living room from the collection "Turban"
from the Maison Coloniale.

Salon de la collection "Turban"
de La Maison Coloniale.

Wohnzimmer aus der Modellreihe "Turban"
von La Maison Coloniale.

Proposal from the Maison Coloniale
combining the models "Butterfly"
and "Cargo".

Proposition de La Maison Coloniale,
combinaison des modèles
"Butterfly" et "Cargo".

Ein Vorschlag von La Maison
Coloniale, bei dem die Modelle
"Butterfly" und "Cargo"
miteinander kombiniert werden.

Table "Pigre" from Misura Emme.

Table "Pigre" de Misura Emme.

Der Tisch "Pigre" von Misura Emme.

Roche Bobois proposes, within the collection Los Contemporáneos, the composition "Fashionista" from S. Joly.

Roche Bobois et la collection Los Contemporáneos, propose la composition "Fashionista" de S. Joly.

Von Roche Bobois wird aus der Modellreihe Los Contemporáneos, die Zusammenstellung "Fashionista" von S. Joly vorgeschlagen.

Within the collection Los Viajeros from Roche Bobois,
we find the composition "Peaceful".

Dans la collection Los Viajeros de Roche Bobois,
on trouve la composition "Peaceful".

Zu der Modellreihe Los Viajeros von Roche Bobois
gehört die Zusammenstellung "Peaceful".

Table "Miyabi" from G. Viganò
for Porada.

Table "Miyabi" de G. Viganò
pour Porada.

Der Tisch "Miyabi", ein Design
von G. Viganò für Porada.

Shelving "Magnetique" from Nils
Holger Moorman. On the right,
Crockery stand "Horizonte" from
Lievore, Altherr, Molina for Muebles
Do+Ce.

Étagères "Magnetique" de Nils
Holger Moorman. À droite, meuble
à vaisselle "Horizonte" de Lievore,
Altherr, Molina pour Muebles
Do+Ce.

Regale "Magnetique" von Nils
Holger Moorman. Rechts
Geschirrschrank "Horizonte",
Design von Lievore, Altherr, Molina
für Muebles Do+Ce.

Collection "Ambiance Chinoise" from the Maison Coloniale.

Collection "Ambiance Chinoise" de La Maison Coloniale.

Modellreihe "Ambiance Chinoise" von La Maison Coloniale.

Inthai proposes these environments with a marked colonial tone.

Inthai propose ces ambiances à l'accent colonial.

Von Inthai wird diese Einrichtungen in ausgeprägtem Kolonialstil vorgeschlagen.

Lights and other objects that contain stories

Auxiliary table from the
"Colección Occa" from Club 8 Company.

Table d'appoint de la "Colección Occa"
de Club 8 Company.

Ein Beistelltisch aus der Modellreihe
"Occa" von Club 8 Company.

Des éclairages et des objets qui racontent...

Licht und Objekte, von denen Geschichten erzählt werden

There are simple objects that awake intense emotions. They provoke associations that send us to other places and to other times, creating in our small home centers of attention that free us of monotony. Some slender orchids on a side table, a carpet of African or oriental inspiration, a woodcarving, a lamp with a paper shade understood to be a unique piece, some fabrics with printings that imitate the freedom of animals in the African savannah... They are all unmistakable symbols of other cultures and of other ways of relating to the world that are created wherever great windows open to the world are found. Each and every one of these objects is, in short, a great storyteller if one knows how to listen.

Il existe de objets simples pouvant réveiller des émotions intenses. Ils provoquent des associations qui nous renvoient à d'autres lieux et d'autres époques et créent, dans notre demeure, de petits centres d'attention capables de nous libérer de la monotonie. D'élégantes orchidées sur une table auxiliaire, un tapis d'inspiration africaine ou orientale, une sculpture en bois, une lampe avec un abat–jour en papier considérée comme pièce unique, des tissus imprimés racontant la liberté des animaux de la savane africaine... Des symboles évidents d'autres cultures et d'autres formes d'intégration à l'environnement, créant de grandes fenêtres ouvertes sur le monde. Chacun de ces objets est, en définitive et si vous savez les écouter, une fontaine d'histoires.

Es gibt schlichte Objekte, die mit starken Emotionen verbunden sind. Sie beschwören Assoziationen herauf, die uns in andere Zeiten und an andere Orte versetzen. Sie verstehen es, unsere Aufmerksamkeit auf sich zu lenken und somit Monotonie aus dem Raum zu verbannen. Eine zarte Orchidee auf einem Beistelltisch, ein von afrikanischer oder orientalischer Kultur inspirierter Teppich, eine Schnitzfigur, eine Lampe mit einem Papierschirm, die als einzigartig anzusehen ist, bedruckte Stoffe, die an die Freiheit der Tiere in der afrikanischen Savanne erinnern: Es sind alles Objekte, die fremde Kulturen und Lebensweisen symbolisieren und dort, wo sie in das Interieur integriert werden, ein großes Fenster zur Welt aufstoßen. Jedes einzelne dieser Dinge erzählt schließlich seine Geschichte – zumindest denen, die zuzuhören verstehen.

Suspended lamps "Minicentra" from David Abad for Dab.

Plafonnier "Minicentra", de David Abad pour Dab.

Hängelampen "Minicentra", entworfen von David Abad für Dab.

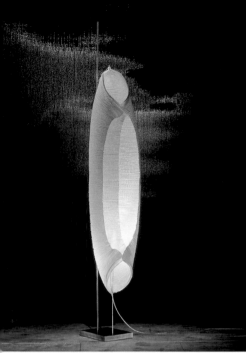

Diverse models of lamps from the collection "The MaMo Nouchies". Designed by Ingo Maurer. From left to right: "Babadul", "Poul Poul", "Wo Tumbu" and "Con Qui".

Différents modèles de lampes de la collection "The MaMo Nouchies", créées par Ingo Maurer. De gauche à droite : "Babadul", "Poul Poul", "Wo Tumbu" et "Con Qui".

Verschiedene Lampenmodelle aus der Modellreihe "The MaMo Nouchies", Design von Ingo Maurer. Von links nach rechts: "Babadul", "Poul Poul", "Wo Tumbu" und "Con Qui".

Lievore, Altherr and Molina are the authors of the design of the table "Irupe" from Muebles Do+Ce. On the right, "Bullshead from Habitat.

Lievore, Altherr et Molina signent la création de la table "Irupe", de Muebles Do+Ce. À droite, "Bullshead, de Habitat.

Von Lievore, Altherr und Molina entworfene Tisch "Irupe" von Muebles Do–Ce. Rechts "Bullshead" von Habitat.

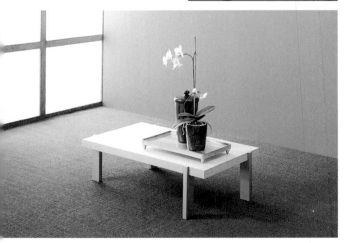

Auxiliary table from the collection 'Occa" from Club 8 Company.

Table d'appoint de la collection "Occa" de Club 8 Company.

Ein Beistelltisch aus der Modellreihe "Occa" von Club 8 Company.

Complements from the collection "Mandalay" from the Maison Coloniale.

Accessoires de la collection "Mandalay" de La Maison Coloniale.

Eine Zusammenstellung aus der Modellreihe "Mandalay" von La Maison Coloniale.

Decorative complements "Atlas" and "Naomi" from Lambert.

Accessoires décoratifs "Atlas" et "Naomi" de Lambert.

Die dekorativen Accessoires "Atlas" und "Naomi" von Lambert.

Textile complements from Insa.

Accessoires textiles de Insa.

Stoffteile zur Ergänzung der Einrichtung von Insa.

Clothes rack "Sciangai" from Zanotta. In the center, "Horse" from Habitat. On the right, screen "Gekko" from Habitat.

Porte–manteau "Sciangai" de Zanotta. Au centre, "Horse" de Habitat. À droite, paravent "Gekko" de Habitat.

Garderobe "Sciangai" von Zanotta. In der Mitte "Horse" von Habitat. Rechts Paravent "Gekko" von Habitat.

"Struktura", "Kassandra" and "Helena" are decorative complements from Lambert. Below, on the right, serving dish "Bastion" from Habitat.

"Struktura", "Kassandra" et "Helena" sont des accessoires décoratifs de Lambert. En bas à droite, plat "Bastion" de Habitat.

"Struktura", "Kassandra" und "Helena" sind dekorative Accessoires von Lambert. Unten rechts die Schüssel "Bastion" von Habitat.

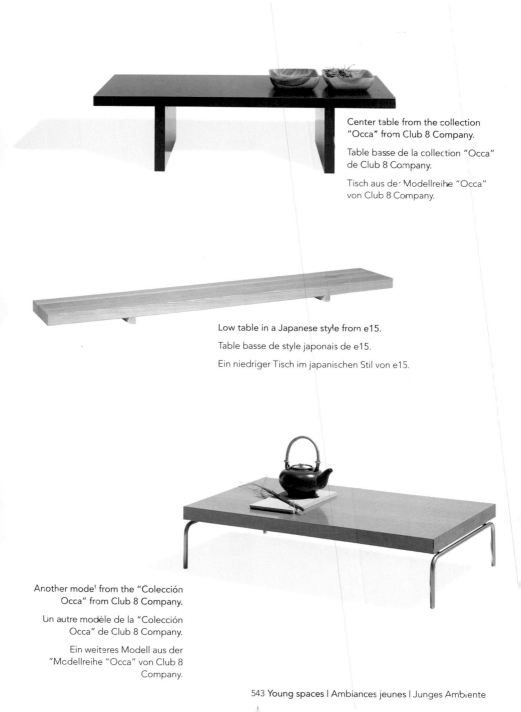

Center table from the collection "Occa" from Club 8 Company.

Table basse de la collection "Occa" de Club 8 Company.

Tisch aus der Modellreihe "Occa" von Club 8 Company.

Low table in a Japanese style from e15.

Table basse de style japonais de e15.

Ein niedriger Tisch im japanischen Stil von e15.

Another model from the "Colección Occa" from Club 8 Company.

Un autre modèle de la "Colección Occa" de Club 8 Company.

Ein weiteres Modell aus der "Modellreihe "Occa" von Club 8 Company.

Proposal from Bis Bis Imports Boston.

Proposition de Bis Bis Imports Boston.

Ein Vorschlag von Bis Bis Imports Boston.

Composition from Bis Bis Imports Boston.

Composition de Bis Bis Imports Boston.

Eine Zusammenstellung von Bis Bis Imports Boston.

Carpets from the collection "África" designed by Antoni Arola. Produced by Nani Marquina.

Tapis de la collection "África" créés par Antoni Arola. Fabrication Nani Marquina.

Teppiche aus der Modellreihe "África", Design von Antoni Arola, hergestellt von Nani Marquina.

Carpets from the collection "Dhurries". Designed and produced by Nani Marquina.

Tapis de la collection 'Dhurries', créés et fabriqués par Nani Marquina.

Teppiche aus der Modellreihe "Dhurries", entworfen und hergestellt von Nani Marquina.

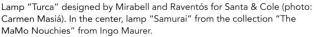

Lamp "Turca" designed by Mirabell and Raventós for Santa & Cole (photo: Carmen Masiá). In the center, lamp "Samurai" from the collection "The MaMo Nouchies" from Ingo Maurer.

Proposal from Bis Bis Imports Boston.

Lampe "Turca" créées par Mirabell et Raventós pour Santa & Cole (photo : Carmen Masiá). Au centre, lampe "Samurai" de la collection "The MaMo Nouchies" de Ingo Maurer.

Proposition de Bis Bis Imports Boston.

Lampe "Turca", von Mirabell und Raventós für Santa & Cole entworfen (Foto: Carmen Masiá). In der Mitte die Lampe "Samurai" aus der Modellreihe "The MaMo Nouchies" von Ingo Maurer.

Ein Vorschlag von Bis Bis Imports Boston.

Stool "Kleiner" from Nils Holger Moorman.

Tabouret "Kleiner" de Nils Holger Moorman.

Der Hocker "Kleiner" von Nils Holger Moorman.

Models from the collection "África" from Antoni Arola for Nani Marquina.

Mocèles de la collection "África", de Antoni Arola pour Nani Marquina.

Modelle aus der Modellreihe "África", von Antoni Arola für Nani Marquina.

Des salles de bain exotiques

Bathrooms with an exotic touch

Badezimmer mit einem exotischen Flair

Composition from the program
"Feng–Shui" from Toscoquattro.

Composition de la gamme
"Feng–Shui" de Toscoquattro.

Eine Zusammenstellung aus der Modellreihe
"Feng-Shui" von Toscoquattro.

The influence from the land of the rising sun and of oriental philosophies such as Zen and Feng–Shui also dominate in the bathroom. The bathroom becomes a homage to water, as an element essential to the existence of nature. A style dominates that seeks luxury in the simplicity of objects, in their textures and their functionality, with an austerity that converts this space into the most adequate place in the home to arrive at a state of authenticity with oneself. They are ideas that satisfy a new way of life, that seek personal gratification and conform to a desire to surround ourselves with materials and colors that exist together in perfect harmony. From these simple compositions an emotional atmosphere is found that induces rest and the purification of body and soul.

Dans la salle de bain, on retrouve également l'influence du pays du Soleil Levant et des philosophies orientales telles que le Zen et le Feng–Shui. Il s'agit d'un hymne à l'eau, considérée comme l'élément vital rendant possible la présence de la nature. Ce qui y prédomine, c'est un style à la recherche du luxe dans la simplicité des objets, dans leurs textures et leur fonctionnalité, et dont l'austérité fait que cette pièce devienne l'endroit idéal pour arriver à un état d'authenticité avec soi–même. Il s'agit de concepts qui satisfont à une nouvelle forme de vie, à la recherche de la gratification personnelle, et qui permettent de s'entourer d'une parfaite harmonie entre les matériaux et les couleurs. Ces compositions extrêmement simples dégagent une certaine atmosphère émotionnelle qui prédispose au repos et à la purification du corps et de l'esprit.

Auch das Badezimmer wird von dem Einfluß des Landes der aufgehenden Sonne und den orientalischen Philosophien wie Zen oder Feng Shui geprägt. Sie verwandeln sich so in Tempel zur Verehrung des Wassers, diesem lebensnotwendigen Element, ohne das ein Überleben der Natur nicht vorstellbar ist. Bei diesem Stil liegt der Luxus in der Schlichtheit der Dinge, in der Einfachheit ihrer Textur und Funktionalität. Die Schmucklosigkeit dieses Raums läßt ihn ideal zur Selbstfindung werden. Mit dieser Konzeption wird eine neue Lebensform unterstützt, die nach persönlicher Erfüllung sucht und den Wunsch nach perfekter Harmonie zwischen Material und Farbe befriedigt. Von diesen schlichten Interieurs wird eine Raumatmosphäre erzeugt, die geeignet ist, Geist und Körper in einen Zustand der Entspannung und Läuterung zu versetzen.

Composition from the collection "Zen" with natural stone washbasins. From Toscoquattro.

Composition de la collection "Zen", avec lavabo en pierre naturelle. De Toscoquattro.

Eine Zusammenstellung aus der Modellreihe "Zen" mit einem Waschbecken aus Naturstein, von Toscoquattro.

Two details from the program "Feng–Shui" from Toscoquattro.

Deux détails de la gamme "Feng–Shui", de Toscoquattro.

Zwei Details aus der Modellreihe "Feng-Shui" von Toscoquattro.

Alternative combination of "Feng–Shui"
from Toscoquattro.

Autre combinaison de "Feng–Shui"
de Toscoquattro.

Verschiedene Zusammenstellungen
von "Feng-Shui" von Toscoquattro.

Detail from the program "Zen"
from Toscoquattro.

Détail de la gamme "Zen" de Toscoquattro.

Detail aus der Molellreihe "Zen" de Toscoquattro.

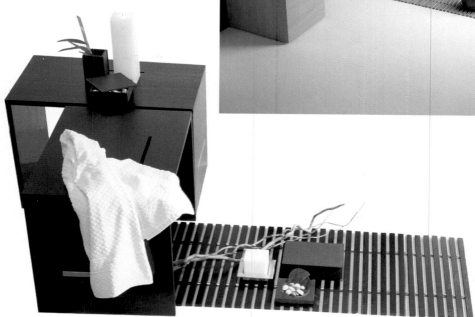

Faucets "Belle de Jour" from Dornbracht. Design from Sieger Design.
On the right, composition from Bis Bis Imports Boston.

Robinet "Belle de Jour" de Dornbracht, création de Sieger Design.
À droite, composition de Bis Bis Imports Boston.

Armaturen "Belle de Jour" von Dornbracht, Design von Sieger Design.
Rechts eine Zusammenstellung von Bis Bis Imports Boston.

Freestanding mirror "Image" from Prospero Rasulo for Glas. On the right, proposal from Bis Bis Imports Boston.

Miroir "Image", de Prospero Rasulo pour Glas. À droite, proposition de Bis Bis Imports Boston.

Spiegel "Image", von Prospero Rasulo für Glas entworfen. Rechts ein Vorschlag von Bis Bis Imports Boston.

The program "Feng–Shui" allows for numerous combinations. From Toscoquattro.

La gamme "Feng–Shui" permet d'obtenir de nombreuses combinaisons. De Toscoquattro.

Die Elemente aus der Modellreihe "Feng-Shui" lassen sich auf verschiedenste Weise miteinander kombinieren. Von Toscoquattro.

Composition with glass washroom from Bis Bis Imports Boston. On the right, program "Feng–Shui".

Composition avec lavabo en verre de Bis Bis Imports Boston. À droite, gamme "Feng–Shui".

Zusammenstellung mit Glaswaschbecken von Bis Bis Imports Boston. Rechts die Modellreihe "Feng-Shui".

Bathroom finished in glass and aventurine mosaic "Le Gemme 20", from Bisazza.

Salle de bain finition mosaïque et verre "Le Gemme 20", de Bisazza.

Badezimmer mit Wandverkleidung aus Glasmosaik und Aventurin "Le Gemme 20" von Bisazza.

Top image, collection "Nagano" from Villeroy & Boch. Below, on the left, faucets "Tara" from Sieger Design for Dornbracht. On the right, detail from the program "Cotta" from Keramag.

Image du haut, collection "Nagano" de Villeroy & Boch. En bas à gauche, robinet "Tara" de Sieger Design pour Dornbracht. À droite, détail de la gamme "Cotta" de Keramag.

Oben Modellreihe "Nagano" von Villeroy & Boch. Unten links Armaturen "Tara", von Sieger Design für Dornbracht entworfen. Rechts ein Detail aus der Modellreihe "Cotta" von Keramag.

Sieger Design is the author
of the design of the faucets
"Belle from Jour" from Dornbracht.

Sieger Design signe la création
du robinet "Belle de Jour"
de Dornbracht.

Sieger Design zeichnet für das
Design der Armaturen
"Belle de Jour" von Dornbracht.

Composition from the program
"Nagano" from Villeroy & Boch.

Composition de la gamme
"Nagano" de Villeroy & Boch.

Zusammenstellung aus der
Modellreihe "Nagano"
von Villeroy & Boch.

Faucets "Obina" from Sieger
Design for Dornbracht.

Robinetterie "Obina" de Sieger
Design pour Dornbracht.

Armaturen "Obina", von Sieger
Design für Dornbracht entworfen.

Washroom "Mohave" with auxiliary furniture in wenge
from Roca. On the right, faucets "Tara" for the shower
from Dornbracht.

Lavabo "Mohave" avec meubles d'appoint en wengé,
de Roca. À droite, robinet "Tara" pour la douche,
de Dornbracht.

Waschbecken "Mohave" von Roca mit Badmöbeln aus
Wengé. Rechts Duscharmaturen "Tara" von
Dornbracht.

Dreaming about other countries

Elegant proposal from the firm Porro.

Proposition élégante signée Porro.

Ein elegante Lösung von der Firma Porro.

Rêver d'autres pays

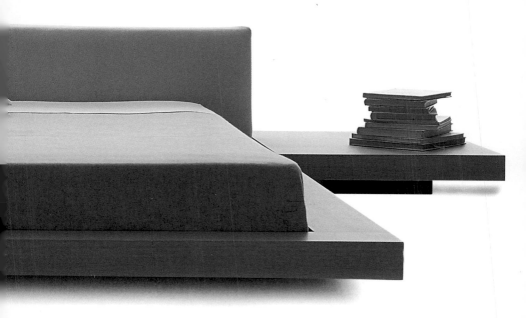

Der Traum von fremden Ländern

The Japanese tradition, first and foremost, and the colonial style, at a certain distance, are the victors in this area. The Japanese custom of sleeping on the floor, in direct contact with the ground, and the characteristic absence of ornaments in the house is being imposed in the West. Some adaptations to western comforts, also of an ancestral nature, such as the use of a mattress are also being included. Low beds, which barely raise above floor level, wardrobes with panels drawn on their fronts imitating paper and sliding doors, moderation, figurative restraint, austere and precise styles, natural colors enhanced by abundant natural light, these are the elements needed to transport us to another way of understanding life that, perhaps, will lead us to a better understanding of the world in which we live.

La tradition japonaise, en premier lieu, et l'esthétique coloniale, suivant de près, sont les grands vainqueurs dans ce domaine. La coutume japonaise consistant à dormir au ras du sol, en contact direct avec la terre, et le vide ornemental caractéristique de la demeure, font leur apparition en occident, s'adaptant néanmoins aux commodités occidentales telles que le sommier. Des lits bas, presque au ras du sol, des armoires dont les portes imitent les portes coulissantes en papier, de la sobriété, un certain maintien figuratif, des lignes précises et austères, des couleurs naturelles mises en valeur par une abondante lumière également naturelle, sont les éléments susceptibles de nous faire voir la vie d'une autre façon, de nous faire comprendre un peu mieux le monde dans lequel nous vivons.

Diese Schlafräume werden in erster Linie von der japanischen Tradition und – in einem etwas geringeren Maße – von dem Kolonialstil geprägt. Die Schlafkultur der Japaner, ihr Bett auf der Ebene des Erdbodens einzurichten, und der Verzicht auf jeglichen ornamentalen Schmuck in ihren Häusern, setzt sich zunehmend in unseren Breiten durch, allerdings wird dabei nicht ganz auf die gewohnte Bequemlichkeit verzichtet und z. B. eine Sprungfedermatratze vorgesehen. Niedrige Betten, die sich kaum vom Boden abheben, Schränke mit Türen, die den japanischen Schiebewänden aus Papier nachempfunden sind, Kargheit, Zurückhaltung in der Formgebung, präzise, schmucklose Linien, natürliche Farben, die durch das reichlich einfallende Tageslicht noch besonders unterstrichen werden, sind einige der Elemente, die wir zum Verstehen einer anderen Lebensform benötigen, die uns vielleicht sogar dabei hilft, die Welt, in der wir leben, besser zu begreifen.

Bedroom "Sichuan", in solid cherry, from the collection Los Viajeros from Roche Bobois.

Chambre "Sichuan" en cerisier massif, de la collection Los Viajeros de Roche Bobois.

Das Schlafzimmer "Sichuan" in massivem Kirschbaum aus der Modellreihe Los Viajeros von Roche Bobois.

Composition from the program "Tao" from Misura Emme. Below, two images from the collection "Moments" from Club 8 Company.

Composition de la gamme "Tao" de Misura Emme. En bas, deux images de la collection "Moments" de Club 8 Company.

Zusammenstellung aus der Modellreihe "Tao" von Misura Emme. Unten zwei Beispiele aus der Modellreihe "Moments" von Club 8 Company.

Model "Senzafine" from Poliform.

Modèle "Senzafine" de Poliform.

Das Modell "Senzafine" von Poliform.

Bed "Pio" from Chi Wing Lo
for Giorgetti.

Lit "Pio" de Chi Wing Lo
pour Giorgetti.

Das von Chi Wing Lo für
Giorgetti entworfene Bett "Pio".

Top image, bedroom from the collection "Basic" from Club 8 Company. Bottom image, wardrobe "Contengo" from Pianca.

Image du haut, chambre de la collection "Basic" de Club 8 Company. Image du bas, armoire "Contengo" de Pianca.

Oben das Schlafzimmer aus der Modellreihe "Basic" von Club 8 Company. Unten der Schrank "Contengo" von Pianca.

Top image, piece of furniture with lamp "Meo" from Chi Wing Lo for Giorgetti. Bottom image, bed "Flat–Kub" from Misura Emme.

Image du haut, meuble avec lampe "Meo" de Chi Wing Lo pour Giorgetti. Image du bas, lit "Flat–Kub" de Misura Emme.

Oben Möbel mit der Lampe "Meo", Design von Chi Wing Lo für Giorgetti. Unten das Bett "Flat-Kub" von Misura Emme.

Bed "Témenos" from
Léon Krier for Giorgetti.

Lit "Témenos" de Léon Krier
pour Giorgetti.

Das von Léon Krier für Giorgetti
entworfene Bett "Témenos".

Bed "Vitto" from Misura Emme.

Lit "Vitto" de Misura Emme.

Das Bett "Vitto" von Misura Emme.

Composition from Giorgetti with the bed "Pio" from Chi Wing Lo as protagonist.

Composition de Giorgetti, avec le lit "Pio" de Chi Wing Lo comme protagoniste.

Zusammenstellung von Giorgetti mit dem Bett "Pio" von Chi Wing als wichtigstes Element.

Composition from the program "Pi" from Juventa.

Composition de la gamme "Pi" de Juventa.

Eine Zusammenstellung aus der Modellreihe "Pi" von Juventa.

Colonial airs in the composition
"Train de Nuit" from the Maison
Coloniale.

De petites notes coloniales dans la
composition "Train de Nui:", de La
Maison Coloniale.

Kolonialstil für die Zusammenstellung
"Train de Nuit" von La Maison
Coloniale.

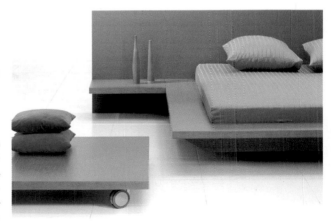

Composition from the program
"Pi" from Juventa.

Composition de la gamme "Pi" de
Juventa.

Eine Zusammenstellung aus der
Modellreihe "Pi" von Juventa.

Bottom, bedroom from the series "Jap" from Zanette. On the left, bed "Hikari" designed by Lodovico Acerbis for Acerbis International.

En haut, chambre de la série "Jap" de Zanette. À gauche, lit "Hikari", créé par Lodovico Acerbis pour Acerbis International.

Oben eine Schlafzimmer aus der Modellreihe "Jap" von Zanette. Links: das Bett "Hikari", das von Lodovico Acerbis für Acerbis International entworfen wurde.

Composition from the collection "Basic" from Club 8 Company.

Composition de la collection "Basic" de Club 8 Company.

Zusammenstellung aus der Modellreihe "Basic" von Club 8 Company.

| Directory · Carnet d'adresses · Adressen

ACERBIS International spa
Via Brusaporto 31
24068 Seriate (Bg), ITALY
Tel. 39 0352 94222
Fax. 39 0352 91454
info@acerbisinternational.com

ADELTA
Friedrich Ebert Str. 96
46535 Dinslaken, GERMANY
Tel. 49 2064 40797
Fax. 49 2064 40798
adelta@t-online.de

ADRENALINA
C.P.99
47841 Cattolica (Rimini),
ITALY
Tel. 39 0721 208372
Fax. 39 0721 209923
adrenalina@adrenalina.it

ALNO AG
88629 Pfullendorf,
GERMANY
Tel. 49 07552 21-0
Fax. 49 07552 21 37 89
mail@alno.de

ALTRO
La Coma 18, A1,
Pl. Pla de Santa Anna
08272 Sant Fruitós del
Bages, SPAIN
Tel.34 902 104 108
Fax. 34 902 104 109
altro@altro.es
www.altro.es

ANDREU WORLD,S.A.
Autovía A3 Madrid-Valencia
Km 323
46370 Chiva (Valencia),
SPAIN
Tel. 34 961 805 700
Fax. 34 961 805 701
aworld@andreuworld.com

ANNIBALE COLOMBO srl
Via delle Betulle 3
22060 Novedrate (Como),
ITALY
Tel.39 0317 90494
Fax. 39 0317 91607
info@annibalecolombo.com

ARCO Meubelfabrieken B.V.
Postbus 11
7100 AA Winterswijk,

HOLLAND
Tel.31 5435 12504
Fax. 31 5435 21395
info@arcomeubel.nl

ARLEX
Pl. Pla de Ilerona, Via Europa
40-42
08520 Franqueses del Vallès,
SPAIN
Tel. 34 938 615 044
Fax. 34 938 615 270
arlex@arlex.es

ARTELANO
57 Rue de Bourgogne
75005 Paris, FRANCE
Tel. 33 1 444 20161
Fax. 33 1 444 20160
artelano@aol.com

ARTEMIDE
Lérida, 68-70
08820 El Prat de Llobregat
(BCN), SPAIN
Tel. 34 934 783 911
Fax. 34 933 707 306
artemide@ict.ictnet.es

ARTQUITECT
Showroom-C/ Comercio, 31
08003 Barcelona, SPAIN
Tel. 34 932 683 096
Fax. 34 932 687 773
artquitect@artquitect.net

AXIA srl
Via delle Querce 9
31033 Castelfranco Veneto
(Treviso), ITALY
Tel. 39 0423 496222
Fax. 39 0423 743733
axia@axiabath.it

B&B ITALIA spa
Strada Provinciale 32
22060 Novedrate (Como),
ITALY
Tel. 39 031 795213
Fax. 39 031 795214
beb@bebitalia.it

BICAPPA ITALIA spa
Via Bergamo 66
24047 Treviglio (Bergamo),
ITALY
Tel. 39 03634 8971
Fax. 39 03634 5917

BIS BIS IMPORTS BOSTON
4 Park Plaza
2116 Boston, USA
Tel.1 617 350 7565
Fax. 1 617 482 2339
info@bisbis.com

BISAZZA
Viale Milano 56
36041 Alte, Vicenza, ITALY
Tel. 39 0444 707511
Fax. 39 0444 492088
info@bisazza.com

B.LUX
Pol. de Eitua, 70
48240 Berriz (Vizcaya), SPAIN
Tel. 34 946 827 272
Fax. 34 946 824 902
info@grupoblux.com

BODEMA
Via Padova 12
20030 Camnago di Lentate
sul Seveso, ITALY
Tel. 39 0362 5572 55-60
Fax. 39 0362 5572 71
bodema@bodema.it

BONALDO spa
Via Straelle 3
35010 Villanova (Padova),
ITALY
Tel. 39 0499 299011
Fax. 39 0499 299000
bonaldo@bonaldo.it

BONESTIL
Santa Teresa, s/n
46691 Vallada (Valencia),
SPAIN
Tel. 34 962 296 014
Fax. 34 962 296 127
bonestil@astro.es

BULTHAUP GmbH
84153 Aich, GERMANY
Tel. 49 8741 800
Fax. 49 8741 80340
www.bulthaup.com

CALLIGARIS
Viale Trieste, 12
33044 Manzano (Udine),
ITALY
Tel. 39 0432 748366
Fax. 39 0432 750104
calligaris@calligaris.it

CARPYEN
Pere IV, 78-84
08005 Barcelona, SPAIN
Tel. 34 933 209 990
Fax. 34 933 209 991
comercial@carpyen.com

CASAMILANO
Via Edison 18
20036 Meda (Mi), ITALY
Tel.39 0362 340499
Fax. 39 0362 341126
info@casamilanohome.com

CASSINA Spa
Via L. Busnelli 1
20036 Meda (Mi), ITALY
Tel. 39 0362 3721
Fax. 39 0362 342246
info@cassina.it

CATTELAN ITALIA Spa
Via Pilastri 15 z.i. Ovest
36010 Carre' (Vi), ITALY
Tel.39 0445 318711
Fax. 39 0445 314289
info@cattelanitalia.com

CERÁMICA BARDELLI
Via Pascoli, 4-6
20010 Vittuone (Mi), ITALY
Tel. 39 0290 25181
Fax. 39 0290 260766
info@bardelli.it

CESANA
Via Dalmazia 3
20059 Vimercate (Mi), ITALY
Tel. 39 0396 082441
Fax. 39 0396 851166
cesana@cesana.it

CIACCI
Via Antonelli, 49
Brugnetto di Ripe, ITALY
Tel.39 0716 620374
Fax. 39 0716 620258
www.ciacci.com

CLASSICON
Perchtinger Strasse 8
81379 München, GERMANY
Tel. 49 089 748133-0
Fax. 49 0897 809996
info@classicon.com

CLUB 8 COMPANY
Fabriksvej, 4 -P.O. Box 74

6870 Ogold, DENMARK
Tel. 45 7013 1366
Fax. 45 7013 1367
club8@club8.com

COR SITZMÖBEL
Nonenstraße 12
D-33378 Rheda-Wiedenbrück,
GERMANY
Tel.49 5242 4102-0
info@cor.de

DADA
Strada Provinciale 31
20010 Mesero, ITALY
Tel. 39 0297 20791
Fax. 39 0297 289561
dada@dadaweb.it

DESALTO
Via per Montesolaro
22063 Cantú (Como), ITALY
Tel. 39 0317 00481
Fax. 39 0317 00112
oma@desalto.it

DIEMO ALFONS
Rosenthaler Straße 19
10119 Berlín, GERMANY
Tel. 49 0308 522975
Fax. 49 0308 5964353

DAB-DISEÑO ACTUAL BARCELONA
Avda. de la Cerdanya, Nau
10; Pol. Ind. Pomar de Dalt
08915 Badalona (Barcelona),
SPAIN
Tel. 34 934 650 818
Fax. 34 934 654 635
info@dab.es

DO+CE-MUEBLES DOCE,S.L.
Pol.Ind.Massanassa C/N.1
Nave 44
46470 Massanassa (Valencia),
SPAIN
Tel. 34 961 252 467
Fax. 34 961 252 554
doce@do-ce.com

DOMUS CENTRAL
Crta. Nacional 332, n° 23,
Km 88
03550 San Juan (Alicante),
SPAIN
Tel. 34 965 943 360
Fax. 34 965 943 361
domus@domuscentral.com

DORNBRACHT
Köbbingser Mühle, 6
58640 Iserlohn, GERMANY
Tel.49 2371 433 0
Fax. 49 2371 433232
mail@dornbracht.de

DURAVIT ESPAÑA
Balmes 184, 4° 1ª
08006 Barcelona, SPAIN
Tel. 34 932 386 020

Fax. 34 932 386 023
info@es.duravit.com

E15 GMBH
Hospitalstraße 4
61440 Oberursel, GERMANY
Tel. 49 6171 582 577
Fax. 49 6171 582 578
asche@e15.com

EDRA spa
Via Livornese Est 106
56030 Perignano (Pisa), ITALY
Tel. 39 0587 616660
Fax. 39 0587 617500
edra@edra.com

ENEA
Ola Auzea, 4
20250 Legorreta (Guipúzcoa),
SPAIN
Tel. 34 943 806 275
Fax. 34 943 806 174

EUROKEYTON
Pol. Ind. Atalayas 85
03114 Alicante, SPAIN
Tel. 34 965 109 150
Fax. 34 965 109 107
informail@eurokeyton.es

FEBAL CUCINE
Via Provinciale 11
61025 Montelabbate, ITALY
Tel. 39 0721 426262
Fax. 39 0721 426284
export@febal.it

FENDI CASA
Via Borelli 1
47100 Forli, ITALY
Tel. 39 5437 91911
Fax. 39 5437 25244
fendi.casa@MEOX.QUEEN.IT

FIAM ITALIA spa
Via Ancona 1/b
61010 Tavullia (Pesaro), ITALY
Tel. 39 0721 20051
Fax. 39 0721 202432
fiam@fiamitalia.it

FONTANA ARTE spa
Alzaia Trieste, 49
20094 Corsico (Milano), ITALY
Tel. 39 0245121
Fax. 39 024512660
info@fontanaarte.it

FREDERICIA FURNITURE
Treldevej 183
7000 Fredericia, DENMARK
Tel. 45 7592 3344
Fax. 45 7592 3876
sales@fredericia.com

GALLOTTI & RADICE
Via Matteoti 17
22072 Cermenate, ITALY
Tel. 39 0317 77111

Fax. 39 0317 77188
info@gallottiradice.it

GAMA-DECOR S.A.
Ctra. Viver-Pto. Burriana,
Km. 62
12540 Villarreal (Castellón),
SPAIN
Tel. 34 964 506 850
Fax. 34 964 506 596
gama-decor@gama-decor.com

GANDIA BLASCO
Musico Vert, 4
46870 Onteniente (Valencia),
SPAIN
Tel. 34 962 911 320
Fax. 34 962 913 044
gandiablasco@gandiablasco.com

GIORGETTI spa
Via Manzoni 20
20036 Meda (Mi), ITALY
Tel.39 0362 75275
Fax. 39 0362 75575
giorspa@giorgetti-spa.it

GIOVANETTI srl
Via Perucciani 2
51034 Casalguidi (Pistola),
ITALY
Tel.39 0573 946222
Fax. 39 0573 946224
giovannetti@ftbcc.it

GLAS
Via Cavour 29
20050 Macherio (Mi), ITALY
Tel.39 0392 323202
Fax. 39 0392 323212
glas@glasitalia.com

HABITAT
P° de la Castellana 79
28046 Madrid, SPAIN
Tel. 34 915 553 354

HABITAT
Colón 34
46004 Valencia, SPAIN
Tel. 34 963 944 112

HABITAT
Diagonal 514
08006 Barcelona, SPAIN
Tel. 34 934 154 455

HABITAT
C.C. El Triangle;
Pl. Catalunya, 4
Barcelona, SPAIN
Tel. 34 933 017 484

INDUSTRIAS COSMIC
Cerdanya, 2-Pol. Ind. La Borda,
P.O. Box 184
08140 Caldes de Montbui,
SPAIN
Tel. 34 938 654 277
Fax. 34 938 654 264
cosmic@icosmic.com

INGO MAURER GmbH
Kaiserstrasse 47
80801 München, GERMANY
Tel. 49 0893 816060
Fax. 49 0893 8160620
www.ingo-maurer.com

INNOVATION RANDERS
Blommevej 38
8900 Randers, DENMARK
Tel. 45 86 438211
Fax. 45 86 438488
mail@inno.dk

INSA srl
Localita' Canova 1
27017 Pieve Porto Morone
(Pavia), ITALY
Tel. 39 0382 727411
Fax. 39 0382 788111
info@insa.it

INTER
Ctra. de Villena Km.2,5
30510 Yecla (Murcia), SPAIN
Tel. 34 968 75 10 11
Fax. 34 968 75 15 88
mobilfresno@bemarnet.es

INTHAI S.A.
Crom, 18 A
08907 Hospitalet de Llobregat,
SPAIN
Tel. 34 933 351 443
Fax. 34 933 355 847
irthai@set.icnet.es

ITRE SRL
Via delle Industrie 16/c
30030 Salzano (VE), ITALY
Tel. 39 0414 82987
Fax. 39 0414 82990
itre@itresrl.com

KAGAN NEW YORK COLLECTION
P.O. BOX 286434
NY 10128 Nueva York, USA
Tel. 1 212 289 0031
Fax. 1 212 360 7307
info@vladimirkagan.com

KELLY HOPPEN INTERIORS
2 Muncen Street
W14 0RH Londres,
UNITED KINGDOM
Tel. 44 020 7471 3350
Fax. 44 020 7471 3351
www.kellyhoppen.com

KERAMAG AG
Kreuzerkamp 11
D-40878 Ratingen,
GERMANY
Tel. 49 2102 9160
Fax. 49 2102 916245
info@keramag.de

KLENK WOHN
COLLECTIONEN
Industriestraße 34
72221 Haiterbach,
GERMANY
Tel. 49 7456 93820
Fax. 49 7456 938240
klenk-collection@t-online.de

LA MAISON COLONIALE
Muntaner 272
08021 Barcelona, SPAIN
Tel. 34 932 413 683
www.lamaisoncoloniale.com

LAGO srl
Via Morosini 22/24
35010 San Giogio in Bosco
(Padova), ITALY
Tel. 39 0495 994299
Fax. 39 0495 994199
info@lago.it

LAMBERT GMBH
Konstantinstraße 303
41238 Mönchengladbach,
GERMANY
Tel. 49 2166 86830
Fax. 49 2166 859638
office@lambert-home.de

LEICHT
Gmünder Straße 70
73550 Waldstetten,
GERMANY
Tel. 49 7171 402 0
Fax. 49 7171 402300
Kontakt@leicht.de

LEOLUX
Kazernestraat 15
5928 Venlo, HOLLAND
Tel.31 7738 77216
Fax. 31 7738 77288
lba@leolux.nl

LIV' IT (GRUPO FIAM ITALIA)
Via Macerata, 9
61010 Tavullia (PS), ITALY
Tel. 39 0721 202709
Fax. 39 0721 202711
www.livit.it

LUBE OVER CUCINE
Dell'Industria 4
62010 Treia, ITALY
Tel. 39 0733 8401
Fax. 39 0733 840115
www.lubeover.it

LUZIFER
Pie de la Cruz, 5-19
46001 Valencia, SPAIN
Tel. 34 963 912 124
Fax. 34 963 913 431
www.luziferlamps.com

MAGIS
Via Magnadola, 15
31045 Motta di Livenza,
ITALY

Tel. 39 0422 768742-3
Fax. 39 0422 766395
info@magisdesign.com

MAISA sas
Corso Garibaldi, 20
20020 Seveso (Mi), ITALY
Tel. 39 0362 500971
Fax. 39 0362 500974
maisa@maisa.com

MARCELLO ZILIANI
Via Amba d'Oro 68
25123 Brescia, ITALY
Tel. 39 0303 63758
Fax. 39 0303 60430
mz@marcelloziliani.com

MATTEO GRASSI
Via Padre Rovanati, 2
22066 Mariano Comense,
ITALY
Tel. 39 0317 57711
Fax. 39 0317 48388
info@matteograssi.it

MAXALTO
Strada Provinciale 32
22060 Novedrate (Como),
ITALY
Tel. 39 0317 95213
Fax. 39 0317 95224
beb@bebitalia.it

METHODO srl
Via Molinetto, 70
31030 Saletto di Breda
di Piave (TV), ITALY
Tel. 39 0422 686132
Fax. 39 0422 686587
info@methodotp.com

MINOTTI CUCINE
Via Napoleone, 31
37015 Ponton (Vr), ITALY
Tel.39 0456 860464
Fax. 39 0457 732678
info@minotticucine.it

MISURA EMME
Via IV Novembre, 72
22066 Mariano Comense(Co),
ITALY
Tel.39 0317 54111
Fax. 39 0317 54111
info@misuraemme.it

MOBILEFFE spa
Via Ozanam, 4
20031 Cesano Maderno (Mi),
ITALY
Tel.39 0362 52941
Fax. 39 0362 502212
info@mobileffe.com

MOBLES 114,S.A.
Riera dels Frarers 24
08907 L'Hospitalet de
Llob.(Barcelona), SPAIN
Tel. 34 932 600 114

Fax. 34 932 600 115
mobles114@bcn1.com

MÖLLER DESIGN
Residenzstraße 16
32657 Lemgo, GERMANY
Tel. 49 5261 9859-5
Fax. 49 5261 89218
info@moeller-design.de

MOLTENI & C. Spa
Via Rossini 50
20034 Giussano (Mi), ITALY
Tel. 39 0362 3591
Fax. 39 0362 852337
www.molteni.it

MONTANA MØBLER
Akkerupvej 16
5683 Haarby, DENMARK
Tel. 45 6473 32111
Fax. 45 6473 3238
montana@montana.dk

MONTIS
Steenstraat 2-postbus 153
5100 AD Dongen, HOLLAND
Tel. 31 1623 77777
Fax. 31 1623 77711
info@montis.nl

NANI MARQUINA
Carrer Església 4-6, 3er D
08024 Barcelona, SPAIN
Tel. 34 932 376 465
Fax. 34 932 175 774
info@nanimarquina.com

NILS HOLGER MOORMANN,
Kirchplatz -Postfach 1145
83229 Aschau, GERMANY
Tel. 49 8052 4001
Fax. 49 8052 4393
info@moormann.de

NITO ARRENDAMENTI SRL
(en España importa y distribuye
en exclusiva Artquitect)
Via E.Mattei, 19
53041 Asciano (Siena), ITALY
Tel. 39 0577 718899
Fax. 39 0577 718733
nitoarredamenti@tin.it

NOBILIA WERKE J. STICKLING
Waldstraße 53-57
33415 Verl, GERMANY
Tel. 49 5246 5080
Fax. 49 5246 508117
nobilia@nobilia.de

NUEVA LINEA
Olalde Urrestilla
20730 Azpeitia, SPAIN
Tel. 34 943 814 525
Fax. 34 943 815 016
nuevalinea@nuevalinea.es

ORGANICA
Rastro San Juan 2
13270 Almagro, SPAIN

Tel. 34 962 861 225
Fax. 34 962 861 225
organica@arrakis.es

OSTER
MÖBELWERKSTÄTTEN
Gewerbegebiet zur Höhe 1
56809 Dohr, GERMANY
Tel. 49 2671 60000
Fax. 49 2671 600090
möbelwerkstätten@oster.de

PEROBELL
Avda. Arraona 23
08205 Sabadell (Barcelona),
SPAIN
Tel. 34 937 457 900
Fax. 34 937 271 500
info@perobell.com

PIANCA spa
(en España, Espacio Pianca de
Mobles Maldà)
Via Capellari 14
31018 Gaiarine (Treviso),
ITALY
Tel. 39 0434 756911
Fax. 39 0434 75330
info@pianca.com

POGGENPOHL
Poggenpohlstraße 1
32051 Herford, GERMANY
Tel. 49 5221 381
Fax. 49 5221 381321
info@poggenpohl.de

POLIFORM spa
Via Monte Santo 28
22044 Inverigo (Como),
ITALY
Tel. 39 0316 951
Fax. 39 0316 99444
info.poliform@poliform.it

PORADA ARREDI srl
Via P.Buozzi 2
22060 Cabiate (Como),
ITALY
Tel. 39 0317 66215
Fax. 39 0317 68386
porada@porada.it

PORRO INDUSTRIA MOBILI srl
Via per Cantu' 35
22060 Montesolaro (Como),
ITALY
Tel. 39 0317 8 0237
Fax. 39 0317 81529
info@porro.com

PREALPI spa MOBILFICIO
Via Pradegnan
31051 Follina (Treviso), ITALY
Tel. 39 0438 970277
Fax. 39 0438 971047
info@prealpi.it

RAFEMAR
Apdo. Correos 98
08240 Manresa, SPAIN

Tel. 34 938 784 810
Fax. 34 938 745 014
rafemar@rafemar.com

RAPSEL
Via Volta, 13
20019 Settimo Milanese
(Milano), ITALY
Tel.39 0233 55981
www.rapsel.it

RATTAN WOOD spa
Via S.Rocco 37
31010 Moriago (Treviso),
ITALY
Tel. 39 0438 966307
Fax. 39 0438 966413
info@rattanwood.it

REGIA
Via Vigevano, Zona Industriale
20053 Taccona di Muggiò
(MI), ITALY
Tel. 39 0392 782510
Fax. 39 0392 782571
info@regia.it

**RIZZA DESIGN
E COMPLEMENTI**
Viale Como 6/6a
20030 Paina (Mi), ITALY
Tel. 39 0362 310075
Fax. 39 0362 311135
info@rizza-design.it

ROBOTS Spa
Via Galvani 7
20082 Binasco (Milano),
ITALY
Tel. 39 0290 54661
Fax. 39 0290 54664
info@robots.it

ROCA
Avda. Diagonal, 513
08029 Barcelona, SPAIN
Tel. 34 933 661 200
Fax. 34 934 194 501
www.roca.es

ROCHE BOBOIS
Muntaner, 266-268
08021 Barcelona. SPAIN
Tel. 34 932 404 056
Fax. 34 934 140 873
www.rochebobois.fr

ROLF BENZ AG &Co.KG
Haiterbacher Strasse 104
72202 Nagold , GERMANY
Tel. 49 7452 601245
Fax. 49 7452 601110
info@rolf-benz.de

SANTA & COLE
Stma. Trinidad del Monte, 10
08017 Barcelona, SPAIN

Tel. 34 934 183 396
Fax. 34 934 183 812
info@santacole com

SCAVOLINI SPA
Via Risara 60-70/ 74-78
61025 Montelabbate, ITALY
Tel. 39 0721 443'
Fax. 39 0721 443404
contact@scavolini.com

SCHIFFINI
Via Genova, 206
19020 Ceparana (SP), ITALY
Tel. 39 0187 9501
Fax. 39 0187 932399
info@schiffini.it

SELVA AG
Via L. Negrelli Str., 4
39100 Bozen, ITALY
Tel. 39 0471 240111
Fax. 39 0471 240112
selva@selva.com

STOKKE
Apdo. Correos 181;
Av. Vizcaya 67
20800 Zarautz, SPAIN
Tel. 34 943 130 596
Fax. 34 943 133 201
stokke_spain@redestb.es

STUA
Pcligono 26
20115 Astigarraga, SPAIN
Tel. 34 943 330 188
Fax. 34 943 556 002
stua@stua.com

**STYLING S.R.L.
(GRUPO BONALDO)**
Via dell' Industria, 2
350'0 Borgoricco, ITALY
Tel. 39 0499 318711
Fax. 39 0499 318700
stylir g@styling.it

TALLER UNO
Balmes 11
17465 Camallera (Girona),
SPAIN
Tel. 34 972 794 127
Fax. 34 972 794 313
info@talleruno.com

TECTA
Sohnreystraße 10
37697 Lauenförde,
GERMANY
Tel. 49 5273 37890
Fax. 49 5273 378933
info@tecta.de

THONET, GEBRÜDER
Michael Thonet Straße 1
35066 Frankenberg,

GERMANY
Tel. 49 6451 5080
Fax. 49 6451 508108
info@thonet.de

TISETTANTA Spa
Via Tofane, 37
20034 Giussano (Mi), ITALY
Tel. 39 0362 3191
www.tisettanta.it

TOBIAS GRAU
Siemensstrasse 35 B
D-25462 Rellingen,
GERMANY
Tel. 49 0 410 13700
Fax. 49 0 410 13701000
info@tobias-grau.com

TOSCOQUATTRO srl
Via Sila, 40 c
59100 Prato, ITALY
Tel. 39 0574 815535
Fax. 39 0574 815384
toscoquattro@toscoquattro.it

TRAMO
Méxic, 17, 3º
08004 Barcelona, SPAIN
Tel. 34 934 796 970
Fax. 34 934 796 973
grupo-t@grupo-t.com

TRIANGOLO
Via Icaro, 10
61100 Pesaro, ITALY
Tel. 39 0721 4253
Fax. 39 0721 268614
ac-t@ac-t.net

TRIP TRAP DENMARK
Havnejev 11
9560 Hadsund, DENMARK
Tel.45 9952 5200
Fax. 45 9952 5229
info@triptrap.dk

VENETA CUCINE spa
V a Paris Bordone, 84
3'030 Biancade (Treviso),
ITALY
Tel.39 0422 8471
www.venetacucine.com

VERARDO SPA
Via Porderone, 28
33070 Tamai (PN), ITALY
Tel. 39 0434 600311
Fax. 39 0434 627155
valentina.b@verardoitalia.it

VIBIA
Barcelona, 72-74
08820 El Prat de Llobregat
(BCN), SPAIN
Tel. 34 934 796 970
Fax: 34 934 796 973
www.vibia.es

VIBIEMME srl
Via Cividale 44
33044 Manzano (Udine),
ITALY
Tel. 39 0432 750473
Fax. 39 0432 740050
vibiemme@vibiemme.it

VICCARBE
Travesia Camí del racó, s/n
46469 Beniparrell (Valencia),
SPAIN
Tel. 34 961 201 010
Fax. 34 961 211 211
viccarbe@viccarbe.com

VILLEROY & BOCH
P.O. Box 1120
D-66688 Mettlach,
GERMANY
Tel.49 0686 481 0
www.villeroyboch.com

**VINCENT SHEPPARD
LLOYD LOOM**
Industriepark Ijzeren Bareel 5
8587 Spiere, BELGIUM
Tel. 32 5646 11111
Fax. 32 5646 1112
sales@vincentsheppard.com

ZANETTE spa
Via Trieste 4
33070 Maron di Brugnera
(Pordenone), ITALY
Tel. 39 0434 623151
Fax. 39 0434 624298
info@zanette.it

ZANOTTA spa
Via Vittorio Veneto 57
20054 Nova Milanese (Mi),
ITALY
Tel. 39 0362 4981
Fax. 39 0362 451038
zanottaspa@zarotta.it

ZENIA HOUSE
Havnegade 2B
DK-8000 Aarhus C,
DENMARK
Tel. 45 8731 0050
Fax. 45 8731 0059
info@zeniahouse.com